SCI/EI 学术论文写作与发表攻略

Strategy to write and publish the SCI/EI academic paper

张建 陈赟 著

机械工业出版社

本书论述了 SCI/EI 学术论文写作与发表攻略，既是囊括通用模板的指导书，又是富含共性词句的手册，单刀直入，直指要害，将繁琐的论文写作工作转变成简单的搭积木游戏，将提心吊胆的专家意见答复工作演绎成谈笑自若的围棋对弈。全书以作者公开发表的三篇 EI 中文论文、三篇 SCI 英文论文为对象，理论联系实际展开论述，内容集中便于学习。

在论文写作部分，指出了整体写作的先后顺序、章节写作的具体内容及模板句，并给出中英文实例分析加深理解，提供中英文实例练习加以巩固；在专家意见答复部分，结合实例分析论述了论文评审一般性知识、评审报告内容及答复要点，并提供了作者公开发表的一篇 EI 中文论文、一篇 SCI 英文论文的投稿、评审和答复实例，供读者借鉴。

本书既可供从事工学、理学、农学等领域的年轻学者参考，也可供这些领域的在校研究生作为教材学习使用。

图书在版编目（CIP）数据

SCI/EI 学术论文写作与发表攻略／张建，陈赟著. —北京：机械工业出版社，2017.12（2023.11重印）

ISBN 978-7-111-58585-5

Ⅰ. ①S… Ⅱ. ①张… ②陈… Ⅲ. ①论文－写作 Ⅳ. ①H152.3

中国版本图书馆 CIP 数据核字（2017）第 295441 号

机械工业出版社（北京市百万庄大街22号　邮政编码100037）
责任编辑：罗晓琪　责任校对：罗晓琪
封面设计：原彬彬　责任印制：李　昂
河北宝昌佳彩印刷有限公司印刷
2023 年 11 月第 1 版第 3 次印刷
184mm×260mm・15.5 印张・387 千字
标准书号：ISBN 978-7-111-58585-5
定价：45.00 元

凡购本书，如有缺页、倒页、脱页，由本社发行部调换

电话服务	网络服务
服务咨询热线：010-88361066	机工官网：www.cmpbook.com
读者购书热线：010-68326294	机工官博：weibo.com/cmp1952
010-88379203	金书网：www.golden-book.com
封面无防伪标均为盗版	教育服务网：www.cmpedu.com

作者简介

张建，1984年出生，江苏沭阳人，教授，博导，双博士，中国船舶科学研究中心博士后。入选国家级青年人才，江苏省杰青，江苏省优青，江苏省优秀科技创新团队带头人，江苏省"333工程"高层次人才，江苏省六大人才高峰高层次人才，镇江市有突出贡献的中青年专家，镇江市十大杰出青年，镇江市出彩教育人。担任国家海事局船舶技术法规专家，国际海洋技术学会会员，美国机械工程师学会专业会员，中国造船工程学会高级会员，中国机械工程学会高级会员，国际仿生学会会员，中国/波兰国家自然科学基金评审专家。担任国际权威期刊 Ships and Offshore Structures 的副主编，国际期刊 American Journal of Mechanical and Materials Engineering、Engineering Science、Modern Subsea Engineering and Technology 的编委，国际权威期刊 Metals、Frontiers in Materials 的客座编辑，以及13本国际权威期刊审稿人。

陈赟，1989年出生，江苏科技大学机械工程学院副教授，中国科学技术大学少年班应用数学专业学士，美国南佛罗里达大学工业工程专业博士。以第一作者/通信作者发表SCI学术论文13篇；授权中国发明专利6件，美国发明专利1件。主持国家及省部级纵向课题3项、委托攻关项目3项。出版学术专著2部，参与撰写英文专著3部。以第一作者获国际会议最佳分会论文奖1项、最佳学生论文奖2项。IE Transactions、Journal of Manufacturing Systems、IEEE Transactions on Automation Science and Engineering、Journal of Intelligent Manufacturing 等SCI期刊审稿人。

前　言

　　SCI/EI 高水平论文写作与发表是一项非常繁琐的工作，困扰着无数年轻学者和研究生，从试验规划、数据分析、论文写作、期刊投稿、同行评审、意见答复、文章录用到最终发表，可谓经历了重重困难，有时评审与答复会反复多次，其中心酸不言而喻。但是，没有高水平论文支撑，年轻学者就无法进入学术俱乐部、提升业内影响力、申报纵向项目，进而阻碍职称晋级和个人发展；没有高水平论文写作与发表经历，研究生就无法养成良好的科研素质、严谨的治学精神、较强的写作能力，甚至影响学位论文评审和顺利毕业。因此，许多人写 SCI/EI 论文是不得已而为之，对其爱恨交加，这也是作者亲眼所见、亲耳所闻、感同身受的体会。

　　静下心来仔细观察，就会发现周围有些人论文高产，像农夫种菜一样一年可以发表四五篇 SCI/EI 论文；还有一些人论文难产，像老牛拉车一样四五年才发一两篇 SCI/EI 论文。于是，作者痛定思痛、苦苦追寻，立志把自己及所指导研究生从"老牛"变成"农夫"。为此，精读了近百篇同行写的高水平论文，研究了数十本关于论文写作方面的中英文教材，学习了"小木虫"、Elsevier、北卡罗来纳大学等网站上论文写作专题，边学边练，小有成效。例如，指导硕士生王明禄同学在两年之内发表 SCI 论文两篇、EI 论文两篇、投稿 SCI 论文两篇，此外发表一篇会议论文获得 2016 年"海洋工程与技术"上海研究生学术论坛一等奖。通过上述学习和实践，发现年轻学者和研究生不缺试验规划、数据分析和期刊投稿能力，缺的是论文写作和答复能力，而现有论文写作的教材和网站要么篇幅庞大、缺乏体系，要么高深莫测、晦涩难懂，搞得年轻学者和研究生无所适从。

　　为了克服现有教材所存在的问题，解决年轻学者和研究生所面临的困惑，作者决定撰写《SCI/EI 学术论文写作与发表攻略》一书，结合自身写作和投稿经历、将繁琐的论文写作工作转变成简单的搭积木游戏，将提心吊胆的专家意见答复工作演绎成谈笑自若的围棋对弈。例如，在论文写作部分，指出了整体写作的先后顺序、章节写作的具体内容及其模板句，并给出中英文实例分析加深理解，提供中英文实例练习加以巩固；在专家意见答复部分，论述了论文评审一般性知识、评审报告内容及答复要点，并提供了作者一篇 EI 中文论文、一篇 SCI 英文论文的投稿、评审和答复实例，供读者参考。全书以作者公开发表的三篇 EI 中文论文、三篇 SCI 英文论文为对象，理论联系实际展开论述，内容相对集中便于读者学习，涉及工学、理学、农学等多个学科。

　　为进一步增加阅读友好性、培养动手能力、提升理论水平，作者邀请美国南佛罗里达大学毕业的陈赟博士撰写本书的第 6 章图表处理，第 7 章文献检索、管理与引用，第 8 章评审与答复，陈博士是中国科技大学少年班毕业，在美国求学六年，论文写作和评审经验非常丰富，2016 年发表 SCI 论文四篇。邀请《Ocean Engineering》副主编崔维成教授、王芳博士担任主审，崔教授是著名科学家、中国深潜英雄、《船舶力学》副主任委员，《Marine Structures》《中国造船》等多家 SCI/EI 期刊编委，两位专家对本书提出了许多宝贵意见。

　　课题组硕士研究生张猛、刘同庆、张莉、花正道、戴永建、廖天岸等在本书的排版、图片处理、文字校核等方面做了很多工作，在此表示感谢。此外，作者特别感谢团队负责人唐文献教授、博士后导师王纬波/吴文伟研究员、博士导师王国林教授的鼓励和支持；感谢江苏省船海机械装备先进制造重点实验室、中国船舶重工集团公司第七〇二研究所船舶振动噪声重点实验室、江苏省道路载运工具新技术应用重点实验室、上海深渊科学工程技术研究中心提供科研条件。

张建
2017 年 4 月

目 录

前言
第1章 写作概述 1
1.1 论文开篇 1
1.2 论文主体（IMRAD） 3
1.3 论文收尾-End of a paper 4
1.4 写作建议-advice for writing 5
1.5 开篇范文分析 6
1.6 实例练习 7
第2章 引言撰写 9
2.1 通用模板 9
2.2 研究重要性模板句 10
2.3 文献综述模板句 13
2.4 存在问题模板句 15
2.5 本文工作模板句 16
2.6 经典范文分析 18
2.7 实例练习 20
第3章 方法撰写 25
3.1 通用模板 25
3.2 方法引言模板句 26
3.3 细节描述模板句 27
3.4 对比引用模板句 29
3.5 问题说明模板句 30
3.6 经典范文分析 32
3.7 实例练习 34
第4章 结果分析与讨论撰写 38
4.1 通用模板 38
4.2 结果引言模板句 40
4.3 图表指示模板句 41
4.4 结果分析模板句 44
4.5 结果讨论模板句 48
4.6 文献对比模板句 51
4.7 问题说明模板句 52
4.8 经典范文分析 55
4.9 实例练习 57
第5章 结论与致谢撰写 63
5.1 结论 63
5.2 致谢 69
5.3 实例练习 71
第6章 图表处理 75
6.1 图表概述 75
6.2 图表的分类 76
6.3 图表的格式 80
6.4 图表的结构组成 80
6.5 一些总结 84
6.6 软件制图实例 84
6.7 实例练习 98
第7章 文献检索、管理与引用 100
7.1 概述 100
7.2 Mendeley 基本情况 100
7.3 Mendeley 操作界面介绍 102
7.4 Mendeley 的主要功能 103
7.5 文档与参考文献的共享 108
7.6 实例练习 109
第8章 评审与答复 110
8.1 论文评审的概念与分类 110
8.2 论文评审报告 112
8.3 论文评审答复 117
8.4 实例练习 125
第9章 写作与发表实例 126
9.1 中文论文实例 126
9.2 英文论文实例 185
参考文献 239

第 1 章　写作概述

学术论文是某一学术课题在实验性、理论性或预测性上具有新的科学研究成果或创新见解和知识的科学记录，或是某种已知原理应用于工程实际过程中取得新进展的科学总结。尽管不同期刊的要求有细微差别，但学术论文的结构遵循一定的格式，按顺序一般包括开篇（preface）、主体（IMRAD）和收尾（end）三个部分。开篇包括标题（title）、作者（author）、关键词（keyword）和摘要（abstract），主体包括引言（introduction）、方法（methodology）、结果（result）、讨论（discussion）和结论（conclusion），收尾包括致谢（acknowledgment）、参考文献（reference）和附件（supplementary material），如图 1-1 所示。写作时，论文的具体格式需要严格依据期刊投稿指南（guide for authors）撰写。本章从宏观角度分析学术论文的一般性架构及其写作要求，重点阐述开篇的内容并分析见刊论文实例，主体和收尾部分将在本书其他章节单独介绍。

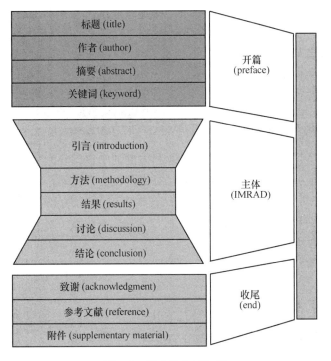

图 1-1　学术论文结构图

1.1　论文开篇

论文开篇（preface of a paper）就像一部电影的宣传海报，直接决定了编辑是否接收文稿并送给同行专家审阅，审稿人是否产生兴趣、耐心评审并给出建设性意见，读者是否下载阅读全文并在其今后发表的论文中引用。

1.1.1 标题

标题（title）是一篇论文的公告，应当清晰准确地描述论文的内容，读者会通过标题来决定是否需要进一步阅读。好的标题吸引读者，糟糕的标题被读者排斥。要让标题变得独特且富有吸引力，需要注意不要将类似于"a study of""investigation into""observations on"这样无法突出重点的词语放在标题中，并且避免使用缩写和专业术语。同时要牢记，文献检索服务需要一个准确的标题，它们从论文标题中提取关键词来交叉互访。一个有效的标题要有以下特点：

1) 点明论文主旨
2) 包含主要论点
3) 准确不含糊、有特色
4) 精炼简洁
5) 有吸引力和趣味性

1.1.2 作者-Authors

论文作者应该是为研究做出智力贡献的人、负责分析数据得出结论的人和最终撰写论文文稿的人。作者顺序要依据不同期刊的要求来排定，通讯作者并不总是第一作者。作者部分应注意以下要求：

1) 包含第一作者和相关作者
2) 不应遗漏相关作者
3) 不应添加无关作者

1.1.3 关键词-Keywords

许多期刊要求作者列出关键词。论文标题和关键词中包含着论文研究的最重要内容。关键词常被用于文献检索，因而，为了能让同行有更多机会查阅到作者的文章，对关键词应当精挑细选。许多外文期刊要求作者在在线投稿过程中填写主题分类（即关键词）来方便编辑选择审稿人。关键词的作用及要求为：

1) 一篇论文的标签
2) 用于文献检索
3) 简洁准确
4) 只可用限定的缩写，如 DNA

1.1.4 摘要-Abstract

摘要一般有字数限制（每个期刊的投稿指南中都有规定），要包括研究问题、研究方法、研究结果和研究结论。与标题对文章内容进行简短概括所不同的是，摘要应当详述论文各个部分。摘要中要给足读者信息来让他们决定是否需要阅读全文。同时，文献检索系统要求文章的标题和摘要独立成段，因此摘要中不应包括图表描述或引用的参考文献。许多作者都在文章主体完成后再撰写摘要，这样可以保证摘要在内容准确的前提下，提高论文的趣味性。对摘要的要求如下：

1) 只写一段

2）总结问题、方法、结果和结论
3）简洁准确
4）有吸引力和趣味性

1.2 论文主体（IMRAD）

1.2.1 引言-Introduction

引言要简洁，一般有 3~4 段内容。在引言中，应清晰地陈述研究的问题、研究背景和研究动机。作者应当综述相关研究进而展现其工作的独特性和所解决难题的重要性。若该难题已被解决，则需陈述对现有研究的质疑或进一步研究。引言中还应简要陈述作者的实验、假设、问题研究和实验大纲，并在之后的讨论部分详细解释这些内容。

1）语言简洁
2）说明研究问题
3）说明现有解决方法及其局限性
4）指出研究目标
5）说明和所投期刊性质相符的观点
6）每篇论文都有其特定的引言

1.2.2 方法-Methodology（Materials and Methods，etc）

方法部分的关键作用是为读者提供能够让他们重复论文研究的所有细节。按一定顺序来解释作者的研究方法、陈述作者的研究过程，避免第一人称出现。详述新方法的创新点和对现有方法的改进点，仅是使用现有方法只需提出并注明引用，还需描述实验器材和实验材料，若实验材料质量参差不齐，还应表明其来源，给出实验中的观察频率，点明所记录的数据类别。准确描述实验方法，包括实验中的错误。为保证作者的数据结果是有效的，要给出作者使用的统计检验方法的名称。如果研究对象有参与人、动物、干细胞或其他对生物有侵犯性的材料，应在道德声明中陈述出来，给出选择研究对象的标准。

1）描述所要解决问题的研究背景
2）详细描述相关信息
3）不要赘述现有研究方法
4）描述试验仪器与试验材料

1.2.3 结果-Results

在结果部分，应当客观地陈述作者的研究发现，并对其描述得尽可能详细。作者要表达出其最新研究发现是如何验证科学理论的，因此清晰、有逻辑性地展现作者的成果至关重要。不要在这个部分直接陈述一些原始数据，绘制表格、图和分析实验现象更有说服力，要描述图表中所有的数据变化趋势。因此，结果部分应当是一系列依据图表对研究难题和研究成果的逻辑性阐述。每一张图表都应标上序号，并在文中相应位置标注。简短地描述每张图来告知读者数据的产生过程。不要进一步解释作者的数据有哪些规律或可以得到什么结论，这些是讨论部分的工作。

1）陈述重要实验数据
2）使用小标题归纳同类结果
3）简洁直观地描述结果
4）着重陈述主要研究发现
5）以意想不到的结果为特色
6）提出数据分析的方法
7）绘制表格和图形

1.2.4 讨论-Discussion

讨论部分用于解释研究结果，关键是解释与前文所述的研究内容相关的研究结果，注意并不是总结文章——这是摘要的内容。在该部分，讨论内容要与引言中提出的问题和假设相呼应，与现有的研究内容相关联，作者应当表明自己的研究结果和现有结果是冲突的、矛盾的或是发展的、递进的。最重要的是，作者要详细阐述出研究结果是如何推进该领域科学理论发展的。不要赘述作者是如何从原始数据获得现有结论的，作者应该依据其所做结论给出一些实用性建议，并大体规划后续研究。

讨论部分要确保：

1）结果有效支撑结论
2）详细且精准描述
3）不讨论无关的新问题
4）与现有成果相比较
5）实事求是

1.2.5 结论-Conclusions

结论部分需要提醒读者读了什么，指出论文有哪些重要结论，一般分为总结段、结论段和方向段。对于总结阶段，用一两句话回顾前文，概述论文写了什么；对于结论段，回顾并提炼出结果分析与讨论中得出的重要结论，点出论文的创新点和潜在应用价值；对于方向段，回顾方法、结果与讨论部分存在的问题，展望下一步研究方向。

1）给出详细具体的结论
2）表明结论的适用领域
3）解释研究成果的先进性
4）陈述后续研究内容并表明是否已经起步
5）避免夸大结论的影响力

1.3 论文收尾-End of a paper

1.3.1 致谢-Acknowledgements

致谢部分一般位于结论之后、参考文献之前，感谢对论文做出贡献但不足以列为作者的人，对论文提供资助的个人、单位或基金，论文校对者、打字员及对论文提出有建设性意见的审稿人，有提醒作者对别人贡献的敬意的作用。

1）致谢指导老师
2）致谢研究资助者
3）致谢校对人员和打字员
4）致谢材料供应商
5）致谢审稿人

1.3.2 参考文献-References

创新研究成果均是建立在现有研究成果基础之上的，应当列出参考文献。在文章中任何非常识性知识或非自己实验所得内容都应属于引用范围。参考文献的标注方法要遵守期刊的投稿指南。若引用内容过长，则该内容要独立成段且要缩进；若引用内容自然呈献于文章中，则应使用引用标注。以上两种情况均需要在文章最后列出参考文献。对参考文献的基本要求如下：

1）参考文献数量不宜过多
2）确保列出所有参考文献
3）勿过多引用自己的论文
4）勿过多引用同一个机构的文献
5）参考文献格式严格遵守期刊的投稿指南

1.3.3 附件-Supplementary material

论文中不能出现所有的原始数据。如果作者觉得这些数据有用，则可放于附件中。随着期刊的网络化和储存补充材料的成本降低，提供全部的原始数据已经很普遍。补充材料可以包含：原始数据表格、录像片段、照片、复杂的三维模型。

1.4 写作建议-advice for writing

学术论文的写作顺序不同于一般文章的写作顺序。如图1-2所示是Elsevier推荐的写作顺序，也是一种在学术界被广泛接受的顺序：把论文写作看成是搭积木盖房屋。首先，铺上最长的图表积木作为房屋地基，即分析实验数据，并通过绘制图表呈现数据分布规律；其次，搭上方法、结果、讨论三块积木，即描述研究方法，叙述研究结果，讨论和分析成果；接着，在三块积木上面搭上结论和引言两块积木，即根据方法、结果、讨论内容，撰写结论和引言；最后，搭上标题、摘要、关键词三块积木作为房顶，即根据方法、结果、讨论、结论和

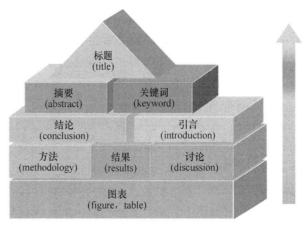

图1-2 学术论文写作顺序图

引言内容，撰写摘要和关键词，在此基础上凝练论文标题。这种论文写作顺序思路清晰、逻辑严谨，可以在学术论文写作中广泛使用。

1.5 开篇范文分析

（1）范文1

深海球形耐压壳力学特性研究（标题）

张建[1,2]，高杰[1]，王纬波[2]，唐文献[1]，周通[1]（作者及单位）

（1. 江苏科技大学，江苏 镇江 212003；2. 中国船舶科学研究中心，江苏 无锡 214082）

摘　要

　　研究了深海球形耐压壳计算方法。（**总结研究问题**）分别建立了球形耐压壳薄壳和厚壳的力学模型、浮力系数求解公式以及壳单元、体单元数值模型。分析1~6km球形耐压壳强度、稳定性、储备浮力特性，并研究网格划分形式、单元类型、密度对数值计算结果的影响。（**研究方法**）研究结果表明，采用厚壳理论、体单元数值分析进行深海球形耐压壳设计与评估更为合理。在设计时，建议先根据内表面应力公式确定耐压壳厚度，再运用厚壳屈曲理论或数值分析校核其稳定性。（**研究结果和研究结论**）

关键词：球形耐压壳；强度；稳定性；厚壳理论

中图分类号：U661.4，TE58　**文献标识码**：A

（2）范文2

Buckling of spherical shells subjected to external pressure: A comparison of experimental and theoretical data（标题）

Jian Zhang[a,b], Meng Zhang[a*], Wenxian Tang[a], Weibo Wang[b], Minglu Wang[a]（作者及单位）

[a]Jiangsu University of Science and Technology, Zhenjiang, Jiangsu, 212003, China

[b]Chinese Ship Scientific Research Center, Wuxi, Jiangsu, 214082, China

Abstract: This paper focuses on spherical shells under uniform external pressure. (**总结研究问题**) Ten laboratory scale models, each with a nominal diameter of 150 mm, were tested. Half of them were manufactured from a 0.4-mm stainless steel sheet, whereas the remaining five shells were manufactured from a 0.7-mm sheet. The geometry, wall thickness, buckling load, and final collapsed mode of each spherical shell were measured, as well as the material properties of the corresponding sheet. The buckling behaviors of these shells were demonstrated analytically and numerically according to experimental data. Analyses involved considering the average geometry, average wall thicknesses, and average elastic material properties. Numerical calculations entailed considering the true geometry, average wall thicknesses, and elastic-plastic modeling of true stress-strain curves. Moreover, the effects of purely elastic and elastic-perfectly plastic models on the buckling loads of spherical shells were examined numerically. (**研究方法**) The results of the experimental, analytical, and numerical investigations were compared in tables and figures. (研究结果和研究结论)

Keywords: spherical shell, 304 steel, buckling, external pressure, numerical solution

1.6 实例练习

运用所学知识,了解并分析自己研究领域内 2~3 篇论文的构架。仿照 1.5 节,分析并改正以下实例中的错误格式:

(1) 实例 1

硬土-软土插桩过程数值分析及验证

张建1,唐文献1,苏世杰1,秦文龙1,王静芳1,刘仁昌2

(1. 江苏科技大学;2. 烟台中集来福士海洋工程有限公司)

基金项目:国家自然科学基金项目 (51005108);江苏省"六大人才高峰"项目 (2011A031)

摘要:基于 Hossain M S 的土工离心模型试验,建立自升式平台插桩过程的数值模型,根据数值计算结果分析插桩过程中土壤流动特性以及插桩深度与插桩阻力的关系,并首次对桩靴底部压力分布规律进行研究。利用 Hossain M S 的试验结果对数值模型进行了验证,数值解与试验值吻合程度较好,说明模型可靠。数值计算结果表明:插桩过程中发生了硬土表面局部隆起、硬土-软土界面变形、空腔形成、土壤回流等现象;硬土、软土的强度比越小,桩靴下方硬土块体积越小,桩靴上方硬土分布越连续、均匀,空腔深度越大;土壤重度越大,桩靴上方硬土回流量越大,空腔深度越小,土壤重度对桩靴下方硬土块形状和体积几乎没有影响;硬土软土的强度比越大、有效重度比越小,发生"刺穿"的可能性越高。桩靴底部压力由内向外先增大、后减小、再增大,证明《海上移动平台入级与建造规范》中桩靴底部压力的线性分布假设与实际不符。

关键词:自升式平台;插桩过程;数值模型;桩靴承载力;桩靴底部压力

中图分类号:TU411　**文献标识码**:A

(2) 实例 2

轮胎硫化过程数值分析及试验研究

张　建^{1,2},王国林^1,唐文献^2,王小娟^3

(1. 江苏大学 风神江大车轮研究所,江苏 镇江 212013;2. 江苏科技大学 机电工程学院,江苏 张家港 2125600;3. 风神轮胎股份有限公司 研发二部,河南 焦作 454003)

摘要:为研究轮胎硫化特性,对其硫化过程进行了数值模拟。提出采用混合定律模型模拟橡胶-帘线复合材料的导热系数、比热容和密度的变化,分别采用三维热参数模型、混合动力模型和无量纲参数公式描述橡胶的热物性参数、硫化动力学特性和焦烧特性,运用 CAE 软件 ABAQUS 及其用户子程序 UMATHT 建立了某子午线轮胎的硫化数值模型,并进行数值分析和试验研究。结果表明:数值结果与试验结果具有良好的一致性,最难硫化的部位在胎肩 N600 处,当胶囊厚度减小 50% 时,N600 的焦烧时间缩短 5.98%,工程正硫化时间降低 11.84%;当初始预热温度增加 66% 时,N600 的焦烧时间缩短 27.05%,而此处的最高温度和工程正硫化时间变化不大；当蒸汽平均温度提高 5% 时，N600 的工程正硫化时间降低 9.29%，而此处的焦烧时间和最高温度变化不大。

关键词：轮胎；硫化；数值分析；热物性参数；硫化动力学；硫化程度；工程正硫化时间

中图分类号：TB333；TQ33　**文献标识码**：A

(3) 实例 3

Investigation on Egg-shaped Pressure Hulls

Jian Zhang[1,2], Minglu Wang[1], Weibo Wang[2], Wenxian Tang[1], Yongmei Zhu[1]

(1 Jiangsu University of Science and Technology, Zhenjiang, Jiangsu, 212003, China;
2 Chinese Ship Scientific Research Center, Wuxi, Jiangsu, 214082, China)

Abstract: Spherical shells are presently the most extensively used shapes for pressure hulls in the deep manned submersible. However, it is known that the spherical pressure hull has disadvantages of difficult interior arrangement/low space efficiency, and is highly sensitive to geometric imperfections. These limitations have prevented further developments of the deep manned submersible to some extent. In order to overcome these limitations, two egg-shaped pressure hulls respectively with the constant and variable thickness are proposed in this paper, where the equivalent spherical pressure hull is also presented for comparison. Buckling of these pressure hulls with geometric imperfections are further studied using numerical analyses at a given design load. It is found that, with respect to hull strength, buoyancy reserve, and space efficiency etc., egg-shaped pressure hulls could be optimally coordinated, which appear to be leading to overall better performance than the spherical pressure hull. Especially, the egg-shaped pressure hull is quite less sensitive to the geometric imperfections, making it more convenient and low costly to form the hull in manufacturing or to open holes in applications. It is anticipated that egg-shaped pressure hulls will play a key role in the future development of deep-sea manned submersibles.

Keywords: pressure hull; egg-shaped shell; buckling; imperfection sensitivity

(4) 实例 4

Buckling of Egg-shaped Shells Subjected to External Pressure

Jian Zhang[a,b], Minglu Wang[a,*], Weibo Wang[b], Wenxian Tang[a]

[a]Jiangsu University of Science and Technology, Zhenjiang, Jiangsu, 212003, China
[b]Chinese Ship Scientific Research Center, Wuxi, Jiangsu, 214082, China

Abstract: The subject of the present paper is a family of egg-shaped shells. The meridian of these shells resembles that of a goose egg. The capacity and mass of the shell were maintained constant. The ratio of the minor B to the major L axis of the shell was determined according to the experimental results of the analysis of 333 goose eggs. Fourteen B/L ratios were determined as follows: 0.4, 0.5, 0.6, 0.65, 0.66, 0.67, 0.68, 0.69, 0.70, 0.71, 0.72, 0.8, 0.9 and 1.0. The effect of the ratio on the buckling behavior of the egg-shaped shell was numerically and analytically analyzed.

Keywords: shell of revolution, egg-shaped shell, goose egg, buckling, external pressure

第 2 章 引言撰写

2.1 通用模板

引言的主要作用在于由浅入深、由宽到窄，将读者带到论文中，讲清楚为什么要开展此项研究、撰写该论文。为此，一篇论文的引言通常由背景介绍、文献综述、本文工作三个部分或者段落组成，本节将着重讲述这三个部分，如图 2-1 所示。

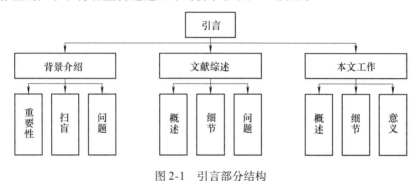

图 2-1 引言部分结构

2.1.1 背景介绍

背景介绍通常为一段话，即引言的第一段，需要依次说明研究重要性、扫盲信息、共性问题三方面内容。

（1）研究重要性

绝大多数学术论文在开篇第一句话，会阐述其研究主题、研究对象或研究领域是有用的、重要的或广受关注的。在学术论文写作时，如果没有指出研究重要性，就会让审稿人或者期刊编辑觉得论文没有发表价值；因此，千万不要太过谦虚，要大胆指出自己的研究很重要、很有用。如果实在写不出研究重要性，建议作者去找一些与自己研究最为相似的、公开发表的高水平论文，把这些论文的第一句话意思组织成自己的语言写出来。

（2）扫盲信息

扫盲信息可以帮助读者了解与研究相关基础知识、基本概念、背景信息或公知常识，为其继续阅读做好充分准备。决定扫盲信息内容的关键因素是论文的目标读者，如果目标读者仅仅是作者的同行，那么扫盲信息可以写得非常专业；但是，作者如果想让更多读者阅读引用，那么扫盲信息就要写得通俗易懂。此外，扫盲信息中的每句话最好附上必要的参考文献作为支撑，这些参考文献可以是一些综述论文或业内经典论文。

（3）共性问题

共性问题可以是当前业内研究热点或者许多学者感兴趣的研究问题，注意不要把共性问题写成论文所解决的具体问题，因为具体问题要在文献综合之后、本文工作之前写出。与扫盲信息一样，共性问题一般也需要引用参考文献来支撑，如果是常识问题，一般不需要参考文献作为支撑。共性问题一般可以从业内经典综述论文、国外学术会议论文或报告，或者业内最新发表的高水平论文中提取，组织成自己的语言写出来。

2.1.2 文献综述

文献综述及其存在问题是引言第二部分，可以是一段话或者分为多段，段落划分取决于内容多少。该部分需要说明别人采用了什么理论或方法、做了什么、还存在什么问题。

（1）文献综述

建议写成总分结构：一个主题句开头，承上启下，其他语句均是为了支持主题句。在综述文献过程中，尽可能避免无序混乱地罗列别人研究成果，最好采用一种逻辑顺序来组织这些文献，例如根据文献发表时间来组织，根据研究方法/理论/模型来分类组织，或采用一般到特殊的顺序来组织。参考文献的标注要严谨，根据描述内容的相关性，可以标在句中，也可以标在句末。

（2）存在问题

该部分目的在于通过文献综述，用 However 或者 Although 来指出当前研究存在的具体问题或空白，从而为引入本文研究内容打下铺垫。存在问题可以是时间问题、研究手段问题、研究对象问题或者提出自己的假设来验证。一方面，必须写出所存在的具体问题来支撑本文工作，给出研究原因；另一方面，用词要有礼貌、委婉表达，充分尊重前人所做工作，给作者自己留有余地，避免被审稿人提出严厉质疑。

2.1.3 本文工作

本文工作目的在于针对上一部分存在的具体问题，圈定研究范围，通常用一段文字，告诉读者本文的主要研究内容。写出论文的研究目标或者关注对象，同时要概述研究方法、所用理论、主要发现等信息，激发阅读兴趣。注意不要对这些方法、理论、发现作详细描述，否则会与以后章节重复。此外，还可以在最后加上一句话来说明研究意义。总之，该部分目的就是让读者把思路集中到要讨论的问题上来，减少不必要的争论。

2.2 研究重要性模板句

（1）备受关注

.... has attracted (received) much attention.

.... has generated considerable recent research interest.

... are attracting widespread interest in fields such as ...

... is of great concern.

... is of growing interest.

Much research has been focused on ...

A major current focus is how to ...

（2）是一个主题或问题

... is a basic subject in regard to ...

... has been the subject of numerous studies ...

... is a basic (major/crucial/common/fundamental) issue in regard to ...

... is a central (current) problem.

... is a challenging area (an interesting field).

... is a essential element.

... key technique (popular method/ powerful tool/ profitable technology).

(3) 时间表达

Today/Nowadays/Recently, ...

For many (a number of years/more than 100), ...

Over the past ten years, ...

During the past two decades, ...

In recent years, ...

Over many decades, ...

(4) 重要作用或泛应用

... play an important (key) role in the development of ...

... play a major part in the development of ...

... find wide applications in ...

... can be used to do ...

... are the most commonly used thin-wall structure geometry.

... primarily used in aerospace application.

经典例句

Understanding and mitigating buckling has long been important to engineers to prevent the catastrophic failure of macroscopic shell structures such as water tanks and submarines.

Many important natural or technological situations require understanding thin, spherical shells.

Buckling of thin-walled shell-like components, frequently found in pressure vessels, has been the subject of numerous studies over many decades.

In many instances, experimental data was used to develop design standards.

Thin-shell structures find applications in many branches of engineering. Typical examples include ......

Whereas, for thicker cylinders usually used in marine and offshore application, ...

Elliptical shells of revolution can be used to close the ends of externally pressurized vessels, and find applications in the submersible and space vehicle industry.

The stability analysis is a basic subject in regard to the designing of thin-walled structures.

The problem of stability of shell structures has been a subject of consideration over the last decades but is still vivid and broadly investigated. It is so because of the many areas where this kind of structures are used, but first of all because of many problems that are still unsolved.

Thick cones are used as structural components in offshore applications, e. g., piles for holding jackets when driven into the sea bed, transition elements between two cylindrical shells of different diameter, and the legs of offshore drilling rigs.

The buckling of unstiffened truncated conical shells under combined loading is of importance to offshore, chemical, and process engineering.

The buckling of conical shells is of interest to the offshore oil and chemical industries.

Cones are important structural components primarily used in the marine and offshore industries.

Conical shells are frequently used as transition elements joining cylinders of different diameters.

For more than 100 years researchers have been observing the stress-strain behaviour of…

Convection heat transfer phenomena play an important role in the development of…

This article examines tabu search—one of three zero-order methods that have become particularly popular over the last few years.

Further details about the measurements and tests can be found in Błachut and Smith (2003).

The stress distribution and static stability of pressure loaded end closures have long history and they have been investigated for many decades.

Recent developments in undersea technology have stimulated interest in research and rescue-type submersible vehicles capable of operating at extreme depths. The need for pressure hulls capable of withstanding the high pressure loadings while providing for adequate interior space has led to a consideration of prolate spheroidal shells for such hull structures.

Domed ends are useful structural components that are lightweight, have an enclosed volume and can withstand external pressure. Typical applications for domes are found in the aerospace and submersible industry, where they can be used to close the forward ends of submarines. The profile of a dome has a profound effect on its ability to withstand external pressure.

The quest for oil/gas and other natural resources has pushed the underwater exploration to deeper and deeper environment. One of the bottle-neck in wider underwater activities is the availability of buoyancy units. This is especially true at greater ocean depth. There are two approaches to buoyancy units.

Search for sensitivity of buckling loads to initial geometrical imperfections has resulted in an enormous research effort for many of recent decades.

Static stability of domed ends has been researched for decades both theoretically and experimentally.

Elliptical shells of revolution can be used in specialized applications, e.g., in pressure hulls for rescue-type submersibles.

Layered structures are widely used in as diverse applications as in aircrafts, thin film deposition in semiconductor devices, heat exchangers, etc.

Structural integrity of externally pressurised domed ends onto cylindrical shells, and made entirely either from steel or from CFRP/GFRP material, has been extensively studied in the past.

This kind of shell is commonly used as a main part of cylindrical vessels.

Advances in computing technology, especially in capabilities of hardware have contributed to rapid development of and success of optimization technology.

The buckling of unstiffened truncated conical shells under combined loading, i.e., axial compression and external pressure acting simultaneously, is of importance to offshore, chemical, and process engineering.

The buckling of shells has long been a canonical problem in the mechanics community.

Thin corrugated shells of circular or noncircular profile are widely used in various areas of engineering and construction such as air engineering, marine structures and piping because of those have high bending and compressive stiffness in the corrugation direction and low stiffness in the transverse direction

Thin shells find application in many engineering areas such as aerospace, marine industries, spacecraft launch vehicles, architecture and beverage industries.

Thin-walled shells of revolution are frequently used as pressure vessels, silos, liquid storage tanks, buoyancy units, etc. In a typical configuration they are built from cylindrical shell capped by two end closures.

Thin-walled cylindrical structures have been widely used in many industrial applications. However, thin cylindrical shells are vulnerable to buckling failures caused by the induced compressive loading.

However, in service these structural elements may lose their load carrying ability under compressive load before the maximum material strength is reached.

Despite of decades of research effort not all aspects of buckling of domed end closures are fully understood and/or codified for practical use.

Conical shell structures are used as structural components in engineering applications within aeronautical, marine, and mechanical industries. They find applications in pressure vessels, pipelines, offshore platforms, and transition elements between cylinders of different diameters.

This calls for a better understanding of the interplay between geometry and friction of the indenter-shell contact in determining the mechanical response.

Thin elastic spherical shells are known to exhibit a buckling instability at a finite external pressure.

Buckling is a ubiquitous phenomenon in thin-walled elastic structures, such as plates and shells.

Elastic capsules are commonly met in nature; prominent examples are red blood cells or virus capsules. Artificial capsules can be fabricated by various methods [1], for example, by interfacial polymerization at liquid droplets [2] or by multilayer deposition of polyelectrolytes [3], and have numerous applications.

2.3 文献综述模板句

（1）开展研究/试验

... carried out (performed/undertook/conducted) the experiment (research/analysis).

（2）研究表明

They claimed (stated/ reported/ concluded/ confirmed/ considered/ discovered/ demonstrated/ indicated/ suggested/ presented /found) that ...

(3) 研究...

... explored (investigated/studied) examined...

经典例句

In recent years there have been serious efforts to synthesize artificial cells consisting of a lipid bilayer and an actin cytoskeleton at the micrometre level and to study their adsorption on surfaces as well as their mechanical properties [11]-[18].

An overview of work in this area can be found in Refs. [1,2].

... is reported in Leon (1971).

Design of a composite bi-sphere pressure hull is discussed in Hall et al. (1991).

Blachut and Eschenauer (2001) details the application of Simulated Annealing method to shape optimisation of bowed out, mild steel, shell. Results

Another theory of the pre-and postbuckling behaviors of ellipsoids was developed by Danielson [7].

A geometry as well as stability of such shells are described in [26]. Results of experimental test are shown in [27].

One of the first studies into the sensitivity of the structures critical load to initial geometric imperfections was carried out by Donnell and Wan [2].

Reference [9] describes an axisymmetric inward bulge introduced into electro-deposited copperwall.

Ref. [3] reports on six buckling tests on unstiffened conical sections between cylinders of different diameters.

It is evident, from literature survey, Ref. [1], that...

Information on additional tests and the relevant theory is available in Refs. [21-29].

... has been extensively studied in the past.

This phenomenon was demonstrated by...

The algorithm has been proposed for these applications...

An alternative approach was developed by...

This in turn generated a large volume of theoretical and experimental studies.

A general discussion on the stability of thin shells is presented by Brush and Almroth [2] and Koiter [3].

The papers devoted to this subject are by Blachut and Wang [9], Blachut [10,11], Barski and Kruzelecki [12] and Krużelecki and Trzeciak [13] where optimization problem is also described.

Details concerning geometry and stability of barrelled shells can be found in papers by Jasion and Magnucki [5] and Magnucki and Jasion [6].

Further details into the above can be found in Refs [6-10].

Results of experiments on a number of barrelled shells combined in one pressure hull are presented by Błachut and Smith [7].

Magnucki [11] proposed a closed shell of revolution composed of a clothoidal and a spherical part. The meridian of this shell is distinguished by a continuous curvature which ensures a smooth stress distribution.

A large number of conference papers in the proceedings are explicitly devoted to buckling experiments.

Euler [1] laid the foundation for the formal analysis of structural stability; a field that has matured to become paramount in engineering design and one of the pillars in the history of mechanics.

In the linear regime, there has been a substantial body of work centered on rationalizing this interplay, from the seminal work of Reissner [16] on spherical shells to the more recent study of geometry-induced rigidity in nonspherical pressurized shells [17, 18].

2.4 存在问题模板句

（1）提出一种新方法、新方向

However, little information(little attention/little work/little data/little research……) (or few studies/few investigations/few researchers/few attempts……) (or no/none of these studies……) has (have) been done on (focused on/attempted to/conducted/investigated/studied(with respect to)) 。

（2）与别人研究类似

However, data is still scarce(rare, less accurate), We need to(aim to, have to) provide more documents (data, records, studies, increase the dataset) . Further studies are still necessary (essential)……

经典例句

Unfortunately, despite its common occurrence in real shells, exactly how inhomogeneity influences the onset of buckling, as well as the shell morphology after buckling, remains to be elucidated. A deeper understanding requires careful investigation of the buckling of spherical shells with tunable, well-defined, inhomogeneities.

… are just a sample of topics still awaiting further investigations.

It appears however that no experimental results are available for composite barrel-type shells.

Little work has been done on the problem of the elastic stability of prolate spherical shells and there are on experimental data to support the few theories.

However, the problem is far from being solved. In fact, the axially compressed cylinder has been considered one of the last classical problems in homogenous isotropic structural mechanics where it remains difficult to obtain close agreement between theoretical prediction and experimental results [1].

It appears that there has been only limited research into buckling performance of conical shells, under the action of combined loads, and within the elastic-plastic range. This has primarily been limited to buckling by external hydrostatic pressure.

However, test results on this subject are scarce, and this is especially true for the case of elastic-plastic buckling.

It appears that there have been no experiments within the elastic-plastic range for unstiffened cones subjected to combined axial compression and external pressure, except for the partial results being reported in Refs [2,3].

Few researchers have addressed the problem of...

There remains a need for an efficient method that can

However, the experimental configuration was far from optimal.

The above questions still remain open ones.

All of these tests have been carried out within the elastic range. Elastic-plastic buckling of cones has not been researched extensively.

It appears that there has been only limited research into buckling performance of conical shells, under the action of combined loads, and within the elastic-plastic range. This has primarily been limited to buckling by external hydrostatic pressure.

On the other hand, the stability studies of corrugated shells resting on elastic medium are very scarce.

However, there seems to be no open literature on the effect of geometrical parameters on critical buckling pressure and mode shape under uniform pressure load, different

Information on externally pressurized toriconical shells, on the other hand, is rare.

The literature survey indicates that detail about elastic-plastic and/or plastic buckling/collapse of conical shells appear to be rare.

In the framework of shell theory, however, a complete picture of the transition into buckled shapes as observed in the experiments is still lacking.

2.5 本文工作模板句

(1) 第一句表达

This current (present) paper (work/study) reports on (concentrate on/examine/provide)...

The purpose (goal/intention/objective/aim) of this paper is to...

In order to...

In this paper (work/study/present work), we aim to (present/perform/introduce)...

(2) 其他语句表达

Furthermore (Moreover, In addition), we will also discuss...

... is organized (set) as follows:

... is presented in detail

经典例句

Throughout this paper, we focus exclusively on spherical shells.

In this paper we investigate the different shapes that appear when a spherical shell is collapsed either under an external pressure or by a volume constraint.

The current paper examines the load carrying capacity of bowed out steel shells subjected to static external pressure.

The current paper presents results of numerical study into the influence of...

The current paper studies elastic-plastic buckling of conical shells subjected to a combined action of axial compression and independent external pressure. This is both a theoretical/numerical and experimental study.

The current paper aims to assess static stability of externally pressurised multilayered metal composite hemispherical and torispherical domes. This is a numerical and experimental work and as such it appears to be the first work of this nature in the open literature.

The paper aims to demonstrate that...

The paper is entirely numerical and it aims at providing a ground for structural optimization followed by selective experimentation at a later stage.

In this paper, investigation into comparison between theoretical prediction and experimental results of buckling load of short mild steel cylindrical shells subjected to axial compression is presented.

The aims of the present investigation are the following: ...

This study is divided into three parts: numerical, experimental, and comparison with current design codes.

The present paper is devoted to the stability analysis of shells of revolution with positive and negative Gaussian curvature.

The goal of this paper is to work out a procedure for design of a whole family of shells of revolution of constant mass and, ...

The subject of the paper is a non-typical shell of revolution. Its meridian is a spline curve composed ...

This paper focuses on ...

The aim of this paper is to examine the load-carrying capacity of spun steel hemispheres under static external pressure.

The aim of this paper is to explore possible advantages of this approach. ...and response of buckling pressures to Force-Induced-Dimples is studied in detail.

The goal of this paper is to work out a procedure for design of a whole family of shells of revolution of constant mass and, as a next step, of constant volume.

Our primary focus is on predictively describing the imperfection sensitivity of the shell to provide a quantitative relation between its knockdown factor and the amplitude of the defect.

This paper is to investigate the influence of the number and amplitude of corrugations on the buckling behavior of un-loaded and radially compressed elliptical cylindrical shells resting on a Winkler foundation.

The current paper provides test data and the corresponding theoretical/numerical results for buckling of externally pressurized mild steel toricones.

Here, we provide an alternative perspective on a burgeoning movement where mechanical instabilities are exploited to devise new classes of functional mechanisms that make use of the geometrically nonlinear behavior of their postbuckling regimes.

Here, we conduct a series of numerical experiments on the indentation of thin elastic shells and take advantage of the predictive power of FEM for this class of problems that we previously validated against our own precision experiments.

In this work, we study the effect of a previously unexplored inhomogeneity that is simple, yet general: a soft spot with a circular boundary in an otherwise uniform spherical shell.

The rest of this paper is structured as follows:

In this letter, we use a combination of experiments, theory, and simulation to study the buckling of spherical colloidal capsules with inhomogeneous shells of non-uniform thicknesses.

In this article, we study the collapse of a three-dimensional spherical capsule via the buckling instability into a fully collapsed state under negative pressure or for reduced capsule volume.

We conclude with potential applications and possible avenues for further research.

2.6 经典范文分析

（1）范文1

深海球形耐压壳力学特性研究

0 引言

根据《中国制造2025》文件，国家将大力推动海洋工程装备突破发展。深海潜水器是大洋勘查与深海科学研究的重要海洋工程装备。（**研究重要性**）在下潜过程中，潜水器的耐压壳起着保障内部设备正常工作和人员健康安全的作用，其重量占潜水器总重的 1/4 ~ 1/2[1]。（**扫盲信息**）

现有的球形耐压壳的设计与分析基于薄壳理论，且已被各国船级社规范认同（**主题句，承上启下**）。潘彬彬等对现有深水球形耐压壳的设计规范进行了对比和分析，指出规范计算中存在的缺陷[2]。然后通过原型试验和非线性有限元分析，建立了预测深海钛合金球形壳极限强度的经验公式。马永前等参考中厚板壳稳定性理论，研究厚球壳的屈曲问题，指出：由于厚度方向的剪切效应，厚球壳的实际临界屈曲载荷低于薄壳理论（Zolley 公式）的结果[3]。王自力、刘涛等的研究表明，随着水深增加，对于耐压壳的分析将从薄壳问题转化为中厚壳问题，然而现有的潜水器规范不适用于深海耐压壳分析，应直接根据有限元计算确定其极限强度[4-5]。（**文献综述**）在有限元建模过程中，模型简化、单元类型、网格密度、网格划分形式、边界条件、求解方法等对球形壳计算结果的影响很大，不同人员对同一问题的计算结果存在差异，数值解的可信度有待商榷。（**存在问题**）

本文从理论分析和数值计算这两方面研究球形耐压壳的强度、稳定性、储备浮力等性能。（**本文工作，主题句**）在 1 ~ 6km 水深条件下，分别按薄壳模型和厚壳模型，分析和对比壳体的强度和稳定性。建立球形耐压壳的壳单元和体单元数值模型，研究单元类型、网格密度对耐压壳强度和稳定性的影响。（**本文工作，具体信息**）

(2) 范文 2

Buckling of Spherical Shells Subjected to External Pressure: A Comparison of Experimental and Theoretical Data

1. Introduction

For more than 100 years, research has been published on spherical shells subjected to uniform external pressure. (*研究重要性*) Knowledge about this type of loading has been widely applied in various engineering fields such as those involving underwater pressure hulls, underground pressure vessels, and underpressure tanks [1-2]. In particular, the spherical configuration is broadly considered an ideal structure for the pressure hulls of deep submersibles. This is due to the extremely efficient stress and strain distributions in the material [3-4]. (*扫盲信息*) Although the theoretical elastic buckling loads are high, the spherical shells have been found to be highly imperfection sensitive and be strongly affected by plastic material properties. The experimental buckling loads are even lower than the theoretical ones. (*共性问题*)

The difference between theory and experiment has prompted numerous studies regarding the buckling of spherical shells loaded by external pressure. (*主题句, 承上启下*) For example, Blachut et al. presented a series of experimental and numerical studies concerning elastic-plastic buckling of spherical[5], torispherical[6], conical[7-8] or barreled shells[9-10] under external pressure. In most of their studies, the material was assumed to be elastic-perfectly plastic. The effects of initial geometric imperfections were also taken into account, which included eigenmode imperfections derived from linear elastic buckling analysis of the perfect geometries or deterministic ones derived from a limited number of measuring points. Moreover, Pan et al. performed a set of experimental and numerical studies on the ultimate strength levels of spherical pressure hulls used in deep submersibles[11, 12]. Their numerical models were elaborated on the basis of initial equivalent geometric imperfections in the shape of the first eigenmode and a local dimple. Their numerical predictions were verified by pressurizing four laboratory scale spherical hulls to collapse. More recently, Quilliet carried out elasticity theory calculations to predict the collapse mode of a spherical shell [13]. Quillet's prediction resembled previously published experimental results. (*文献综述*) However, little attention has been paid to true geometry, including deterministic imperfections, derived from a more precise measurement. And the effects of plastic material properties including or excluding yield strengths and hardening parameters on the buckling of spherical shells were rarely investigated as well. Further study is still necessary in this branch of mechanics. (*存在问题*)

For investigating the buckling of spherical shells loaded with external pressure, (*本文工作, 主题句*) spherical shells were manufactured from 304 stainless steel sheets through stamping and butt-welding processes. The geometries and thicknesses of these shells were obtained using a highly accurate three-dimensional optical scanner and an ultrasonic probe, respectively. And their buckling properties were also demonstrated by a series of hydrostatic tests. The buckling and postbuckling behaviors of these shells were then determined numerically and verified experimentally. The numerical analysis was based on deterministic imperfections obtained from measured geometric shapes and elastic-plastic modeling of true stress-strain curves. Furthermore, the effects of constitutive models, such as purely elastic and elastic-perfectly plastic modeling of material, on the buckling loads were studied numerically. (**本文工作 具体信息**) This paper aims to provide a rational approach to predicting the real load-carrying capacities of spherical shells. (**论文主要发现、或研究意义**)

2.7 实例练习

运用所学知识，仿照 2.6 节，分析以下实例。

（1）实例 1

硬土-软土插桩过程数值分析及验证

0 引言

当在硬土-软土结构的海底安装自升式钻井平台时，若某个桩靴突然发生无法控制的穿透，将导致桩腿屈曲、平台退役，甚至导致平台倾倒，这种灾难性的事故称为"刺穿"。为了避免发生"刺穿"事故，需要研究平台的插桩性能，包括插桩过程中桩靴周围土壤的流动特性、桩靴承载力（即插桩阻力）与插桩深度的关系、桩靴底部压力分布规律等。插桩过程中桩靴和土壤间的固定度决定了桩腿、固桩架和船体在作业和自存工况下的力学响应特性；插桩深度的大小决定了桩腿的设计总长；可靠的桩靴承载力设计是保证平台安全工作、避免发生"刺穿"事故的重要保障；桩靴底部压力分布规律不仅是桩靴强度校核的关键，也是对桩靴周围土壤剪切失效和"刺穿"失效进行分析的重要信息 [1-5]。

近年来，数值方法逐渐成为研究平台插桩性能的重要工具，小应变有限元法（SSFE）和大位移有限元法（LDFE）被广泛用于研究自升式平台插桩性能。但上述两种方法的运用需要丰富的工程经验，求解结果严重依赖网格划分和参数设置，且在研究深插桩过程时计算效率低、收敛困难 [6]。欧拉-拉格朗日耦合法（CEL）非常适合求解经典有限元法不能求解的大变形土工问题，Tho K K 等首次运用 CEL 法进行了插桩过程数值模拟 [7]，Qiu G 等通过试验法、数值分析 LDFE 法和解析法验证了 CEL 法的有效性 [8-9]。

Hossain M S 利用土工离心模型试验模拟了直径为 6m 的桩靴在硬土-软土中的插桩过程 [10]，本文基于 Hossain M S 的土工离心模型试验，采用 CEL 法建立插桩过程的数值模型，并利用 Hossain M S 的试验结果对数值模型进行验证，然后根据数值计算结果分析插桩过程中土壤的流动特性以及插桩深度与插桩阻力的关系，并首次对桩靴底部压力分布规律进行研究。

（2）实例 2

轮胎硫化过程数值分析及试验研究

0 引言

硫化是轮胎制造过程中的最后一道工序，在这个极其重要的阶段，轮胎在平板硫化机上形成最终理想形状。在硫化机上，热量通过含有高压热水的胶囊和高温蒸汽的金属模具传入轮胎内部，过热水和蒸汽不断循环以保证介质较高的温度。这些传入的热量促使橡胶化合物发生化学反应，最终形成一种超弹性耐久材料，以满足轮胎的性能要求。对轮胎硫化过程进行研究不仅有助于制造高质量的轮胎，而且可以节约制造成本。

与其他材料（如金属）相比，橡胶的热扩散系数非常低，轮胎内部每一点的温度历程都不一样，导致温度和硫化程度分布不均，简单的等温硫化曲线已经不能用来评价橡胶的硫化程度。可以使用两种方法解决此问题，一种是通过热电偶测出轮胎内部关键点处的温度历程，如胎肩、胎冠和胎圈等较厚的地方，再应用合理的动力学模型把各点温度转化为硫化程度，以此确定硫化的必要时间。但配方设计和边界温度的改变将影响硫化反应过程，进而影响橡胶的最终交联密度和机械性能。而且每次试验后，必须把轮胎割开，找出热电偶的位置，因此，成本高、时间长。另一种方法是基于计算机仿真的数值技术，可以预测出轮胎内部每一点的温度和硫化程度，有助于减少轮胎开发成本和缩短研发周期。

Toth[1]首次使用有限元法模拟了轮胎的硫化过程，并研究了初始温度对硫化的影响。Han[2]建立了在平板硫化机上轮胎硫化的二维轴对称模型，使用自己开发的软件求解系统方程，之后Han[3]使用这个模型优化了轮胎硫化工艺。White[4]开发了一款模拟轮胎硫化过程的商业软件VACAM-LAB，利用FE技术计算产品在升温和降温过程中温度变化的不均匀性。闫相桥[5]开发了轮胎硫化有限元计算软件，模拟某卡车轮胎的硫化过程，采用各向异性模型模拟钢丝-帘线符合材料的热物性参数变化。Ghoreishy[6-7]使用HSTAR软件建立了一套完整的轿车轮胎硫化的二维轴对称模型。其中，硫化动力学方程由自编软件求解，模型包括胶囊和金属模具，并与测温试验比较。Ghoreishy[8]综述了橡胶硫化有限元分析中的若干问题，并以某子午线轮胎为例，对其进行了有限元模拟。然而，上述研究缺少对橡胶材料和橡胶-帘线复合材料的热物性以及硫化动力学模型等问题的深入研究，尤其橡胶-帘线复合材料的热物性变化规律。

为此，本文结合作者在橡胶硫化领域现有研究成果，研究建立橡胶-帘线复合材料的热物性参数模型，并运用有限元技术对某全钢子午线轮胎硫化过程进行现场测温试验和数值模拟，分析轮胎焦烧、温度和硫化程度等参数的变化，研究了轮胎预热温度、蒸汽温度和胶囊厚度对轮胎硫化性能的影响。

（3）实例3

Investigation on Egg-shaped Pressure Hulls

1. Introduction

The deep-sea manned submersible plays an important role in oceanic exploration and deep-sea research. As one of the most critical components in a deep manned submersible system, the pressure hull provides a safe living and working space for crews and some non-pressure-resisting/non-water-repellent equipment. The weight of the manned pressure hull ac-counts for almost 1/3 of the total weight of a submersible. Therefore, the pressure hull should be designed to optimally coordinate safety, buoyancy reserve, space efficiency etc. [1-4].

As is well known, due to its efficiency to bear the external high hydrostatic pressure in deep sea, spherical pressure hull is the most extensively used structure for the deep manned submersibles, where the stresses and strains are equally distributed throughout when the pressure hull is subjected to high hydrostatic pressure in deep sea. In brief, the spherical pressure hull has advantages of good mechanical properties, low buoyancy factor and efficient material utilization [5, 6]. However, the spherical pressure hull is meanwhile with difficult interior arrangement, and especially it is a highly imperfection-sensitive structure [7,8]. Any small changes in geometry such as a tiny imperfection may lead to a significant drop of the buckling load. These limitations have prevented to some extent from making a breakthrough on design for the better overall performance of a pressure hull of deep manned submersibles.

In order to resolve these deficiencies, since some years ago, researchers have proposed many kinds of novel and unconventional geometric forms of shells, such as toroidal structure [9], teardrop shaped hull [6], connected spheres [10] and shaped circular cylinder [6] etc. However, as we know, due to the manufacturing difficulties in welding and machining these novel shaped metal body made of either HY steel, or titanium alloy, or aluminium alloy, and required with very high accuracy standard, these novel structural geometries have not been extensively applied, and most of these investigations and designs were theoretical research, or say, mostly just on "paper work" stage. With the rapid development of new materials, e. g. fiber reinforced composite material, and also with related new manufacturing techniques, the above manufacturing difficulty does not possess any longer as big a problem on such like novel/unconventional forms of pressure hull structures as in the "metal age" before. For example, with the modern winding technique in fiber reinforced composites, you can easily manufacture any revolving shell structures even with variable thickness of optimised design. These developments in material area have provided a big space to improve the optimisation of design for pressure hull, including geometry design.

Eggshell is a thin-walled shell of revolution, with multifocal surfaces of positive Gaussian curvature [11]. It has advantages of amazing weight-to-strength ratio, proper span-to-thickness ratio, rational streamline, satisfactory aesthetics and reasonable material distribution [12, 13]. Eggshell can withstand extremely high loads by membrane actionwhen subjected to uniform pressure, for the material is used to its full strength [14e16]. For example, the eggshell provides the egg with anexternal support using the dome principle to obtain enough strength and stability, with economy in building material and without requirement of ribs [14, 16]. Likewise, the pressure hull is also a thin-walled shell structure subjected to hydrostatic pressure, requiring excellent characteristics such as safety, material economy, inner space and hydrodynamics [17]. Obviously the eggshell could provide effective biological information for the design of the pressure hull with unconventional geometry. Authors' previous research work has demonstrated that the goose egg-shaped pressure hull has a favorable pressure resis-tance, which could provide guides for the development of a new type of the manned pressure hull [17, 18]. These findings prompt us to further explore the design method and properties of egg-shaped pressure hulls.

The manned pressure hull is a shell structure with closed space. One of the limit states considered during its design process is the loss of stability, which generates considerable recent interest. There are mainly three ways to tackle this problem: analytical formulations, numerical simulations and experimental investigations. Analytical solutions have the advantage to use abacuses and simple formulae to give the global and local buckling load of shell. However, this method is not appropriate for shells with complex shapes, boundary conditions and loadings. And it is difficult to analyze imperfect shells considering geometrical and material nonlinearity [19, 20]. As a result, analytical approaches always lead to apparent discrepancies be-tween theoretical and experimental results. Numerical simulations are then commonly applied to undertake buckling ana-lyses of shell structures, for which reliable analytical solutions are not available in current literature. The realistic buckling resistance of a shell structure with imperfections can be determined by both geometry and material nonlinear analysis (GMNIA) [21]. Finally, experimental investigations are straightforwardways to perform buckling analysis for shell structures. However, it is impossible to directly investigate buckling behavior of a shell structure by experiments during the early design stage. Moreover, experimental investigations are time consuming and require high cost and complex equipment. Consequently, the use of numerical simulations is widely considered as a replacement of experimental investigations, although some complex physical problems can be only solved by combination of experimental and numerical activities [22].

Based on previous bionic research work [17], this paper proposed two goose egg-shaped pressure hulls respectively with constant and variable thickness. The yielding loads and buckling loads of pressure hulls with geometric imperfections are specially investigated by numerical analyses. The egg-shaped pressure hulls are also compared with the equivalent spherical pressure hull on overall performance of strength, stability, buoyancy reserve, space efficiency. Buckling loads of these different types of pressure hulls, respectively with similar geometric imperfections, are further studied to estimate their imperfection sensitivities. It seems that the egg-shaped pressure hull is quite less sensitive to the geometric imperfections, for which it is convenient to be manufactured and to open holes on the hull.

(4) 实例4

Buckling of Egg-shaped Shells Subjected to External Pressure

1. Introduction

Shells of revolution have received considerable attention for applications such as underwater pressure hulls, space vehicles, pressure vessels, and pressure tanks. The most frequently investigated structures are cylindrical, conical, and spherical shells and their combinations [1,2]. Non-typical shapes such as ellipsoidal [3], parabolical [4], and hyperboloidal [5] shells have also been studied. However, such shells tend to lose stability when subjected to external pressure [6].

An effective means for increasing the load carrying capacity of shells is the incorporation of a shell of revolution that has a positive Gaussian curvature. For example, a spherical shell is widely accepted to be an ideal solution because of the extremely efficient stress and strain distributions in the material [7-9]. However, it has been found to be highly imperfection sensitive; moreover, the spherical configuration renders the housing of equipment or human beings difficult. A substantial quantity of research has focused on shells of revolution with non-typical meridional configurations [10].

The barreled shell is an apt example that combines the advantages of spherical and cylindrical shells. It is a cylindrical shell that has a meridional curvature. The buckling of barreled shells has been inves-tigated in recent years. Jasion and Magnucki, for instance, proposed a set of barreled shells with the Cassini oval [11], clothoidal-spherical [12], and circular arc meridians [13]. They provided buckling results for these shells that were obtained using analytical or numerical methods. Furthermore, Blachut detailed the results of the numerical and experimental study into the buckling behavior of barreled shells that have meridians in the form of circular arcs [14] and generalized ellipses [15]. Close agreement between the numerical predictions and the experimental data was obtained.

The eggshell is a desirable configuration for supporting uniform pressure by membrane action. It has advantages such as an excellent load capacity, weight-to-strength ratio, span-to-thickness ratio, and aesthetic appeal [16]. In previous studies, we have proposed a set of egg-shaped pressure hulls based on the geometric functions of various bird eggshells [17, 18]. We have found that goose egg-shaped shells could meet the requirements of safety, space utilization, riding comfort, and hydrodynamics. However, previous research has considered only elastic buckling; moreover, the size of the shell was selected according to experience. The effect of the shape index (SI) on the buckling behavior of egg-shaped shells was not investigated.

This paper focuses on a family of egg-shaped shells that have a constant capacity and mass. The geometric properties of these shells were determined on the basis of the geometric properties of goose eggs. Their linear buckling behavior was analyzed numerically and analyti-cally. The nonlinear buckling behavior of such shells, including the initial geometric imperfections, was analyzed using the finite element method. This paper presents a new design method for non-typical shells of revolution based on a bionic perspective.

第 3 章 方法撰写

3.1 通用模板

方法的主要作用在于告诉读者"What do you do?",提供试验或者建模的详细信息,以便读者可以重复论文方法并得出相似结果。更重要的是,作者还应分享自己对所用方法的观点或看法,让读者理解并接受该方法。为此,一篇论文的方法通常应包括方法引言、细节描述、对比引用、问题说明四个方面内容,如图 3-1 所示。

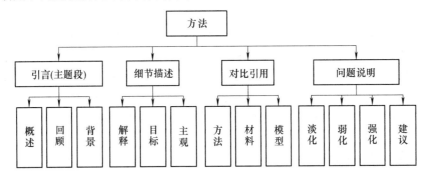

图 3-1 方法部分结构

3.1.1 方法引言

为了增加阅读友好性、将读者带入该部分,针对方法部分写出一段引言(即方法部分的主题段)是非常有必要的。写法如下:①概述试验次数、材料数量等工作总量,或者说明研究的目的,给读者留下总体印象;②介绍材料或者研究对象的背景、来源、成分等;③回顾前言部分的研究目标,或者希望解决的问题。总之,通过引言的给出,方法部分会呈现出总分结构,增加阅读友好性。

3.1.2 细节描述

方法部分不但要详细描述做了什么,还应指出为什么要这样做。对于细节描述,其信息量越多、越全面越好,由于作者对论文试验的材料、剂量、设备、软件、步骤等非常熟悉,这就很容易遗漏方法中一些的关键信息,进而无法保证读者可以重复论文的试验、得到相似结果,这样审稿人或者读者就很容易对论文结果提出质疑。

同样地,论文中这样做的原因对作者自己来说是心知肚明,而对读者来说则一无所知,带来一些无谓的猜想,进而可能让读者无法认同所用方法,对论文产生较差的印象。有时候,可以提供一些背景信息来说明为什么这样做,例如,指出选择某一材料的原因在于该材料具有哪些特性,选择某一设备、模型或软件的原因在于它们具有哪些特定的功能或者希望达到什么效果。

此外，在细节描述语句中，应加入大量生动而主观性的词汇（形容词、副词），来体现作者已对其试验有了非常专业的认知，非常小心谨慎地完成了其试验。这些词汇包括：小心地（carefully）、紧紧地（tightly）、精确地（accurately）。

3.1.3 对比引用

鉴于论文所用方法不可能全是作者自己创造的，或多或少会参考现有文献中的方法。在这种情况下，适当引用这些文献有助于简化对方法的描述，使得审稿人或读者认为作者具有良好的学术道德。另一方面，即使加上参考文献引用，为了扩大读者群，作者也要适当描述试验流程、设备、材料等内容，避免让读者再去花时间和精力查阅引文内容。此外，还应通过合适的语句，向读者说明自己所用方法与现有文献的相似性和差异性。

3.1.4 问题说明

理论上，每种方法都或多或少存在缺点或问题。在方法中指出这些问题，可以给审稿人或读者比较好的印象，避免他们提出严厉的质疑，这样做也可以表明作者自己的专业性，同时为解释结果中可能存在的不足打下伏笔。此外，指出问题也可以为下一篇论文或下一步试验提供参考，推动科学研究不断进步。需要注意的是，还应通过合适的语句来说明问题，尽量向"淡化问题""弱化责任""强化优点""提出建议"4个方面努力。

3.2 方法引言模板句

All/both/each/many/most/the majority (of) (the) tests/(the) samples/(the) trials/(the) experiments/(the) equipment/(the) chemicals/(the) models/(the) instruments/(the) materials【主语】is/are (was/were)【谓语】commercially available/ acquired (from/by)/carried out/chosen/conducted/collected/devised/found in/generated (by)/ modified/ obtained (from/by)/performed (by/in)/provided (by)/ purchased (from)/supplied (by)/used as supplied/investigated

经典例句

All reactions were performed in a 27 mL glass reactor…

In the majority of the tests, buffers with a pH of 8 were used in order to…

Both experiments were performed in a greenhouse so that…

The material investigated was a standard aluminium alloy; all melts were modified with sodium.

Topographical examination was carried out using a 3-D stylus instrument.

The experiments were conducted at a temperature of 0.5℃.

Five pairs of laboratory scale domes were tested. Each pair had nominally identical geometry.

Four pairs of nominally identical cones, (C1, C2), (C3, C4), (C4, C5) were tested under hydrostatic pressure, axial compression, and arbitrarily chosen combined loading, respectively.

Buckling tests on 10 laboratory scale cones were carried out in order to benchmark the numerical predictions of the load carrying capacity.

A number of coupons of 12.5mm width and 50mm gauge length were prepared in accordance with BS EN 10002: 2001 [21],

All domes were measured at 10 mm intervals along the meridian for 16 meridians. ...

All the domes were measured for both shape and thickness.

Material properties of steel were obtained experimentally by testing standard 10mm diameter round coupons cut out from the billet.

This study involved sampling and analyzing 10 spherical shells to determine their buckling behaviors.

Analysis of a shell structure should cover three states: pre-buckling, buckling and post-buckling state.

All seven shells were hemispherical, without any cylindrical flange.

3.3 细节描述模板句

（1）指明原因（目的）

because *	provide a way of (+ -ing)
by doing..., we were able to	selected on the basis of...
chosen for (+ noun)	so as to (+ infinitive)
chosen to (+ infinitive)	so/such that
for the purpose of (+ -ing or noun) **	so (+ -ing)
for the sake of (+ -ing or noun)	thereby (+ -ing)
in an attempt to (+ infinitive)	therefore *
in order to (+ infinitive)	thus (+ -ing)
it was possible to (+ infinitive)	to (+ infinitive)
offer a means of (+ -ing)	to take advantage of
one way to avoid...	which/this allows/allowed etc.
our aim was to (+ infinitive)	with the intention of (+ -ing)

经典例句

For the sake of simplicity, only a single value was analysed.

The purpose of the circumferential strain gauges was to observe the experimental buckling modes in the circumferential directions.

The cylinder was constructed from steel, which avoided problems of water absorption.

For this purpose, we assume that the buckling modes have the form of Legendre polynomials with an exponential function as a modulating factor. Since

The advantage of using three-dimensional analysis was that the out-of plane stress field could be obtained.

Domes were machined in pairs, to demonstrate repeatability of the experiment and also act as a safeguard should one of the pair be damaged

It is customary to use the eigen shape as the possible shape of initial geometric imperfection and scale it as a function of the wall thickness.

Four round specimens were also cut from the same tube, along its axial length, <u>in order to establish the material properties.</u>

Nonlinear analysis based on an incremental method <u>permits</u> to create equilibrium paths.

<u>A big advantage of the nonlinear analysis is that it allows us to introduce</u> geometrical imperfections into the model and

The model has been subjected to uniform external pressure p <u>that is a typical load for</u> submersibles, underground tanks or aboveground tanks during emptying process.

<u>The most comprehensive approach adopted in the current paper uses the FE models</u> based on measured geometry and on measured wall thickness.

The post-buckling analyses have been <u>performed with the use of the arc length method available in the ANSYS code.</u>

The linear analysis performed in such a system <u>gives us not only the value of a critical load but also the picture of a buckling shape.</u>

The polyvinyl alcohol solution is less dense than the oil; <u>as a result</u>, after the droplets are produced and collected, the light inner water droplets gradually rise within them.

（2）主观描述

Accurately/always/appropriately/at least

Carefully/completely/constantly/correctly/directly

Exactly/entirely/firmly/frequently/freshly/fully/gently

Immediately/independently/individually/precisely

Randomly/rapidly/reliably/repeatedly

Rigorously/separately/smoothly/successfully/suitably

Tightly/thoroughly/uniformly/vigorously

经典例句

The thicknesses of each sample were measured <u>at least three times.</u>

The specimen was <u>monitored constantly</u> for a whole period.

The samples were <u>slowly and carefully pressurized</u> to collapse.

Each dome was thermoset between <u>accurately machined</u> male and female aluminium alloy moulds.

Failure of each dome was <u>accompanied by a small bang, together with a small spurt</u> of water.

The cylinder is assumed to <u>be fully clamped at one end.</u>

It would be interesting to <u>see carefully conducted</u> experiments in order to check validity of the FE predictions.

The shell wall pieces had to be cut from the sheets <u>as precisely as possible</u>, <u>in order to get exact</u> circumferential lengths along their end circles.

In the first phase a <u>high-precision</u> extensiometer was used which produced <u>exact</u> stree-strain curves.

Before testing, the domes <u>were carefully measured</u> for any variations in shape and thickness.

The boundary conditions at the base of the dome <u>were set to fully clamped.</u>

This arbor was then mounted in a lathe, coated with a releasing agent, preheated, and then slowly rotated as the liquid epoxy resin mixture was poured evenly over its surface.

A shell is loaded with uniform external pressure only.

From the PSD the root mean square (rms) of the amplitude can directly be calculated as the square root of the area under the spectrum.

One has to separately check the sensitivity in spherical cap and in the knuckle.

3.4 对比引用模板句

（1）与现有方法完全一样

according to	can be found in
as described by/in	details are given in
as explained by/in	given by/in
as in	identical to
as proposed by/in	in accordance with
as reported by/in	the same as that of/in
as suggested by/in	using the method of/in

注意：in 后面接别人工作（in Blachut et al. (2008)）；by 后面接人或者团队（by Blachut）。

（2）与现有方法部分相似

a (modified) version of	(very) similar
adapted from	almost the same
based in part/partly on	essentially the same
based on	largely the same
essentially identical	practically the same
in line with	virtually the same
in principle	with some adjustments
in essence	with some alterations
more or less identical	with some changes
slightly modified	with some modifications

（3）与现有方法差别很大

a novel step was…	partly based on
adapted from	although in many ways similar
in line with	although in some ways similar
loosely based on	although in essence similar
partially based on	with the following

注意：当所用方法与现有方法差别很大时，需要特别指出具体相差的内容。

经典例句

More details can be found in Ref. [17].

And it is designed according to Ref. [15].

A number of coupons of 12.5mm width and 50mm gauge length were prepared in accordance with BS EN 10002:2001 [21].

An intermediate method is re-commended as a "less onerous" approach, which is based on a combination of LBA and MNA.

... using eigenvector-affine imperfection. Adapted from Ref. [48].

These expressions are identical to the relations used in Refs. 1, 4, and 5 except for the extra terms.

The volume of water contained in the tank is considered constant (3500m^3), adopting a different maximum fluid level for each of the models analysed (however, modifications at the upper level are small).

It leads to shells with the thickness described by smooth functions, and the present paper will, in principle, be confined to such structures.

The problems are solved by a modified method of finite differences eliminating rigid displacement errors.

The coupons for this work were designed and tested according to Chinese Standard (GB/T 228.1-2010) [15], which is in line with ISO 6892-1: 2009 [16].

The protein was overexpressed and purified as reported previously. 10, 12.

In our implementation we followed Sato et al. (1998) by using a discrete kernel size.

The size of the Gaussians was adjusted as in [2].

Our numerical model is similar to ones used in other studies of the buckling of both uniform and nonuniform shells under pressure.

We fabricate monodisperse thin-shelled capsules using water-in-oil-in-water (W = O = W) droplets prepared by microfluidics [24, 25].

3.5 问题说明模板句

(1) 淡化问题

did not align precisely	minor deficit
only approximate	slightly disappointing
it is recognized that	negligible
less than ideal	unimportant
not perfect	immaterial
not identical	a preliminary attempt
slightly problematic	not significant
rather time-consuming	

(2) 弱化责任

limited by	inevitably

necessarily	(it was) difficult to
impractical	unavoidable
as far as possible	impossible
(it was) hard to	not possible

(3) 强化优点

acceptable	quite good
fairly well	reasonably robust

(4) 提出建议

future work should…	currently in progress
future work will…	currently underway

注意:"future work should"表明作者指出了未来的工作方向,邀请同行来共同研究;"future work will"表明作者下一步的工作计划。

经典例句

Inevitably, considerable computation was involved.

The observed discrepancy between measured and calculated results is inevitably attributed to the imperfections of shells.

Unfortunately crack formation due to the rheological phenomena occurring in concrete is unavoidable, but whenever compression prevails in the shell mechanical behaviour cracks tend to close and their dissemination is more limited.

Only a brief observation was feasible, however, given the number in the sample.

Although centrifugation could not remove all the excess solid drug, the amount remaining was negligible.

Within the elastic domain it is immaterial what the loading path is.

Although testing produces a reliable assessment of their, it is often time consuming and expensive.

These tests indicated some tendency for the material to creep but it was felt that this had negligible effect on our test results.

Solutions using ($q = 1$) differed slightly from the analytical solutions.

Continuing research will examine a string of dc-dc converters to determine if the predicted efficiencies can be achieved in practice.

While the anode layer was slightly thicker than 13 μm, this was a minor deficit.

Even with this limitation, the RSA can be implemented in special purpose finite element codes to estimate reasonably accurate know-down factors that could be acceptable in most applications.

However, most FDM systems provide good, acceptable accuracy and surface finish for most engineering design applications

In a certain range of the amplitude a, the effect of neglecting the quartic terms in the expression of the energy functional will be small and will be acceptable for engineering.

3.6 经典范文分析

（1）范文 1

深海球形耐压壳力学特性研究

2 球形耐压壳有限元数值研究

以对载人球形耐压壳在 6km 水深的工作条件下进行计算，设计厚度为 75mm。考察网格划分形式、单元类型和单元密度等因素对计算结果的影响。*(方法引言)*

2.1 壳单元方案

采用 pro/e 软件，进行三维 CAD 建模，并抽取中面，采用 ANSA 前处理软件，进行网格划分。计算载荷以均布压力形式施加在耐压壳表面。耐压壳理论上是不受任何约束的，为了消除模型的刚性位移，选择三个点，限制其六个自由度的位移。求得的各约束反力接近 0，说明所施加的约束为虚约束，仅限制了方案的刚体位移。*(问题说明·淡化问题)* 现对 2 种工况进行分析：（1）线性准静态分析；（2）线性屈曲分析。采用 ABAQUS/Standard 进行计算，并运用 ABAQUS/Viewer 进行后处理。采用单因素控制变量法建立不同网格划分形式、单元类型、单元密度下的数值方案，进行分析计算。*(细节描述)*

采用随机划分、钱币划分、网球划分三种划分形式，它们分别对应于方案 1、方案 2、方案 3。单元类型为 4 节点完全积分线性壳单元（S4），网格单元数量约为 6500。对于单元类型，采用 4 节点完全积分线性壳单元（S4）、4 节点减缩积分壳单元（S4R）、每个节点 5 个自由度的 4 节点减缩积分壳单元（S4R5）、8 节点双曲厚壳单元（S8R）、每节点 5 个自由度的 8 节点双曲厚壳单元（S8R5），它们分别对应于方案 3、方案 4、方案 5、方案 6、方案 7。这些方案均采用网球划分的形式，单元数、节点数与方案 3 一致。对于数值方案，需要进行网格的收敛性检查来验证方案结果的正确性。分别采用平均尺寸为 200mm、120mm、100mm、70mm、60mm、45mm、35mm、20mm 的网格进行计算，分别对应于方案 8、方案 9、方案 10、方案 11、方案 3、方案 12、方案 13、方案 14，单元类型均为 S4，均采用网球划分，具体信息如表 1 所示。*(细节描述)*

2.2 体单元方案

体单元网格方案可以通过壳单元网格沿厚度方向偏移 4 层单元得到，其中的载荷、边界、工况与壳单元一致。*(主题句)* 首先，根据方案 3 的网格，建立体单元方案，单元类型设定为三维 8 节点体单元（C3D8）、三维 8 节点减缩积分体单元（C3D8R）、三维 8 节点非协调模式体单元（C3D8I）、三维 20 节点体单元（C3D20）、三维 20 节点减缩积分体单元（C3D20R），它们分别对应于方案 15、方案 16、方案 17、方案 18、方案 19。此外，分别采用周向平均尺寸为 200mm、120mm、100mm、70mm、45mm、35mm、20mm 的网格进行计算，分别对应于方案 20、方案 21、方案 22、方案 23、方案 24、方案 25、方案 26，这些方案的网格分别由方案 8、方案 9、方案 10、方案 11、方案 12、方案 13、方案 14 的网格沿厚度方向偏移所得，单元类型均为 C3D20R，具体信息如表 2 所示。*(细节描述)*

(2) 范文2

Buckling of Spherical Shells Subjected to External Pressure: A Comparison of Experimental and Theoretical Data

2. Materials andmethods

This study involved sampling and analyzing 10 spherical shells to determine their buckling behaviors. A series of tests were performed to obtain the geometric and buckling properties of these shells in addition to their material properties. (*方法引言*)

2.1. Shell manufacturing and testing

Each spherical shellwas manufactured using the tungsten inert gas butt welding of two coupled hemispherical shells, after which the excess of the weld has been removed by grinding and then been polished. (*主题句*) Each hemispherical shell was cut and stamped from 304 thin stainless steel sheets with a nominal thickness of either 0.4 mm or 0.7 mm. Ten spherical shells with a nominal diameter of 150 mm were manufactured for the tests. Five of them were fabricated from a 0.4-mm-thick sheet and were denoted as t0.4-1, t0.4-2, t0.4-3, t0.4-4, and t0.4-5. Five other shells were fabricated from a 0.7-mm-thick sheet and were denoted as t0.7-1, t0.7-2, t0.7-3, t0.7-4, and t0.7-5. In addition, all the shells were not stress relieved during the manufacturing process because the ratios of the wall thickness to the nominal diameter were very low. (*问题说明*) Before the spherical shells were tested, the wall thickness and geometric shape were measured for all the shells.

……

2.2. Material properties

In cases of uniform external pressure, the buckling behaviors of spherical shells are determined according to the compression stress-strain behavior of the relevant material. However, experiments to demonstrate such behaviors with thin-walled structures are extremely difficult to conduct. Therefore, the compression behavior of steel is assumed to be the same as its tension behavior. (*方法引言, 问题说明*) This hypothesis has been frequently used in the buckling prediction of various shells of revolution loaded by external pressure [7, 9, 14]. (*对比引用*) Thus, the material properties of steel sheets can be established by testing a series of flat tension coupons.

The coupons for this work were designed and tested according to Chinese Standard (GB/T 228.1-2010) [15], which is in line with ISO 6892-1: 2009 [16]. (*主题句, 对比引用*) They were cut along the rolling directions of the same sheets that were used to manufacture spherical shells for ensuring accurate material data. Five coupons were selected for each thickness and subjected to uniaxial tension. Two of them were strain-gauged in the transverse and longitudinal directions to obtain Poisson's ratio (ν) for the material and to verify the extensometer readings. (*细节描述 - 主观词汇 + 指明原因/目的*) The average values were 0.277 for the 0.4-mm-thick sheet and 0.291 for the 0.7-mm-thick sheet. Other coupons were tested to obtain accurate stress-strain curves, which can be demonstrated in the following form: …… where E is Young's modulus, σ_{yp} is the yield strength based on 0.2% proof stress, and n and k are the strain hardening parameters. The values of these coefficients, as well as the average values, are listed in Table 3. The testing coupons were numbered and named according to the thickness and coupon number; one name, for example, was t0.4-c1, where t0.4 indicates that the thickness of the sheet was 0.4 mm, and c1 indicates that the coupon number was one. The variance of coefficients for each thickness was very small. *（细节描述－主观词汇）*

3.7 实例练习

运用所学知识，仿照 3.6 节，分析以下实例。
（1）实例 1

硬土-软土插桩过程数值分析及验证

2 数值模型

2.1 模型建立

基于 Hossain M S 土工离心模型试验 [10] 建立插桩过程数值模型（见图2），分为桩靴、欧拉区、硬土、软土4部分，由于结构、边界条件的对称性，采用1/4模型建模，在对称面上施加对称边界。①由于桩靴变形非常小，故定义为刚体模型，并在刚体参考点上施加 0.2 m/s 恒定速度来进行插桩过程的准静态分析，桩靴直径为 D。②在硬土层上方定义高度为 D 的欧拉区（该区域材料为空），以模拟土面隆起现象。③采用三维减缩积分欧拉单元模拟土壤，土体尺寸为径向 6D、垂向 10D [10]。为了保证数值计算的稳定性，泊松比取为 0.49，弹性模量对插桩结果影响不大 [8-9，11]，取为土壤剪切强度的 500 倍 [6，11]。此外，在模型中施加土壤有效重度所产生的初始应力场。

为了解决土壤大变形所导致的网格扭曲问题，采用欧拉网格离散土壤、采用拉格朗日网格离散桩靴。在对土壤进行离散时，在桩靴可能经过的区域采用小尺寸网格，越远离该区域的部分网格尺寸越大。

目前大多数研究者将插桩过程中桩靴和土壤间的接触简化为完全光滑接触或完全粗糙接触，这2种情况下计算出的插桩阻力最大相差5%，对土壤流动过程几乎没有影响 [7-9]，因此，本文不考虑桩靴和土壤间的摩擦，采用加强沉浸边界法模拟桩靴和土壤间的相互作用。

（2）实例 2

轮胎硫化过程数值分析及试验研究

2 轮胎硫化试验

为了验证数值模型的正确性，基于热电偶轮胎硫化测温法，使用轮胎硫化测温系统（图2（a）），结合 T 型热电偶进行轮胎硫化测温试验，热电偶的测试精度为 ±0.5℃，试验中每20s记录一次数据。待测轮胎为某全钢子午线轮胎，直径、断面宽和断面高分别为 1048，268 和 263mm。在主成型毂上把 6 个热电偶埋入轮胎内部（图3），其中，1#为反包端部，2#为胎侧外部，3#为垫胶中心，4#为带束层端部，5#为胎冠中心表面，6#为胎冠中心底部. 将成型后的水胎放入平板硫化机内进行硫化（图 2 (b)）。金属模具 2 和 3、胶囊 1 和轮胎的初始温度分别为 120、100 和 30℃，机内硫化时间为 52min，胶囊在前 5min 水温由 180℃线性降至 170℃，而后温度保持不变；加热金属模具的蒸汽温度在前 6min 保持 120℃恒温不变，后 8min 由 120℃线性升至 151℃，之后的 38min 保持 151℃恒温不变。轮胎出模后置于 40℃空气中，橡胶在余热的作用下继续进行交联反应。硫化测温系统用于记录轮胎 6 个测试点在平板硫化机内升温硫化过程以及在空气中后硫化过程的温度历程。

(3) 实例 3

Investigation on Egg-shaped Pressure Hulls

2 Material and methods

The current investigation involves the egg-shaped pressure hull with the constant thickness (EPHC), the egg-shaped pressure hull with the variable thickness (EPHV), and the spherical pressure hull (SPH). These pressure hulls are designed with the same volume, equivalent yield strength and material for the purpose of comparison. On the one hand, contour and size of the three pressure hulls are determined referring to Chinese deep manned submersible 'JiaoLong' [23]. On the other hand, equations for thickness and buoyancy factor of each pressure hull are provided by analytical formulations.

2.1 Contour and size of pressure hulls

It is well known that many of the spherical pressure hulls in current deep manned submersibles are with radius of around 1m, such as 'Jiaolong' of China for example [23]. This size provides a suitable working condition for crews of three and necessary equipment. This size is then used to be equivalent reference for designing the compared egg-shaped pressure hulls. The contour of egg-shaped shells (EPHC/EPHV) is determined based on the goose egg-shaped function developed by Narushin [26], as shown in Equation (1). The size of the EPHC/EPHV is designed to be the same as the volume of the spherical pressure hull with radius of 1m. According to Equation (1), the length L and the width B of the EPHC/EPHV are 2.453 m and 1.836 m, respectively. Fig. 1 shows the contour of the EPHC/ EPHV.

For the spherical pressure hull (SPH) subjected to the hydrostatic pressure, stress is equally distributed, so the thickness is designed to be constant. But for the egg-shaped pressure hull with the constant thickness (EPHC), stress of the material along the major axis is variable. Therefore, both of the EPHV and the EPHC were proposed in this paper. For the EPHV, in order to save material and reduce buoyancy factor, thickness in the middle part is designed to be variable, so as to make the von Mises equivalent stress in this part constant. The thickness of each pressure hull is detailed in section 2.2.

In addition, the design load of pressure hulls is calculated with Equation (2) [24]. Since some reduction factors are included in this equation, it is suitable for classical design of pressure hulls. It should be noted that no additional reduction factors will be added when geometry and material nonlinear analyses with imperfections (GMNIA) are implemented to determine the buckling load of the pressure hull.

It should be pointed out here that, although the final aim of our research work is to make the application of carbon fiber reinforced polymer (CFRP), which is well known as layered, orthotropic material, such material behaviour can be readily dealt with at the expense of introducing much more parameters into the problem. However neither the physical principles involved in the analyses nor the general character of the results will change. For simplicity reasons the properties of the pressure hull material are assumed homogeneous, linearly elastic. The material property data of pressure hulls is then still temporarily referring to that of Ti-6Al-4V(TC4), which has been frequently used in deep manned submersibles [25]. Its mechanical parameters are as follows: …. And the relationship between stress and plastic strain of TC4 can be found in Fig. 2 [25].

2.2 Design of egg-shaped pressure hulls

In this section, yielding and buckling load of a perfect egg-shaped shell are analyzed firstly. Then, thickness and buoyancy factor of egg-shaped and spherical pressure hulls are determined.

2.2.1 Strength and stability of a perfect egg-shaped shell

In accordance with membrane theory in shells of revolution under external pressure [24], the meridional stress $\sigma_\varphi(x)$ and the circumferential stress $\sigma_\theta(x)$ of the egg-shaped shell are calculated with Equations (3) and (4), respectively. Then, the von Mises equivalent stress $\sigma_{r4}(x)$ of the egg-shaped shell is obtained from Equations (3) and (4), listed in Equation (5).

……

(4) 实例4

Buckling of Egg-shaped Shells Subjected to External Pressure

2. Geometry of the egg-shaped shell

The geometry of a typical eggshell is illustrated in Fig. 1. It consists of a sharp end, equator, and blunt end arranged along the major axis (axis of revolution).

The radius of the circumference of a shell of revolution is provided in Cartesian coordinates by Eq. (1), which is an egg-shaped equation proposed by Narushin [19, 20]. This equation has been widely applied for describing the contour of eggshells. Consequently, this equation is used to define the geometry of the middle surface of the egg-shaped shell. To facilitate the creation of a family of egg-shaped shells, the following variable for determining the SI (i.e., the ratio of the minor B to major L axis) is introduced: $SI = B/L$. This parameter determines the geometry of the egg-shaped shell. As shown in Fig. 2, for $SI = 0$, the egg-shaped shell is an infinitely long cylindrical shell. When $0 < SI < 1$, an egg-shaped shell is obtained. For $SI = 1$, the egg-shaped shell approximates a spherical shell. Therefore, the cylindrical shell and spherical shell, which are described by the dashed lines in Fig. 2, can be treated as particular instances of the egg-shaped shell.

Egg SIs differ greatly among the world's bird species [21]. Our previous studies have demonstrated that the goose egg can provide a guide for developing a new type of manned pressure hull [18]. The range of *SI*s in this study was determined on the basis of the experimental results of 333 eggs (6 days old) from 2-year-old geese. The eggs were selected from Jiangshan farm, located in Zhejiang Province, China. To obtain the *SI*s, the major L and minor B axes of the eggs were carefully measured using a digital caliper. The *SI* results are shown in Fig. 3; they approximate a normal distribution. The *SI* value is most frequently in the 0.65 to 0.72 range. This range was selected for creating a family of egg-shaped shells with a constant capacity and mass. Besides, to extend the range of *SI*, the shells with *SI*s of 0.4, 0.5, 0.6, 0.8, 0.9 and 1 were also proposed.

3. Capacity and mass of the egg-shaped shell

The capacity of the egg-shaped shell is determined in accordance with Mohsein [22], as follows:

$$V = \frac{\pi}{6}LB^2. \tag{4}$$

The mass of the egg-shaped shell is calculated using the following relationship:

$$m = At\rho, \tag{5}$$

where t is the shell thickness, and ρ is the mass density of the material. The surface area A is determined using a modified version of Mohsein [22]:

$$A = k\pi(LB^2)^{\frac{2}{3}}, \tag{6}$$

where $k = 1.02$ is a correction coefficient. Using (4), (5), and (6), the major (L) and minor (B) axes are calculated as follows:

$$L = \sqrt[3]{\frac{6V}{\pi(\text{SI})^2}}, \tag{7}$$

$$B = \sqrt{\frac{6V}{L\pi}}. \tag{8}$$

Thus, L and B are respectively determined using (7) and (8) by retaining the capacity (V) and mass (m) of the egg-shaped shell constant. It is assumed that $V = 3.1809 \text{m}^3$, $A = 10.4598 \text{m}^2$, $t = 15 \text{mm}$. According to (7) and (8), a family of egg-shaped shells with a constant capacity and mass can be created by calculating the major L and minor B axes. The meridian of this family of shells is identified in Fig. 4.

To verify Narushin's eq. (1) and Mohsein's functions (4) and (6), the contours of 50 goose eggs were carefully measured using the optical 3D scanning method (the eggs were randomly selected from the 333 samples). The experimental contours were expressed in the form of point clouds and automatically transformed into 3D CAD models. The meridians, volumes, and surface areas of the selected eggs were determined and compared with Narushin's and Mohsein's formulas. The difference between the experimental results and Narushin's predictions was determined by Pearson's correlation coefficients, as listed in Table 1. The agreement between the experimental egg shape and the fitted one is very close. Table 2 compares the volumes and surface areas of goose eggs obtained by the tests with those obtained using the formula (4) and (6). As can be seen, the calculations are in close agreement with the experimental data. It may be noted that the difference between the mean surface areas obtained from tests and Eq. (6) is only 0.19%, while the difference would be as many as 2.15% using the original Mohsein's formula, which does not include the correction coefficient k.

第4章 结果分析与讨论撰写

4.1 通用模板

结果分析与讨论是一篇论文最重要的部分,其主要作用在于告诉读者 "What do you find, comment and discuss?",与读者分享自己的试验结果,给出对这些结果的看法,并提出结果问题所在。为此,一篇论文的结果分析与讨论应包括结果引言、图表指示、结果分析、结果讨论、文献对比、问题说明六个方面内容,如图4-1所示。

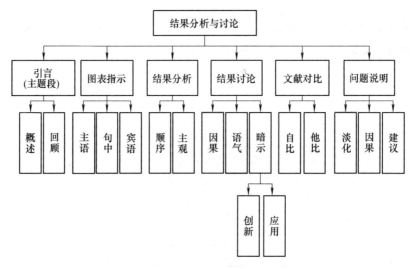

图4-1 结果分析与讨论结构

4.1.1 结果引言

与方法引言相似,为了增加阅读友好性、将读者带入该部分,针对结果分析与讨论部分写出一段引言(即主题段)是非常有必要的。写法如下:①概述该部分的主要内容,引导读者对该部分留下与作者一致的总体印象或观点,从而避免读者通过阅读单个结果,形成自己的、与作者意愿相背的观点;②回顾前文内容,如前言中的共性问题、具体问题、文献综述、研究目标等,以及方法部分的主要内容,提醒读者前面讲了什么。总之,通过引言的给出,结果分析与讨论部分会呈现出总分结构,增加阅读友好性。

4.1.2 图表指示

大部分论文以图表形式来展示其主要研究成果,正所谓一图胜千言,从图表信息即可初步判断论文质量,图表的重要性不言而喻。图表质量、逻辑顺序、呈现方式等对一篇论文来说至关重要。一般地,期刊编辑、审稿人或广大读者会最先阅读论文标题和摘要,其次就是通篇浏览图表，看完图表，可初步决定初审可否通过、审稿是否同意发表、同行能否继续阅读或引用。因此，本书有专门一章来详细阐述学术论文图表处理问题。

然而，仅仅列出图表是远远不够的，作者还需要说出自己对这些图表的看法，向读者一一解释图表，使其同意作者提出的观点、得出的结论，这就需要用文字形式来表达。通过在结果分析与讨论部分指示图表，邀请读者浏览某幅图、某张表，达到图文结合的效果，避免读者通过看图形成与作者不一致的意见。

4.1.3 结果分析

作者应对结果内容进行总体规划，按照一定的逻辑或时间顺序，陈述结果并对其分析，并根据各个结果的重要程度，决定对某些结果进行大篇幅讨论分析。值得注意的是，在详细陈述、分析最为重要的结果之前，需要简要陈述一些潜在的、与重要结果相关的结果，由浅入深，均匀过渡，进而达到高潮。

语言的功能非常强大，可以呈现出图表本身所无法表达的信息。这就要求作者不仅要客观分析图表内容，还应在图表分析中运用大量主观词汇，与读者分享自己对这些图表的看法，引导读者接受作者的观点。例如，理论计算与试验结果相差15%，如果作者说高达15%（as many as），说明误差很大，读者会认为吻合度不高；反之，如果作者说仅为15%（only），说明误差较小，读者会认为吻合良好。

4.1.4 结果讨论

该部分是论文的中枢神经、精华所在，一篇论文之所以称之为论文，其原因在于它包含了大量、细致的讨论。一方面，作者应讨论导致某些结果、出现某些现象或规律的原因，可从材料、方法、结构、工艺等方面讨论，给出因果关系；另一方面，作者还应对讨论进行升华，尝试说明该试验结果表明、暗示、指示或者预示了什么，有什么启示或者言外之意。当然，讨论部分不乏出现大量的情态动词，可以弱化这些讨论的语气，避免审稿人或读者对论文提出严厉的质疑。

4.1.5 文献对比

既然引言部分进行了文献综述、阐述了研究现状，那么这里就要通过与现有文献对比分析来呼应引言，向读者说明自己研究与他人研究的关系，这是作者义务。因此，除了分析与讨论作者自己的试验结果，还需对这些结果进行定位，通过与现有试验结果、理论结果进行对比分析，找出异同点，体现论文的研究意义与价值。

4.1.6 问题说明

与方法部分类似，每篇论文的结果都或多或少存在一些缺点或问题，这就需要在结果分析与讨论中指出这些问题，可以给审稿人或读者比较好的印象，避免他们提出严厉的质疑，这样也可以表明作者自己的专业性，同时为下一篇论文或下一步试验提供方向或建议。需要注意的是，还应通过合适的语句来说明问题，尽量向"淡化问题""给出原因""提出建议"3个方面努力。

4.2 结果引言模板句

(1) 结果概述

generally speaking/in general,

in most/all cases,

in the main/ on the whole

in this section, we compare/evaluate/present…

it is apparent that in all/most/the majority of cases,

it is evident from the results that…

the overall response was…

the results are divided into two parts as follows:

using the method described above, we obtained…

经典例句

In general, these imperfections are unknown in the design phase, thus patterns and amplitude have to be assumed.

In general, a minimum configuration of supports provides an imperfection sensitivity factor near to one.

In all cases, buckling is considered as a static process.

In most of the cases, the failure of stiffened shell structures occurs due to elastic buckling.

For all three cases the worst possible scenario is sought through the application of structural optimization.

Over the whole domain, the results are in very good agreement with those obtained using the concept of a shell of uniform stability.

It is evident from the assumption $d < r$, which corresponds to a sharp edge of the indentation, that the scaling law holds only for sufficiently small bending resistances.

It is evident that the nonlinear response of FGM toroidal shell segments with immovable simply-supported edges under thermoemechanical loads is quite different from the one of movable simply-supported FGM toroidal shell segments subjected to only mechanical loads.

Generally speaking, the pressure on the external shell surface at the windward side varies according to the velocity pressure, apart from the upper region with its edge disturbance.

In this section, the general theory on which this report is based will be described.

In this section, we start by describing the rapid prototyping technique used to fabricate our elastomeric shells containing a well-defined dimplelike defect at their pole.

In this section, the conical shell model has the same geometry and boundary conditions as considered in the preceding section.

A summary of all of the validation results is then presented, followed by an assessment of the numerical accuracy using the probabilistic methodology described above.

More realistic cases of thinning can then be studied using the validated numerical methods.

The statistical methods described above can be used to back calculate the level of confidence associated with a PSF of 1.1 for the mean curve, giving a value of approximately 90%.

(2) 前文回顾

as discussed previously,
as mentioned earlier/before,
as outlined in the introduction,
as reported,
in order to…, we examined…
it is important to reiterate that…
it is known from the literature that…

it was predicted that…
our aim/purpose/intention was to…
since/because…, we investigated…
to investigate…, we needed to…
we reasoned/predicted that…
the aforementioned theory/aim/prediction

经典例句

As previously stated, the strength is also affected by the ratio between the portion of the cross section filled with respect to…

As discussed earlier, hot and cold weather challenges animals in the area of reproduction.

It is predicted from the results of one of the concentric loading tests that the average fracture stress under internal pressure should be 12.6 MPa.

As mentioned earlier, there is a separation of rigid body motions from the total displacements.

As was mentioned earlier, this gives the largest reduction in strength for a given amplitude of shape deviation.

As outlined in section 2, the meridional radius of curvature and the area of meridional cross section of the EPHC/EPHV are 1.30 m.

It is important to reiterate that for some shell stability problems, a linear bifurcation analysis may not adequately represent the shell behavior.

This hypothesis is confirmed by the aforementioned simulations and by experiments, in which shapes with a single dimple are usually observed.

As aforementioned, the imperfection amplitude in this long axial wavelength mode needs to be impractically large to reach the lower bounds to the nonlinear buckling loads.

Using the aforementioned algorithm, we find that for many actuators the energy can suddenly decrease upon inflation.

As predicted, there was a significant positive relationship between mean cuckoo gens eggshell thickness and the rate of egg rejection shown by its host species.

In this case, it is reasoned, as in the theory of beams and thin plates, that the transverse shear stresses are parabolically distributed across the thickness of the shell. Assuming

4.3 图表指示模板句

(1) 图表作为主语

Fig. 1 or Table 1 contains/corresponds(to)/demonstrates/displays/gives/illustrates/lists/plots

Fig. 1 or Table 1 provides/reports/represents/reveals/shows/summarises/presents

经典例句

Figs. 8 and 9 plot the best fit meridian together with the measured data points for C4 and C5.

Table 6 contains the comparison of experimental and theoretical values for shells S3 and S3a. Similar

The figure corresponds to the right part of the plot provided in Fig. 5

Fig. 3 demonstrates a representative schematic dis-tribution of wind pressure based on the above formulations, as well as the uniform wind pressure.

In addition the figure displays the actual response of the real column, which begins to depart from the elastic curve at point.

Table 1 gives a sample of values for the wall thickness, t, and also the amount of barrelling at the equator, D, for several combinations of (n1; n2; n3) values.

Table 1 lists and describes the stages.

Fig. 5 plots the pressure of the buckling transition.

Table 3 provides comparison of numerical results obtained from ABAQUS and BOSOR5 codes corresponding to different modelling of the same barrel.

Fig. 6 reveals that the vertical velocity of leading node 3419 rose with time.

Figs. 9-11 show the vertical dis-placement, velocity and acceleration history of leading node 3419 and trailing node 1783.

Table 2.3 presents some sample critical load parameters furnished by the above stability criterion.

Figure 1 displays typical evolutions for the pressure difference: first a linear increase followed by a drop at first buckling, after which pressure difference varies in a much lesser extent.

Figure 3 presents values of ($\Delta V/V$) from numerical simulations, as a function of a combination of γ and ν translated in 3D parameters.

(3) 图表括在句中

(data not shown)　　　　　　　　　　(see Fig. 1)

(Fig. 1)　　　　　　　　　　　　　　(see Figs. 1-3)

(see also Fig. 1)

经典例句

Semimajor axis of prolate spheroid (Fig. 1)

The undeformed middle surface R (Fig. 1).

The length of all equivalent cylinders is the same and it equals to the length of slant, L (see Fig. 1).

Depending on the structure and loading, the secondary path may be symmetric orasymmetric, and it may rise or fall below the critical buckling load (see Fig. 1.1).

The strain components of the composite conical shell in S, q and z directions are defined as u, v and w, respectively (see, Fig. 1).

As a further complication, the membrane stress distributions often differ considerably from those of the fundamental load cases "uniform axial compression", "uniform circumferential compression" and "torsional shear" (Fig. 1).

In order to illustrate the application of the proposed design method to existing shell structures first consider tank no. 1 in an LNG carrier (see Figs 1 and 4).

Radius of knuckle in torispherc (see Fig. 1a)

The different patterns may have been used together on different individual examples in the same SU, but have never been found combined on fragments from the same piece or refitting set (Figs. 5-7).

An inspection of the contours of thickness for E1 and E3 (see Figs. 13(a) and 13(b)) reveals that at the base, there are three areas of increased thickness and three areas of decreased thickness.

The difference in the two overall shapes is not that great (see Fig. 8e).

In both cases considered the final result is a local dent (see Figs. 11a and b).

This point is detected by a continuous decrease of the load in the force-deformation diagram (see Fig. 1).

In comparison with the curved plate model we find a qualitative agreement (cf. Figs. 8 and 9): The wrinkle amplitude has a prominent peak which is centred in the region of compressive hoop stress, and decays rapidly outside this region.

(3) 图表作为宾语

according to Fig. 1
as can be seen from/in * Fig. 1
as detailed in Fig. 1
as evident from/in the figure
as illustrated by Fig. 1
as indicated in Fig. 1
as listed in Fig. 1
as shown in Fig. 1
as we can see from/in Fig. 1…
can be found in Fig. 1
can be identified from/in Fig. 1
can be observed in Fig. 1
can be seen from/in Figure 1

comparing Figs. 1 and 4 shows that…
data in Fig. 1 suggest that…
displayed in Fig. 1
evidence for this is in Fig. 1
from Fig. 1 it can be seen that…
inspection of Fig. 1 indicates…
is/are given in Fig. 1
is/are represented (etc.) in
is/are visible in Fig. 1
in Fig. 1 we compare/present etc.…
results are given in Fig. 1
we observe from Fig. 1 that…

注意：from 含有推断的意思，而 in 则是显而易见的。

经典例句

According to Fig. 1 the shell is described by two main radii of curvature.

According to Fig. 1 the radius R1 will be later denoted as R.

Comparing Figs. 5 and 7 show that the predicted final failure mode is highly consistent with the experimental one.

It is seen from Fig. 5 that for L ABAQUS does not predict bifurcation and predicted failure of the cylinder is by axisymmetric collapse.

It can be seen from the plots that with decreasing of y1 the buckling pressure increase.

First, the thickness of each wall was measured using an ultrasonic probe at 13 equidistant points along a meridian for eight equally spaced meridians, <u>as detailed in Fig. 1</u>.

<u>As is evident from the figure that</u> the four buckling curves merge with each other and have identical modes.

The roof support system typically consists of a set of radial rafters, ring rafters, and columns, evenly distributed in the conical roof, <u>as illustrated in Figs. 1 and 2</u>.

When a cone is subjected to uniform external pressure acting over the whole surface, <u>as illustrated in Fig. 2b,</u> it represents a case of combined stability.

In most cases the cones lose stability by bifurcation buckling with the number of hoop waves <u>indicated in Fig. 6</u>.

As indicated by the authors and <u>can be observed in these figures</u>, the experimental results agree with the numerical ones.

<u>It can also be observed from the figure</u> that to this plateau lower bound, the reductions from the minimum classical critical stresses are moderate.

<u>Comparing Figs. 8-10 it is seen that</u> the increase in the magnitude of collapse load is associated with the progress of plastic straining primarily in the flange and in the shell wall in close vicinity of the flange.

We observe the abrupt formation of localized indentations in the shells, <u>as shown in Fig. 1(b)</u>. For each osmotic pressure investigated, the fraction of the capsules that buckle increases over time, eventually plateauing, <u>as shown in Fig. 1(c)</u>. We quantify this behavior by fitting this increase to an empirical exponential relationship, exemplified by the smooth lines <u>in Fig. 1(c)</u>.

Moreover, surprisingly, roughly 30% of the very inhomogeneous capsules begin to buckle through the formation of one, then two, adjacent indentations, <u>as exemplified in Fig. 2(c)</u>.

4.4　结果分析模板句

（1）主观词语

abundant(ly)	essential(ly)	marked(ly)
acceptable(ably)	excellent	measurable(ably)
adequate(ly)	excessive(ly)	mild(ly)
appropriate(ly)	exceptional(ly)	minimal(ly)
brief/(ly)	extensive(ly)	more or less
clear(ly)	important(ly)	most(ly)
comparable(ably)	in particular	negligible(ibly)
consistent(ly)	in principle	noticeable(ably)
distinct(ly)	inadequate	obvious(ly)
dominant(ly)	interesting(ly)	overwhelming(ly)
dramatic(ally)	large(ly)	poor(ly)
drastic(ally)	low	remarkable(ably)
equivalent	main(ly)	resembling

satisfactory	simple(ply)	sufficient(ly)
scarce(ly)	smooth(ly)	suitable(ably)
serious(ly)	somewhat	surprising(ly)
severe(ly)	steep(ly)	tendency
sharp(ly)	striking(ly)	the majority of
significant(ly)	strong(ly)	too + adjective
similar	sudden(ly)	unexpected(ly)

经典例句

The peanut shell is the <u>abundant</u> by-product produced in the process of the peanut production.

However, most FDM systems provide good, <u>acceptable</u> accuracy and surface finish for most engineering design applications.

The values are rather conservative and the structural behaviour of compositematerial is not considered <u>adequately</u>.

It is possible to reduce the edge effects through the <u>appropriate</u> lamination stacking.

Plastic loads based on the apex deflection were found to be <u>comparable</u> to those calculated by using volumetric changes.

Therefore, higher quality 3D printers and more detailed investigation into the MakerBot MakerWare printing settings are recommended if <u>consistent</u> material properties or geometries are required.

The status of calculations of the stability of elastic shells is <u>distinctly</u> different.

Out of all these imperfections, the geometrical imperfections are more <u>dominant</u> in determining the load carrying capacity of thin cylindrical shells.

These results suggest that the shell-indenter frictional contact can be tuned to <u>dramatically</u> modify the mechanical response of the shell under indentation.

First, buckling relaxes in-plane constraints, and causes a <u>drastic</u> drop of the inside/outside pressure difference.

An approximate solution of the equilibrium Eq. (2.310a) by Galerkin's method is then <u>equivalent</u> to an approximate minimization of the second variation of the potential energy by the Rayleigh Ritz method.

Note that the primary equilibrium paths obtained from these two approaches show an <u>excellent</u> agreement.

It does not lead to an <u>excessively</u> large computational cost and the obtained results have an acceptable error.

The aspiration criterion allows removal of the tabu restriction if a specific configuration yields <u>exceptionally</u> good return.

FDM process software allows <u>extensive</u> possibilities of tool path build styles used in each layer by altering appropriate process variables.

One should not expect that complicated structural stability problems involving thin-walled plate and shell components, where nonlinear effects play an <u>important</u> role, can be solved routinely without much effort and thought by any of the many codes that are currently available.

In particular, the wall thickness is found for vessels being loaded by the weight of its content and placed on two supports.

Thus the structural analyst must, in principle, always deal with two sets of equations.

The discrepancy between the experimental and the theoretical predictions can beattributed to an inadequate assessment of the material properties.

Interestingly, the sequences of bifurcations and stable capsule shapes differ for prescribed volume and prescribed pressure.

Similarly, in situ, considerable volume increase goes on, but at a rate which diminishes rapidly until reduced to negligible proportions by the increasing rigidity and impermeability of the shell.

It also becomes apparent from the results displayed in Figure 2.39 that for $n = 4$ or less there is a noticeable difference between the predictions.

Obviously, it is unnecessary to consider $M > 1$ for this geometry.

Another remarkable difference among VTE same-stress and VGE designs prebuckling deformed shapes is the deformation in the more curved regions.

As can be seen, the agreement between theoretical and experimental results is generally satisfactory.

Depending on the outcome of the review, approval to proceed to the next stage could be given, or, in the case of serious deficiencies rework would be required.

It is shown that both inward and outward imperfections can significantly reduce the load carrying capacity.

Until recently, however, there have been several somewhat different systems of organization that were preferred by some journals and some editors.

Strikingly, the results of the linear analysis give a buckling load which is lower than the geometrically non-linear analysis.

The first question was answered by using the code BOSOR4 and the errors in the buckling load were found to be sufficiently small.

It is somewhat surprising to see in Fig. 13 that the barrel S3 is marginally less sensitive than the equivalent cylinder S1.

It is from this coating that the samples gain the majority of their strength and toughness depending on the penetration into the layers.

However, results are presented that show how certain reinforcement configurations can cause an unexpected increase in the magnitude of local deformations and stresses in the shell and cause a reduction in the buckling load.

（2）数量修饰

表明该数很大

a great deal (of)	at least	marked
a number (of)	considerable	more (than)
as many as (45)	greater (than)	most

| numerous | plenty | substantial |
| over (half/25%) | much | significant |

表明该数很小

a few	few	negligible
a little	fewer (than)	only
as few as 45	little	slight
barely	less	small
below	marginal	under

修饰大小

easily (over/under)	extremely (high/low)	so (high/low)
even (higher/lower)	far (above/below)	well (under/over)
exceptionally (high/low)		

强度接近

| approximately | nearly |
| close (to) | slightly |

经典例句

As may be seen, the imperfections in the form of Legendre polynomials give the lower collapse pressures but there is not a great deal of difference between them.

A large number of geometric and material variables prohibit the traditional experiment-based lower-bound design method for metallic shells from being extended to composite ones.

The difference would be as many as 2.15% using the original Mohsein's formula, which does not include the correction coefficient.

Each set contains at least five specimens of different thickness including 10 mm, 20 mm, 30 mm, 40 mm and 50 mm.

Small imperfections will lead to a considerable reduction of the value of 2ma x mentioned in connection with Fig. 9.

There are numerous publications dedicated to demonstrate the applicability of the method to elastic-plastic systems.

The second was to verify that optimizing a dome's geometry, while keeping the weight constant, can bring substantial increases in the buckling strength.

Preliminary design studies indicate that implementation of these new knockdown factors can enable significant reductions in mass and mass-growth in these vehicles.

A large number of permissible shapes can be attained with as few parameters as possible.

In the distance of barely several grains there were observed strong gradients of stresses which took the extreme values from the calculated stress range.

Throughout, we find that the maximum principal strains remain below 6%.

Numerical results indicated that the effect of rotation on the magnitude of collapse load was marginal.

Therefore, considering the supports as perfectly rigid, introduces a negligible error.

Negligence of this parameter lead to a 15% increase of the corresponding model bias while geometric imperfections made up for <u>only</u> 3%.

Unwanted load eccentricities by columns, <u>slight</u> deviations from flatness by plate assemblies or minute waviness along the generator of a cylindrical shell are all examples of initial (geometric) imperfections.

Only a <u>small</u> portion of experiments has been carried out within the elastic-plastic range.

Cuckoo density in this Hungarian population is extremely <u>high</u>.

For the smooth rim the elastic energy scales whereas for the polygonal indentation we find a much smaller exponent, <u>even</u> smaller than the exponent 1/6 that is predicted for stretching ridges.

The conventional SDF are found to be accurate within <u>approximately</u> 20%, with 95% confidence, for intact pressure hulls.

Eggshell formation is amongst the most rapid mineralisation processes known, occurring daily during a period of <u>approximately</u> 18 h.

Within the studied range, this could be <u>nearly</u> five times more severe than in the case of geometric imperfections in the shell's generator.

The rigid surface is defined as an analytical surface, in the form of flat disk of <u>slightly</u> larger diameter than that of the cylinder.

It is shown in Fig. 2 that the RS critical loads can generally predict <u>close</u> lower bounds for buckling into the short axial wavelength modes showing more severe imperfection sensitivity.

4.5 结果讨论模板句

(1) 因果关系/联系

因果关系

(be) a/the cause of	create/(be) created
(be) a/the consequence of	derive/(be) derived
(be) a factor in	effect/(be) effected
(be) a/the result of	elicit/(be) elicited
(be) due to	give rise to
(be) correlated with	generate/(be) generated
account for/(be) accounted for	influence/(be) influenced
affect/(be) affected	initiate/(be) initiated
arise from	originate in
ascribe to/(be) ascribed to	produce/(be) produced
attribute to/(be) attributed to	result from
bring about/(be) brought about	result in
cause/(be) caused	stem from
come from	trigger/(be) triggered
connect to/(be) connected to *	yield
contribute to	

因果联系（因果关系不明确、需要弱化）

associate/(be) associated   relate/(be) related

accompany/(be) accompanied   link/(be) linked

It appears/ seems that + 因果关系

It is (very/highly/extremely) probable/likely that + 因果关系

It is (widely/generally) accepted that + 因果关系

It is/may be reasonable to suppose/assume that + 因果关系

It is/may be thought/recognised/believed/felt that + 因果关系

It is/may/can be assumed that + 因果关系

There is a clear/good/definite/strong possibility that + 因果关系

There is evidence to indicate that + 因果关系

This implies/seems to imply/may imply that + 因果关系

It is thought/said/recognised that + 因果关系

（2）情态动词—弱化表达

一般现在时：may/might/could/can

一般现在时否定式：may not/might not

一般过去时：may have/might have/could have

一般过去时否定式：may not have/might not have

（3）言外之意

imply/implies that   it is conceivable/ logical that

indicate/indicating that   it is inferred that

suggest(ing) that   it is evident that

it is apparent that   it is thought/believed that

经典例句

However, at the same time, the reduction of collapse and yield pressures <u>caused by</u> the wall thinning was 20% and 40%, respectively, when compared to intact models.

Low phosphorus levels <u>can cause</u> the production of soft-shelled eggs.

The joint flexibility <u>may cause</u> the buck-ling of the structure prematurely and the member capacities cannot be utilized.

<u>As a consequence</u> of the Legendre transformation, the two regions shaded gray in the p(V) diagram have the same area at p = pc (Maxwell construction).

In particular, the formation of folds or stretching ridges, which are also characteristic for crumpled sheets, is <u>a direct consequence of</u> the inextensibility due to a large stretching modulus.

Stress analysis using modern computer modelling techniques indicated that the shell should fail in tension <u>as a result of</u> the accumulation of stress at its inner most surface.

It is worth to remember that an unsuccessful arc-length analysis can be <u>as a result of</u> too large or too small arc-length radius.

<u>Due to a lack of</u> adequate analytical results, current practices in industry put heavy reliance on experinlennri testing and empirical data to supplement theoretical analysis.

Due to the complex structure and the amorphous/crystal phase interactions, the heating at about 500 8C texturizes the crystals orienting them mainly along the c-axes normal to the inner eggshell surface.

In other cases the shape of the egg has been correlated with the dimensions of the embryo developing inside it.

Overall collapse pressures were more severely affected by corrosion damage than interframe collapse pressures.

These modes arise from an alternative set of solutions which are the same as Eqs. (25).

The deviations to the exact results can be attributed to the crude simplification of the buckling pattern.

The second was to verify that optimizing a dome's geometry, while keeping the weight constant, can bring substantial increases in the buckling strength.

The changes in forces consists of two parts that come from change in the natural forces at a fixed configuration.

The top paperclip was connected to a load cell, which moved upwards with a constant speed of 15mm/min.

At a critical level of stress one or more of these radiating cracks becomes unstable and this is accompanied by the characteristic relaxation in the force deformation curve normally associated with shell failure.

It indicates that KS of shell membranes is associated with the breaking strength of the shell.

However, this increase amounts to a fraction of only about 1/3-2/3 of the increase which is effected by rigid support conditions.

Distributed model error give rise to distributed error in the assessed external loads.

Their connection might give rise to technological difficulties and therefore such designs would not be suitable.

Structures located near underground ammunition facilities may be subjected to ground motions generated by accidental explosions.

This process can be strongly influenced by structural inhomogeneities in the capsule shells.

The direction of crack growth maybe influenced by the curvature of the shell and variations in shell thickness.

The high-speed movies of Esslinger [16] showed that the loss of stability is initiated by a local single buckle.

The differences in the obtained results can stem from the consideration of the material anisotropy and from use of different safety levels.

An analysis of the shape equations constructed around this elasticity model revealed that wrinkling can be triggered by the onset of the hard-core interactions.

The percentage reduction in overall collapse pressure, compared with intact experimental models, was found to be closely related to the percentage depth of thinning.

However, once the elastic buckling loads are determined in this way, it was felt that the remaining two steps of the design procedure should be linked to the elastic buckling loads in a unique manner.

It appears to suggest that certain portions of such a vessel under uniform external pressure may behave in a manner similar to that of a complete vessel.

There is, in fact, much evidence to indicate that eggshells or secondary egg envelopes were, in the first place, evolved because of the proloinged retention of the eggs.

This indicates that our results are applicable beyond elastomeric shells and can be extended to other materials that remain in the elastic regime up to a few percent strain, provided that no plasticity takes place.

This finding suggests that our results should be relevant and applicable for engineering scenarios across a wide range of length scales.

This finding, in conjunction with the observation of increased load-bearing capability for rough shell-indenter contact, could have implications for the design of engineering shells with enhanced resistance to localization by roughening their surfaces.

These observations directly demonstrate that the deformations of a capsule after it buckles are sensitive to the shell inhomogeneity.

It may be inferred that some interaction between interframe and overall failure modes occurred, even though the latter mode was dominant at collapse.

It is also evident that this increase in volume—presumably due to osmotic swelling—occurs during the early phases of shell deposition.

It is apparent that the buckling behavior has two distinct forms.

It is conceivable that nonaxisymmetric bifurcations could occur for this system.

4.6　文献对比模板句

compare well with	confirm
consistent with	match
in line with	prove
is/are in good agreement	support
is/are identical (to)	validate
is/are parallel (to)	verify
is/are similar (to)	correlate

经典例句

They also compare well with the experimental collapse load of aluminium model no.

The results for frequency of vibration compare favorably with the available literature.

Previous studies have shown that the embryonic survival of ostrich chicks was impaired in eggs that were stored for seven days and longer (Brand et al., 2007), which was consistent with the findings of Ar & Gefen (1998), Deeming (1996), Wilson et al. (1997) and Horbańczuk (2000).

… which is consistent with previous findings [5, 8].

This failure mode is consistent with previous experimental results regarding shells of revolution with a positive Gaussian curvature.

This is consistent with the energy scaling observed by Lidmar et al for icosahedral shells [7].

The strains-to-failure of the panels were consistent with those of the small fastener specimens representing the panel critical elements.

These values are in line with the values of the static modulus mentioned by other investigators.

The results for the SPH are in line with previous findings given in [2].

Among the existing theories Budiansky [1], Weinitschke [2], Thurston [3] and Archer [4], using various techniques, have obtained critical pressures for axisymmetrical buckling in a surprisingly good agreement with one another.

The F(V) and p(V) diagrams are in good agreement with previous work based on triangulated surface models.

The present results show good agreement with the existing analytical and finite element solutions.

These expressions are identical to the relations used in Refs. 1, 4, and 5 except for the extra terms.

The base radius and radius of circular top region are identical to that considered in the previous case for the characteristic parameter value.

His investigation resulted in the identification of a third, higher modal branch, although the two lower branches were nominally identical to those of Kalnins [2].

Eggshell formation in Caryophyllaeus laticeps and Caryophyllaeides /ennica (Cestoidea: Caryophyllaeidea), as shown by histochemical tests for proteins, phenols, and polyphenol oxidase, is similar to that of D. latum, Ligula sp., and Schistocephalus

These graphs are very similar to those obtained by Król et al. [24].

Our thin elastic shells were manufactured by coating a spherical mold with a polymer solution, following a protocol similar to that introduced in a previous study [22].

Our study is well aligned with efforts currently underway by NASA and others interested in large shell structures to replace the old empirical knockdown factors employed in design codes by an approach

Moreover, we find E for the experimental capsules [solid line, Fig. 1(d) inset], in good agreement with our theoretical prediction.

These results qualitatively agree with our experimental observations.

4.7 问题说明模板句

(1) 淡化问题

not always reliable   not identical
not always accurate   not completely clear
not ideal   not perfect

not precise	reasonable results were obtained
not significant	room for improvement
less than ideal	slightly (disappointing)
less than perfect	(a) slight mismatch/limitation
negligible	somewhat (problematic)

经典例句

But the level of preloading and the magnitude of perturbation are case dependent, and <u>the method is not always able to provide a reliable estimate of</u> buckling (as will be discussed later).

The drawback is that the analyst is required to make choices about each of those aspects of the model, and the correct choice <u>is not always obvious</u>.

Thus, this type of element <u>cannot always provide accurate results</u> when used for the bending analysis of plates. <u>However,</u> because of its simplicity, this polynomial is used in engineering practice.

The guidelines assume that the evaluator is trained in ship structural analysis and design, <u>but is not necessarily expert in FEA. Ideally the guidelines would be provided as</u> part of the job specifications (or statement of work, statement of requirements, etc.) to the analysts.

For example, the imperfection sensitivity of axially compressed cones <u>is not thought to be identical to</u> that of cylinders but its exact nature has not been quantified.

Fortunately, the thickness profile of our experimental samples varied slightly along the meridian of our shells due to limitations of our fabrication procedure; the male and female parts of the molds were <u>not perfectly aligned during casting</u>.

The determination of the transverse shear stresses from their resultants <u>is not as precise</u>, even within the framework of the present theory.

Because tangential edge conditions <u>have not usually been precisely</u> controlled in buckling tests, some of the scatter of test results can be attributed also to this source.

For stiff structures, where the deformations <u>do not significantly affect</u> the action of the loads, the stresses, strains and displacements are always linear functions of the load (as follows from the linearity of the basic differential equations and boundary conditions of the classical theory of elasticity).

Outside these regions, the displacements <u>are negligible</u>; these regions are referred to as G2 (for the rest of the dimple) and G1 (for the rest of the undeformed part).

The spherical dome is loaded with a uniform pressure and the shell's self-weight is not taken into account, because the weight of the very thin shell is <u>negligible</u> compared to the pressure load which is applied.

Consequently, the correction due to higher-order multiple scattering, according to Ye (1995) and Kargl (2002), was <u>negligible</u> and could be ignored.

By comparing the magnitude of the direct and bending stresses, it can be argued that FLB relations contain many terms which are <u>negligible</u> for thin shells.

Tests were conducted on solid cylindrical specimens of 4 mm length and 4 mm diameter as well as 6 mm length and 6 mm diameter. Reasonable agreement is obtained between the two.

Their fundamentals are still used today. However, there is always room for improvement.

The numerical pressure-strain responses are in good agreement, except that initial yielding is delayed in the FE models so that the predicted compressive strains are somewhat smaller than the measured strains in the nonlinear portion of the curves leading up to collapse.

（2）给出原因

beyond the scope of this study	unpredictable
difficult to (simulate)	not the focus of this paper
hard to (control)	not within the scope of this study
inevitable	not explored in this study
unavoidable	it should be noted that…

经典例句

It should be emphasized that prediction of material strength properties is currently beyond the scope of simplified mathematical theory.

Meanwhile, the third thumbnail shows the termination of the large amplitude homoclinic, which is beyond the scope of our present discussion.

Considering a variable geometry lattice with attached thin layers, say, composite layers, within which the fiber angles could also vary with position is considered a very complex problem, one beyond the scope of the present study.

Hence, it is difficult to interpret the significance of $n = 4$ lobes obtained in the experiment.

The work is difficult to automate as it requires a great deal of human feedback to sense the recovery success, yet it is highly limited by underwater conditions that are very harsh on the divers.

While hairline cracks are considered inevitable, cracks of appreciable width are undesirable because of the long-term detrimental effects.

Practically it is impossible to obtain a prescribed mismatch, because small uncontrolled tolerances are unavoidable in machine shop practice.

As a result, the true pressure at which uniform shells lose stability can be unpredictable.

When the cracks appear the axisymmetry is lost and it is unpredictable what happens.

It should be noted that the shape of the shell was assumed perfect for these analyses.

It should be noted that the numerical result is influenced, among others, by the support conditions which, on the other hand, influence the buckling shape.

It should be noted that the graph used has been obtained for shells with the base ring clamped completely, when in fact the clamped supports are located in some isolated points of the base ring of the tower.

（3）提出建议

further work is planned

future work should…

future work will…

in future, care should be taken

in future, it is advised that…

经典例句

Much work should be devoted to systematic investigation of properties evaluation for candidate titanium alloys for submersible structures.

Future work should also include the application of group theoretic techniques to simplify, the analysis of the dynamic shell problems as well.

There are still many aspects to be considered during the design, and the related design rules should be specified. These will be investigated in our future work.

For the present analysis, we used average values of these parameters, because we restricted our investigation into the variability of marine floats to experimental factors. Future work will address the analytical variations.

Future work should be directed at studying how effective s-e curves could be generated starting from a realistic nonlinear material curve with strain hardening.

Special care should be taken when making samples from the RP machine as the level of coating penetration plays an important role in the final strength of the RP sample.

When the hyperboloid relation f /L is over 0.16, it is convenient to adopt a conical geometry, which has significant constructive advantages, but care should be taken to check the value of the maxi-mum tensile stresses acting on the wet surface.

To put improved procedures to immediate use, however, the designer is advised to be alert to new developments in shell-stability analysis.

As most domes in practice have geometric imperfections in them, it is of interest to know how the results in this paper change for imperfect shells. The authors hope to answer this question in the near future.

It is hoped that applications of shell structures in the latter areas will become more frequent already in the near future.

Based on the used numerical model, other geometries than domes and other load patterns should be examined, enabling the design of complex GFTR-IPC shell geometries which will be realised in the future.

4.8 经典范文分析

(1) 范文1

深海球形耐压壳力学特性研究

2.3 数值结果分析

2.3.1 壳单元数值结果

根据式 (1) 和式 (8),6km 水深下球形耐压壳的理论中面应力和理论临界屈曲载荷分别为 653.33MPa 和 733.67MPa。对表 1 中列出的 14 个壳单元数值方案的计算结果及与理论中面应力和理论临界屈曲载荷偏差列于表 3。**(图表指示)** 由方案 1、方案 2、方案 3 的结果可知，在强度方面，随机形式的平均应力结果与理论值最为接近，钱币划分和网球划分形式的平均应力与理论值相差也较小，不足 0.1%；*(结果分析－主观，文献对比－他比)* 但随机划分的最大最小应力相差太大，出现明显的应力集中，网球划分和钱币划分的最大最小应力相差很小，较为符合球形耐压壳的等强度特性。在稳定性方面，网球划分的临界屈曲载荷与理论值相差最小，为 0.049%，而随机划分和钱币划分的临界屈曲载荷与理论值相差较大，分别为 1.782%、0.167%。*(文献对比－他比)* 因此，从强度和稳定性两方面考虑，采用网球划分为球形耐压壳建模的最佳选择。*(结果讨论－暗示)*

由方案 3、方案 4、方案 5、方案 6、方案 7 结果可知，在强度方面，无论是否采用减缩积分单元，得到的平均应力结果与理论值相差都非常小，几乎可以忽略不计；*(结果分析－主观)* 而从最大最小应力差值考虑，减缩积分单元 S4R 和 S4R5 较为理想。陆蓓、潘彬彬等在进行球形耐压壳数值分析时，也采用了 S4R 和 S4R5 单元。*(文献对比－他比)* 在稳定性方面，S4 计算精度最高。因此，从强度和稳定性两方面考虑，4 节点完全积分线性壳单元 (S4) 为球形耐压壳建模的最佳选择。*(结果讨论－暗示)*

网格疏密对数值模拟的准确度影响很大。先进行网格无关性检验。只有当网格数的增加对计算结果影响不大时，这时的仿真结果才具有意义。*(结果引言－回顾)* 单元密度的选取要综合考虑计算时间和精度[10]。*(文献对比－他比)* 对表 1 中的方案 8、方案 9、方案 10、方案 11、方案 3、方案 12、方案 13、方案 14 的计算结果，绘制应力误差曲线、屈曲临界载荷误差曲线，分别如图 3(a)、(b) 所示。图 3(a) 所示为球形耐压壳中面上最大应力，*(图表指示－句中)* 最小应力和平均应力与理论强度应力的比值曲线，当单元平均尺寸与球形耐压壳半径比为 0.07 时，数值方案得到的结果就开始收敛，且网格尺寸越小，数值方案的平均应力越趋近于理论值，而最大最小值的差值也越来越小，趋于解析解。

……

图 4 所示为方案 3 计算所得的中面应力云图、内外表面应力云图、1 阶屈曲振形图。*(图表指示－主语)* 显然，采用壳单元进行数值模拟时，中面和内外层面的应力相差仅仅不到 1%，*(结果分析－主观)* 这与理论结果相差甚远，*(文献对比－他比)* 表明采用壳单元进行厚球壳强度分析是不合理的。*(结果讨论－暗示＋弱化)*

(2) 范文 2

Buckling of spherical shells subjected to external pressure: A comparison of experimental and theoretical data

3. Results and discussion

Previous studies have indicated that the experimental buckling loads of spherical shells are lower than theoretical predictions [4, 17]. This phenomenon may result from inevitable geometric imperfections and from nonlinear material properties. This problem of classical mechanics is far from being solved; the buckling analysis of spherical shells remains to be vivid and is still challenging. *(结果引言－回顾)*

This section reports how the buckling loads and final collapsed modes of a family of spherical shells were determined from hydrostatic tests. The results of analytical and numerical investigations into these shells are presented and compared with the experimental findings. The effects of constitutive models on the buckling load are discussed. (结果引言-概述)

3.1. Experimental and analytical results analysis

The experimental buckling loads are listed in column 2 of **Table 4**, and graphed in **Fig. 4**. Photographs of the final collapsed modes for 10 spherical shells are presented in **Fig. 5**. (图表指示-宾语) Notably, the buckling load of the t0.7-2 spherical shell was not recorded because of an incorrect operation during the testing process. (问题说明) However, the final collapsed mode of this shell was still obtained. The buckling loads of the 0.4-mm-thick spherical shells ranged between 1.330 and 1.956 MPa, whereas the 0.7-mm-thick shell buckling loads ranged between 3.178 and 4.692 MPa. The buckling loads of the 0.7-mm-thick shell loads were more than twice those of the 0.4-mm-thick shell loads. (结果分析,文献对比-自比较) This variance mainly affected by the ratio of the average wall thickness (t_{ave}) to the average radius (r_{ave}), as illustrated in Fig. 4. (结果讨论-因果关系) The experimental buckling load increased monotonically with an increase in t_{ave}/r_{ave}. As shown in Fig. 5, the final collapsed modes of all shells are identical, and all of them have the form of a local dent because of the high ductility of stainless steel and the initial geometric imperfections of the shells. This failure mode is consistent with previous experimental results regarding shells of revolution with a positive Gaussian curvature, such as those for spherical shells reported by Quilliet [13], for ellipsoidal shells reported by Healey [18], and for barreled shells reported by Blachut [9, 10]. (文献对比-他比)

Atheory derived by Zoelly [19] predicts the elastic buckling load (p_{cr}) of spherical shells, which is obtained using Eq. (1). This analytical formula is widely accepted in ocean and aerospace engineering as a rule for designing spherical shells [4, 20, 21]. (文献对比-他比) The results of Eq. (3) are listed in column 3 of Table 4, followed by the ratio of the experimental load p_{test} to the elastic buckling load p_{zoelly} in parentheses. (图表指示-宾语) As shown in the table, (图表指示-主语) the experimental load of a spherical shell was as little as 15.07%-24.55% of that shell's elastic buckling load, (结果分析-主观,文献对比-他比) confirming that the spherical shell is a highly imperfection-sensitive structure. A small imperfection may lead to a substantial decrease in the magnitude of the buckling load. (结果讨论-暗示+弱化) Furthermore, the average ratio of the experimental load p_{test} to the elastic buckling load p_{zoelly} for 0.4-mm-thick spherical shells was approximately 3% lower than the ratio for 0.7-mm-thick shells. (结果分析-主观,文献对比-自比) It appears that the nonlinear properties of spherical shells' materials may play a major role in the buckling behaviors of shells with various wall thicknesses. (结果讨论-暗示+弱化)

……

4.9 实例练习

运用所学知识,仿照4.7节,分析以下实例。

(1) 实例1

硬土-软土插桩过程数值分析及验证

3 插桩性能分析
3.1 土壤流动特性

土壤流动特性对插桩过程影响很大，桩靴上部回流或坍塌的土壤将导致桩靴所受载荷陡然增加，使插桩深度迅速增大。图4为采用数值模型计算的土壤速度矢量图及变形过程图，为了清楚显示土壤变形，图中隐藏了桩靴。

由图4可知：初始阶段，桩靴周围的土壤仅有少量向上流动，桩靴下方少量土壤向下运动，硬土表面发生局部隆起，在桩靴上部形成空腔，硬土-软土界面也向下变形；随着插桩深度增加，土壤主要向下垂直流动，不再向上运动，硬土表面不再变形，形成了垂直剪切面，在桩靴下方形成了倒锥形硬土块；当桩靴底插到初始硬土-软土界面时，硬土块被压入软土层中，土壤流动集中在桩靴下方，由于锲形土的作用，硬土-软土界面开始轻微向上隆起，桩靴上方的空腔仍然完全敞开；当空腔深度超过硬土层厚度后，土壤开始回流，硬土逐渐回流到空腔内；当桩靴完全被硬土包围时，出现局部土壤流动现象，限制了空腔深度进一步增加，被压入软土层的硬土开始在桩靴边缘处与硬土层分离，稳定空腔深度与土壤开始回流时的空腔深度一致。

为了分析土壤特性参数变化对插桩过程的影响，采用数值模型模拟了硬土、软土的不排水剪切强度和有效重度改变后土壤的最终变形情况。

对硬土参数变化后土壤最终变形图（见图5）进行分析可以发现：①硬土不排水剪切强度减小时，桩靴下方硬土块体积减小，桩靴上方硬土形状由圆形变为锥形且分布更加连续、均匀，空腔深度增大。硬土不排水剪切强度增大时反之。②硬土有效重度增大时，桩靴上方硬土回流量增大且分布更加连续、均匀，空腔深度减小，而桩靴下方硬土块形状和体积基本没有变化。硬土有效重度减小时反之。

软土不排水剪切强度增大时土壤最终变形情况与硬土不排水剪切强度减小时相似，可见，硬土、软土的强度比越小，桩靴下方硬土块体积越小，桩靴上方硬土分布越连续、均匀，空腔深度越大。软土有效重度增大时土壤最终变形情况与硬土有效重度增大时相似，可见，土壤重度越大，桩靴上方硬土回流量越大，空腔深度越小，而桩靴下方硬土块形状和体积基本没有变化。

3.2 插桩深度和插桩阻力关系

图6为采用数值模型计算的插桩深度与插桩阻力的关系（包括硬土参数变化后的结果）。由图6可知：①对原始模型而言，在桩靴最大截面入土后，受土壤分布的影响，插桩阻力出现峰值，之后随着插桩深度的增加，插桩阻力缓慢减小，这种变化非常容易导致刺穿事故，在插桩设计时，需要避免这种情况。②硬土不排水剪切强度增大时，同一插桩深度的插桩阻力增大，更容易发生"刺穿"。硬土不排水剪切强度减小时反之。③土壤有效重度对插桩深度与插桩阻力间关系的影响比较复杂，因为土壤有效重度不仅影响土层自重应力分布，也影响土壤流动特性，但总体来说硬土有效重度减小时更容易发生"刺穿"。

软土不排水剪切强度减小时插桩深度与插桩阻力间关系的变化趋势与硬土不排水剪切强度增大时相似，软土有效重度增大时更容易发生"刺穿"。可见，硬土、软土的强度比越大、有效重度比越小，发生"刺穿"的可能性越高。

3.3 桩靴底部压力分布规律

《海上移动平台入级与建造规范》[12]中假设作用在整个桩靴底部的压力呈线性分布，一端为 0，另一端为平均值的 2 倍。为了验证该假设的合理性，采用数值模型计算 6 个插桩位置处桩靴底部和土壤间的接触压力（见图 7）。由图 7 可知：① r（桩靴底部某一点到桩靴中轴线的垂直距离）小于 1.50m 时，压力（p）逐渐增大；r 在 1.50~2.55m 时，压力逐渐减小；r 大于 2.55m 时，压力迅速增大。可见，《海上移动平台入级与建造规范》中关于桩靴底部压力线性分布的假设与实际情况不符。② 桩靴底部压力由内向外先增大、后减小、再增大。插桩深度为 1.080D 时，压力波动最大，最外端压力近似为平均值的 4.5 倍，此时采用《海上移动平台入级与建造规范》进行桩靴设计可能造成安全事故。

（2）实例 2

轮胎硫化过程数值分析及试验研究

3 结果分析与讨论

以上述试验轮胎为例，运用有限元法进行硫化过程的数值模拟。轮胎是由多层橡胶和/或钢丝橡胶复合体叠加而成的复杂变厚结构，故采用网格划分软件 HyperMesh 对其进行结构离散。鉴于模型的对称性，只分析半个轮胎，离散后的数值模型包含 1679 个轴对称传热单元（97% 为四边形单元），1769 个节点。将试验确定的相关边界条件施加到图 3 所示的轮胎硫化模型中，在平板硫化机内的升温阶段施加 Dirichlet 边界条件，在空气中的后硫化阶段施加 Fourier 边界条件，在胎冠处的对称边界上施加对称边界条件，硫化数值计算的时间严格按照试验时间设定。图 4 显示了在硫化过程中 6 个特征点试验与数值计算的温度历程，可见，在机内硫化阶段，与金属模拟接触的轮胎外表面测点 2[#] 和 5[#] 温升最快，在 800s 左右温度接近蒸汽温度并保持不变，而轮胎内部越厚的地方温升越慢，如测点 4[#] 的温升最慢，测点 3[#] 和测点 6[#] 次之，且两点的温度历程较为接近，1[#] 的温升最快；在后硫化阶段，机内硫化过程中温升越快的测点温度下降越快，温升越慢的测点温度下降越慢。数值计算结果与试验结果具有良好的一致性，说明本文所用的数值分析方法是正确的。

3.1 轮胎硫化分析

图 5 为 6 个典型硫化时间点上轮胎内部温度场分布情况．由图 5 可知，在机内硫化阶段，与平板硫化机直接接触的轮胎内外表面温度首先升高，其中，与含有 170℃ 循环水的胶囊接触的内衬层温度高于其他部位，尺寸越薄的地方温升越快；在后硫化阶段，与空气直接接触的轮胎内外表面的温度首先下降，尺寸越薄的地方降温速度越快。整个轮胎在硫化过程中的温度变化规律与试验结果一致。

通过无量纲参数可以知道橡胶是否由焦烧期进入热硫化期，图 6 显示了轮胎开始发生交联反应（55.6s）、胎侧进入热硫化期（303.7s）、胎圈、胎侧和胎冠区进入热硫化期（379.7s）以及整个轮胎进入热硫化期（407.7s）时的无量纲参数云图。可见，温升较快的轮胎内外表面首先开始发生交联反应，其次是尺寸较薄的胎侧，接着是胎冠和胎圈，最后开始发生交联反应的是最厚的胎肩。

图 7 显示了 6 个时间点的轮胎硫化程度分布，当硫化程度为 1 时，表明此处的硫化反应

已经完成。由图 7 可知,与平板硫化机接触的轮胎内外表面(特别是与胶囊接触的胎侧内表面)最先完成硫化反应,其次是温升较快的胎侧,而后是胎圈和胎冠,最后完成硫化反应的是尺寸最厚的胎肩。

由数值计算可知,胎肩最难硫化的部位是 600 号节点(图 7(f),N600),此处的焦烧时间最长、温升最慢、硫化反应最后完成。在进行硫化工艺设计时,把 N600 的硫化程度达到 70% 时的时间(即工程正硫化时间,其余 30% 的硫化程度靠出模后的余热来完成)作为轮胎在平板硫化机内的硫化时间更加有效可靠。因此,可以把 N600 焦烧时间(t_i)、硫化时能够达到的最高温度(T_{max})、硫化程度达到 70% 时刻的时间(t_{70})作为评价轮胎硫化性能的指标。

3.2 胶囊厚度、初始温度和蒸汽温度对轮胎硫化性能的影响

为缩短轮胎硫化时间,根据硫化工程师的建议,研究胶囊厚度减小 50%(1#方案)、初始预热温度增加 66%(2#方案)以及蒸汽平均温度提高 5% 时(3#方案),t_i、T_{max} 和 t_{70} 的变化情况见表 1。由表 1 可知,当胶囊厚度减小 50% 时,N600 的焦烧时间缩短 5.98%,N600 的最高温度提高 1.83%,工程正硫化时间降低 11.84%;当初始预热温度增加 66% 时,N600 的焦烧时间缩短 27.05%,N600 的最高温度提高 0.2%,工程正硫化时间降低 2.83%;当蒸汽平均温度提高 5% 时,N600 的焦烧时间缩短 1.52%,N600 的最高温度提高 3.65%,工程正硫化时间降低 9.29%。可见,增加轮胎预热温度有利于缩短焦烧时间,而较小胶囊厚度和提高蒸汽温度有利于降低工程正硫化时间。

(3)实例 3

Investigation on Egg-shaped Pressure Hulls

3 Results and discussion

3.1 Mechanical properties of pressure hulls

Yielding load and buckling load are both very important parameters to evaluate safety of a pressure hull. Fig. 5 shows different classical yielding loads and critical elastic buckling loads of the egg-shaped pressure hull with constant thickness (EPHC), the egg-shaped pressure hull with variable thickness (EPHV) and the spherical pressure hull (SPH). For the EPHV, abscissa is the maximum thickness, and for the other two pressure hulls it is the real thickness.

It is evident from the results that there exists an intersection between classical yielding load and critical elastic buckling load for each pressure hull. Before the intersection, buckling is the main factor, in which case elastic or elastic-plastic buckling might lead to collapse of the pressure hull. After the intersection, strength is the main factor, in which case the maximum stress reaches the yield condition and then might lead to collapse of the pressure hull. The results for the SPH are in line with previous findings given in[2].

For the EPHC, the load and thickness at the intersection are 28.81 MPa and 0.01982 m, respectively. If the design load is less than 28.81 MPa, the thickness is calculated by Equation (14), otherwise by Equation (11). For the EPHV, the load and thickness at the intersection are 30 MPa and 0.02064 m, respectively. If the design load is less than 30 MPa, the thickness is calculated by Equation (27), otherwise by Equation (24). For the SPH, the intersection point is 20.7 MPa and 0.01247 m.

In addition, under the same critical elastic buckling load, the thickness of the EPHV (here it actually means the maximum value at the whole span along axis, as thickness of EPHV is variable) is the maximum, then the EPHC is following, and the thickness of the SPH is the minimum. And under the same yielding load, the thickness of the SPH is less than the thickness of the EPHC that is equal to the maximum thickness the EPHV.

Buoyancy factor is an index to evaluate buoyancy reserve of a pressure hull. Fig. 6 shows the buoyancy factor versus the design load for the EPHC, the EPHV and the SPH. It can be seen in Fig. 6, the buoyancy factor of each pressure hull is non linear with respect to the design load before the intersection point in Fig. 5, and is linear with respect to the design load after that. The buoyancy factor of the EPHC is always higher than that of the EPHV by approximately 10%. When the design load is less than 20.7 MPa, the buoyancy factors of both EPHC and EPHV are higher than that of the SPH. However, when the design load is more than 30 MPa, the buoyancy factor of EPHV becomes lower than SPH, by approximately 3.2%, meanwhile the buoyancy factor of EPHC is higher than SPH by approximately 7.6%. Therefore, it is expected that the buoyancy reserve of EPHV can be better than that of SPH in deep sea.

……

(4) 实例4

Buckling of Egg-shaped Shells Subjected to External Pressure

4. Numerical results and discussion

To examine the effect of eggSI on the load carrying capacity of egg-shaped shells, both linear buckling analysis and nonlinear buckling analysis with imperfections included were performed. Fourteen egg-shaped shells with a constant capacity and mass were analyzed. The analysis was performed using the finite element method in Abaqus. The fully integrated S4 shell element was selected to avoid hourglassing. The number of elements was determined using mesh convergence analysis. Thus, the finite element model of each egg-shaped shell has the same shell elements of 7584 and nodes of 7586. The uniform pressure $p_0 = 1$ MPa was externally applied to the whole surface area of the egg-shaped shells. This is a typical load for underwater pressure hulls, underground pressure vessels, and underpressure tanks. To avoid rigid displacements, for example of the egg-shaped shell with SI of 0.69, constraints were applied at three random spatial points and the support condition of each point from left to right as follows: Uy = Uz = 0, Ux = Uy = 0, Uy = Uz = 0, as shown in Fig. 5; this was identical for all analyzed egg-shaped shells. These constraints were in line with CCS2013 [23] and did not cause excessive constraint of the models because the pressure was equally applied. The reaction forces at these points were zero. Ti alloy (Ti-6Al-4V) was used to construct the egg-shaped shells. The relationship between stress and strain for this material is defined as follows: …… where n is the strain hardening parameter (59.327), E is the Young's modulus

(110GPa), and σ_y is the yield stress (830 MPa). These parameters were determined according to the experimental results of numerous tension coupons tested according to Chinese Standard (GB/T 228.1-2010) [24]. Test details were reported in [25]. The Poisson's ratio was assumed to be 0.3.

4.1. Linear buckling analysis

This section focuses on the linear buckling loads and modes of egg-shaped shells. Linear eigenvalue buckling analysis was conducted numerically using a Lanczos eigensolver implemented in Abaqus/Standard. A semianalytical formula developed by Mushtari [26] was adopted for calculating the elastic buckling loads; thus, …… where $\overline{R_1}$ is the mean value of the principle meridional radius of curvature for the shell section bounded by the nodal curves of the local buckling forms; likewise, $\overline{R_2}$ is the mean of the principle circumferential radius of curvature. Details of this formula are provided in [27-29]. According to these previous studies, (10) can be used to predict the linear buckling load of the thin, convex shells of revolution with a membrane stress and with a number of waves along the parallels. When $R_1 = R_2$, (10) can be simplified to the equation used for the classical buckling problem of spherical shells developed by Zoelly [30]. However, when $R_1 = \infty$, p_{cr} is zero and does not correspond to the elastic buckling load of infinitely long cylindrical shells. In all analyses, only the elastic properties of the material were used. The numerical and analytical results are shown in Fig. 6 and Table 3.

Using the analytical and numerical approaches, the linear buckling load was found to increase monotonically in conjunction with increases in the SI, as shown in Fig. 6. The analytical calculations underestimated the numerical buckling loads by 0.5%-12.2%. When the egg SI increased, this difference initially decreased and then slightly increased. In all cases, the buckling mode exhibited the similar form. As can be seen from Table 3, the shells with SIs of 0.4, 0.5, 0.6, 0.8, 0.9 and 1.0 take the form of ($n =$) 5, 7, 8, 10, 11 and 12 circumferential waves, respectively; the shells with an SI ranging from 0.65 to 0.72 take the same form of nine circumferential waves ($n = 9$). All of the egg-shaped shells analyzed take the same form of one meridional half-wave ($m = 1$) at the equator. These are typical buckling modes for axisymmetric shells with positive Gaussian curvature, such as barreled shells [11, 12].

第 5 章　结论与致谢撰写

5.1　结论

结论部分需要提醒读者读了什么，指出论文有哪些重要结论，一般分为总结段、结论段和方向段，如图 5-1 所示。对于总结段，用一两句话回顾前文，概述论文做了什么；对于结论段，回顾并提炼出结果分析与讨论中得出的重要结论，点出论文创新点和潜在应用价值；对于方向段，回顾方法、结果分析与讨论中存在的问题，展望下一步研究方向。

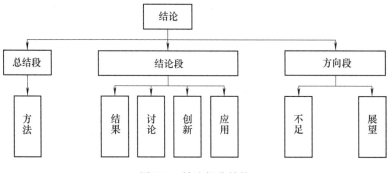

图 5-1　结论部分结构

5.1.1　总结段经典例句

We have reported results from experiments on the critical buckling load of spherical elastic shells under pressure loading, with an emphasis on how their knockdown factors are affected by an engineered dimple like imperfection.

We present results from a numerical investigation of the localization of deformation in thin elastomeric spherical shells loaded by differently shaped indenters.

We have presented systematic results of an FEM numerical exploration on the large deformation of indented thin elastic spherical shells.

This study shows that the Force-Induced-Dimple (FID), concept provides a safer estimate of buckling strength than the other two approaches which have been widely used in the past (eigenmode-type and increased-radius patch).

Computations have shown that buckling pressures of toricones with small (r/D)-ratio can be significantly smaller than buckling pressures of cones alone, i.e., without the knuckle portion.

The study reveals complicated nature of imperfection sensitivity of buckling pressure to the initial deviations from perfect shape, in externally pressurised domed end closures.

Although the above results are purely numerical, several conclusions can be drawn for design purposes.

Imperfection analyses on axially compressed CFRP, GFRP and aluminium cylindrical shells through the finite element simulations were presented.

The results of test and numerical analysis indicate that this new deterministic approach has the potential to provide an improved and less conservative shell design in order to reduce weight and cost of thin-walled shell structures.

Short conical shell with constrained radial displacements and rotations at both ends show significant sensitivity of buckling loads to the initial geometric imperfections.

The paper highlights several issues associated with plastic buckling of steel cones subjected to axial compression, external pressure or both.

This paper reports on the first experimental results on the combined stability of relatively thick metallic cones.

Comparison of experimental data with numerical estimates of buckling loads has revealed the following:

Two nominally identical cones failed at the same magnitude of pressure, hence confirming good repeatability of the experimental data.

This paper has, through experiment and numerical calculations (both axisymmetric and 3D), revealed a number of difficulties which exist when dealing with layered metallic shells.

The paper shows that experiments related to static buckling of pressure vessel components have remained relevant to a wide range of industries over the last decade or so.

It has been shown that bowed out shells can support much higher external, hydrostatic pressure than mass equivalent cylinders.

It appears that the use of bowed-out cylindrical shells for multi-segment pressure hull offers several benefits.

Barreling out of cylindrical shells offers a means for increasing their buckling strength when the shells are subjected to static external pressure.

Two sets of nominally identical cylinders (1mm and 2mm wall thickness) failed at almost the same magnitude of collapse force.

The present series of tests, on externally pressurized, near-perfect machined torispherical and hemispherical shells having $R_s/t \ll 300$ and made from mild steel has shown that:

Several conclusions can be drawn from this work.

This paper presents the numerical investigation of elastic stability of shells of revolution.

A simple procedure to create a family of shells of revolution of constant mass and constant volume has been shown.

In the paper the problem of elastic stability of the barreled shell under radial pressure is discussed.

In the present paper the results of the theoretical and numerical (FEM) study on the strength and stability of shells in the form of Cassini oval are presented. The study covers the pre-buckling, buckling and post-buckling state.

In the paper the results on stress and stability analysis of the clothoidal shell of revolution are presented.

In summary, by combining experimental and numerical tools we have shown that snap-through instabilities at constant volume can be triggered when multiple fluidic segments with a highly nonlinear pressure-volume relation are interconnected, and that such unstable transitions can be exploited to amplify the response of the system.

Our analysis shows that a circular thin region in a spherical shell, although a simple inhomogeneity to describe, strongly influences the buckling properties in important and subtle ways.

Our simulations have shown that the shape of a shell that is collapsed by an external pressure depends on the deformation rate as well as on the Föppl-von Kármán number.

5.1.2 结论段经典例句

（1）创新点

To the best of our knowledge, this is the first time that experimental results on the knockdown factors of imperfect spherical shells have been accurately predicted, through both finite element modeling and shell theory solutions.

A new approach is presented to analyze the buckling behavior of an orthotropic elliptical cylindrical shell due to the effect of radial loads and resting on a Winkler-type foundation.

It is also surprising to see virtually no sensitivity of buckling loads to the initial shape imperfections for the case of lateral pressure, only.

This is the first study into elastic-plastic buckling of unstiffened truncated conical shells under simultaneously acting axial compression and an independent external pressure.

Our study opens avenues for the design of the next generation of soft actuators and robots in which small amounts of volume are sufficient to achieve significant ranges of motion.

（2）作用/应用/运用/用途

This observation is particularly important for estimates of buckling strength at the design stage where the worst possible scenario is being adopted to be followed by the knock down factor(s).

It provides designers with a safe design at the preliminary stage (providing the worst possible scenario).

We hope that our results will instigate a resurgence of interest on the mechanics of thin spherical shells and motivate future explorations on the effect of other types of imperfections on their buckling behavior.

The critical pressure and mode shapes obtained from the present study can be utilised for the design of actuators for control components and pressure sensing elements.

The SPLA demonstrated attractive ability for designing imperfection in axially compressed composite cylindrical shells and promoted a desirable technique in a preliminary design process or an evaluation of a buckling failure.

Considering that the SPLA can be applied on perfect cylindrical shells, this methodology could be a good guideline for pre-design of cylindrical shell structures prone to buckle.

The new concept shall be expanded to stiffened shells and dynamic loading.

Yet, these loading paths are of practical relevance.

Suggestions have been made for the possible inclusion of such domes into the current design codes: ASME VIII, PD55000, and ECCS recommendations.

Although here we have focused specifically on controlling the nonlinear response of fluidic actuators, we believe that our analysis can also be used to enhance the response of other types of actuators (e. g., thermal, electrical and mechanical) by rationally introducing strong nonlinearities. Our approach therefore enables the design of a class of nonlinear systems that is waiting to be explored.

Besides contributing to our fundamental understanding of buckling transitions in inhomogeneous shells, our results can be applied to designing capsules with tunable shapes.

This property could be exploited for applications, such as release of encapsulated materials under specific environmental conditions, that require precise control over the pressure at which buckling happens.

These and many more shell shapes and inhomogeneities can be explored using numerical simulations of the type used in this work.

This generic behaviour also applies to other types of deformation, for example when a dimple is formed by indenting the capsule with a point force [6, 7, 9], when the capsule is pressed between rigid plates [7] or when the capsule adheres to a substrate [10].

Our capsules may be used to guide colloidal self-assembly; for example, a colloidal particle can spontaneously bind to the indentation formed during buckling through a lock-and-key mechanism [39]. This mechanism is typically applied to a homogeneous colloidal particle, which buckles through the formation of a single indentation at a random position on its surface.

5.1.3 方向段经典例句

(1) 不足/缺点/缺陷/问题

Finally, variable wall thickness, embedded manufacturing stresses, true path of fibres, and other lamination stacking were not addressed here.

Finally, these numerical results are based on the FE calculations and it would be desirable to benchmark them against experimental data.

Failure loads were well defined during experiments but their numerical predictions can, in some cases, carry large errors (up to 31%) which, is surprising for carefully conducted tests in the laboratory.

The effect of residual stresses on possible shape distortion(s) and on the magnitude of buckling loads has not been examined.

The influence of embedded residual stresses was not part of this investigation. Both, cones and round coupons cut for material properties have not been stress relieved. Hence the effect of residual stresses remains unknown.

But it needs to be stressed that the above scatter is not unusual for buckling/collapse tests on pressure vessel shell components.

As there is no other available experimental data in the literature <u>it is difficult to generalise the findings of the paper.</u>

<u>One specific drawback seems to be associated with,</u> the <u>asyet,</u> low success in parallelization of the method.

<u>Some drawbacks associated with the optimal geometries have been identified in the paper.</u>

（2）展望

<u>We hope that</u> our exploratory numerically study <u>will help catalyze further theoretical efforts in this direction.</u> Moreover, our work has focused on elastic systems and <u>it would be interesting to perform a similar analysis for</u> metallic shells that undergo elastic-plastic deformation.

This is therefore an area of mechanics research <u>that is as relevant as ever and deserves further attention.</u>

Knowing these information for perfect shells, <u>further study can be carried out to</u> find out the effects of imperfections present in this type of shells, and on the post buckling behaviour of these shells.

This clearly would <u>justify further examination.</u>

The lower-bound approach has been verified by available experimental data but in view of a number of modelling possibilities of FID <u>it would be interesting to see carefully conducted experiments in order to check validity of the FE predictions.</u>

As these results are based on the consideration of two different shells only, <u>further parametric studies must be addressed in order to</u> increase the data pool.

<u>This in turn might indicate the need for</u> other profiles to be included into modelling in order to secure the worst possible response.

<u>This clearly would warrant a further investigation.</u>

Under repeated loading the situation is less clear and <u>it warrants further investigation.</u> The imperfection sensitivity of buckling strength along the combined stability path <u>remains an open issue also worth further study.</u>

The role of residual stresses <u>needs to be examined as</u> all four cones reported here were not stress relieved at all.

<u>This awaits further investigation in view of</u> the large sensitivity of buckling load to radial constraints at barrel edges.

<u>Whilst promising, this observation requires further investigation as no conclusion could be made at this stage.</u>

<u>It might be beneficial if</u> variation of the wall thickness is allowed in order, for example, to mitigate the edge effects.

Effects of initial geometric imperfections on the buckling strength multi-segment arrangements, and imperfections in the transfer of axial load from segment to segment <u>would also need to be addressed.</u>

Equally, only constant wall thickness was used in the paper; but a variable wall thickness would be another possibility for further studies.

In view of obtained results, it would be worth exploring the performance of multi-segmented barreled pressure hulls.

The effects of initial imperfections on the overall conclusions of this paper will be reported in a future paper.

Interesting results can be given by the examination of the influence of the radius r_0 on the buckling shape.

The authors hope to answer this question in near future.

5.1.4 结论范文分析

(1) 范文1: 球壳力学特性

深海球形耐压壳力学特性研究

3 结论

(1) 强度是厚球壳设计的主要影响因素。中面应力与内表面应力差值随着 t/R 增加而逐渐增大, 当 t/R 增加到 0.075 时, 两者差值达到最大为 10.4%, 即使 t/R 为 1/20 时, 两者差值也达到了 7.1%。建议以内表面应力为基准设计和评估深海球形耐压壳。Zolley 公式误差随着 t/R 增加而逐渐增大, 当 t/R 为 0.075 时, 两者差值达到最大为 2.1%, 薄壳理论可用于厚球壳稳定性初步评估。经验法求解球形耐压壳浮力系数偏于保守, 其误差随着 t/R 增加而逐渐增大, 当 t/R 达到 0.075 时, 误差达到 10.1%, 即使 t/R 为 1/20 时, 误差也高达 6.8%。(*总结段*) 建议采用解析法评估深海球形耐压壳的浮力系数。(*方向段*)

(2) 综合考虑计算精度和效率, 建议采用网球划分、4 节点完全积分线性壳单元、单元平均尺寸 $0.07R$, 建立球形耐压壳的壳单元数值方案。建议采用网球划分、三维 20 节点减缩积分体单元、周向单元平均尺寸 $0.07R$、厚度方向 4 层单元, 建立球形耐压壳的体单元数值方案。壳单元数值方案、薄壳理论方案可用于浅海耐压壳设计与评估, 体单元数值方案、厚球壳理论方案可用于深海耐压壳设计与评估。(*总结段*) 建议船级社在进行深海耐压壳设计规范修订时, 采用内表面应力、厚壳临界屈曲载荷作为评价指标。(*方向段*)

(2) 范文2: 球壳屈曲

Buckling of Spherical Shells Subjected to External Pressure: A Comparison of Experimental and Theoretical Data

4. Conclusions

In the present work, the results of experimental, analytical, and numerical study into the buckling behaviors of spherical shells are presented, as well as the effects of constitutive modes on the buckling loads of these shells. (*总结段*) The experimental buckling load increased monotonically with an increase in t_{ave}/r_{ave}, which was as little as 15.07%-24.55% of the elastic buckling load determined using Zoelly's equation. The experimental collapsed modes of all the shells were identical; all of them assumed the form of a local dent, which is typical of shells of revolution with a positive Gaussian curvature. (*结论段*)

Geometrically and materially nonlinear buckling analyses were performed on the spherical shellsfor deterministic imperfections. Very good correlation was obtained between the numerical buckling loads and the experimental ones. The path of each spherical shell had an unstable characteristic typical of shell structures. All the shells buckled within an elastic-plastic range. The buckling and postbuckling modes of all the analyzed shells were similar and assumed the form of a local dent, which was in very good agreement with the experimental results. (*结论段*)

The effects of constitutive models on the buckling of spherical shells were demonstrated numerically according to the buckling load. The failures of spherical shells varied gradually from elastic buckling to elastic-plasticbuckling as the wall thicknesses increased. Very good agreement was obtained among the elastic-plastic, elastic-perfectly plastic, and experimental results. The elastic-perfectly plastic assumption resulted in a highly accurate prediction. The elastic assumption yielded a fairly large increase in the magnitude of the buckling load above the elastic-plastic assumption and experiment. (*结论段*)

This work therefore indicates that the real load-carrying capacity of a spherical shell can be obtained numerically from measured geometric shape and average wall thickness, as well as from the assumption of elastic-perfectly plastic material properties. The current approach appears to be effective for other shells of revolution with typical meridional profiles, such as cylindrical and conical shells, as well asfor shells of revolution with nontypical meridional profiles, such as barreled and egg-shaped shells. (*结论段*) However, some limitations merit attention. Although the predicted buckling loads and final failure modes were verified experimentally, the critical buckling modes were not examined through testing. Moreover, the manufacturing process caused some variance in the wall thicknesses, and that variance exerted an effect on the buckling of spherical shells; however, this effect was not studied. These limitations require further investigation in the near future. (*方向段*)

5.2 致谢

致谢是感谢对该项研究、论文构思、撰写工作提供帮助的个人、项目、单位，体现作者具有良好的学术道德和对别人贡献的敬意。其中，个人包括为参与试验、论文构思、撰写但不足以列为作者的团队人员，对论文提出建设性意见的同事、专家或审稿人，以及为该项研究提供资助的自然人；项目包括企业项目、政府项目、实验室项目等课题；单位包括为该项研究提供资助、试验场地、参考资料等组织机构。目前，致谢技术贡献者、政府基金和审稿人最为普遍，如图 5-2 所示。

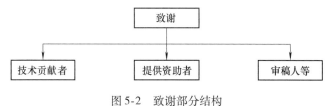

图 5-2　致谢部分结构

5.2.1 第一人称写法经典例句

We are grateful to Professor Gustavo Guinea, who provided us with preliminary data on the response of arterial tissue from patients affected by Marfan's syndrome. The authors acknowledge support from the Ministerio de Cienciae Innovación in Spain under the Project reference DPI2008-03769 during the preparation of this work.

We are grateful to Ashkan Vaziri and Amin Adjari for fruitful discussions. A. N. acknowledges the support of NSF through a Graduate Research Fellowship (1122374) and MIT through an Asher H. Shapiro Graduate Fellowship. P. M. R. thanks support from the National Science Foundation, CMMI-1351449 (CAREER).

We thank J. Hutchinson for helpful discussions on shell theory, F. Spaepen for pointing us towards relevant literature on elastic instabilities, E. Katifori and G. Vliegenthart for guidance with numerical simulations, S. Datta for general discussions, and the anonymous referees for constructive suggestions and corrections. We acknowledge support by the National Science Foundation via Grant DMR1005289 and through the Harvard Materials Research Science and Engineering Center via Grant DMR0820484.

We thank Jens Hohage and Christian Wischnewski for their numerical simulation results.

We thank David R. Nelson, Jayson Paulose (Harvard University) and Rudolf Merkel (Forschungszentrum Jülich) for many fruitful discussions.

We thank Martin Brinkmann for discussions and bringing Ref. [26] to our attention. We acknowledge financial support from the Mercator Research Center Ruhr (MERCUR).

Our sincere thanks to Dr. Ing. Bodo Geier for his advice and discussions. Special thanks to the test team of the Institute of Composite Structures and Adaptive Systems.

5.2.2 其他人称写法经典例句

This work was supported by Amore-Pacific, the NSF (DMR-1006546), and the Harvard MRSEC (DMR-0820484). Work by D. R. N. was also supported by NSF Grant No. DMR-1005289. S. S. D. acknowledges funding from Conoco Phillips. It is a pleasure to acknowledge H. A. Stone for communicating the lubrication theory solution used here; D. Vella for stimulating discussions and for helpful feedback on the manuscript; G. M. Whitesides for comments that motivated some of this work; and the anonymous referees for valuable feedback on the manuscript. The computer programs used to conduct numerical simulations are based on code generously provided by E. Katifori. S. S. D., S. -H. K., and J. P. contributed equally to this work.

This work was supported by the National Science Foundation (CAREER CMMI-1351449).

The author would like to express his thanks and appreciation to the anonymous reviewers whose substantial and constructive comment significantly improved the paper. (感谢审稿人)

The author wishes to thank Dr O. Ifayefunmi for his help whilst preparing this paper.

The authors would like to express sincere gratitude to Politeknik Sultan Salahuddin Abdul Aziz Shahand thank the Ministry of Higher Education, Malaysia, through the High Impact Research Grant (UM. C/625/1/HIR/MOHE/ENG/33).

The research leading to these results has received funding from the European Community's Seventh Framework Programme (FP7/ 2007-2013).

The author wishes to acknowledge and thank Messrs S. Pennington, L. Ruong and P. Smith for their inputs into this paper.

The authors are thankful to the Technical University of Poznan and the University of Liverpool for providing financial assistance to one of them (K, M.).

The author wishes to acknowledge help he has received from Mr. P. Wang in obtaining some of the experimental data.

The author will also like to acknowledge the financial support received from the Faculty of Engineering Technology, Universiti Teknikal Malaysia Melaka under the auspices of UTeM short terms funding.

The authors wish to thank Mr. S. Pennington and Mr. Z. Yan for their help and assistance in conducting the experimental work.

The work has been supported by Ministry of Science and Higher Education Grant no. N N501 038535.

The authors acknowledge support from the Ministerio de Ciencia e Innovación in Spain under the project reference DPI2011-26167 during the preparation of this work. The authors would like to thank the anonymous reviewers for their valuable comments.

The authors acknowledge support from the Ministerio de Ciencia e Innovación in Spain under the project reference DPI2014-58885-R.

5.3 实例练习

运用所学知识，仿照 5.1.4 节、5.2 节，分析以下实例。

（1）实例 1

硬土-软土插桩过程数值分析及验证

4 结论

基于 Hossain M S 土工离心模型试验，采用 CEL 法建立了自升式平台插桩过程的数值模型。利用 Hossain M S 的试验结果对数值模型进行了验证，结果表明：数值解与试验值吻合程度较好，验证了数值模型的可靠性。

采用数值模型计算了插桩过程中土壤速度矢量图及变形图，以分析土壤流动特性。结果表明：插桩过程中发生了硬土表面局部隆起、硬土-软土界面变形、空腔形成、土壤回流、局部土壤流动等现象。为了分析土壤特性参数变化对插桩过程的影响，采用数值模型模拟了硬土、软土参数改变后土壤的最终变形情况。结果表明：硬土、软土的强度比越小，桩靴下方硬土块体积越小，桩靴上方硬土分布越连续、均匀，空腔深度越大；土壤重度越大，桩靴上方硬土回流量越大，空腔深度越小，而土壤重度对桩靴下方硬土块形状和体积几乎没有影响。

采用数值模型计算了插桩深度与插桩阻力的关系。结果表明：硬土、软土的强度比越大、有效重度比越小，发生"刺穿"的可能性越高。

采用数值模型计算了桩靴底部压力分布。结果表明：桩靴底部压力由内向外先增大、后减小、再增大，证明《海上移动平台入级与建造规范》中关于桩靴底部压力的线性分布假设与实际情况不符。

（2）实例2

轮胎硫化过程数值分析及试验研究

4 结论

1）采用混合定律模型进行轮胎硫化过程数值模拟，计算结果与试验结果具有良好的一致性，轮胎最难硫化部位是胎肩处的600号节点，通过N600处的焦烧时间、最高温度、工程正硫化时间的数值可以确定轮胎硫化工艺设计参数。

2）当胶囊厚度减小50%时，N600处的焦烧时间缩短5.98%，N600处的最高温度提高1.83%，工程正硫化时间降低11.84%；当初始预热温度增加66%时，N600处的焦烧时间缩短27.05%，N600处的最高温度提高0.2%，工程正硫化时间降低2.83%；当蒸汽平均温度提高5%时，N600处的焦烧时间缩短1.52%，N600的最高温度提高3.65%，工程正硫化时间降低9.29%。

3）本文运用的建模方法和分析思路有效可靠，可用于分析其他类型的轮胎及复杂橡胶件的硫化过程。

致谢：

感谢风神轮胎股份有限公司和江苏省道路载运工具新技术应用重点实验室对论文的资金和试验支持，感谢江苏科技大学图书馆张鑫老师提供的相关论文信息。

（3）实例3

Investigation on Egg-shaped Pressure Hulls

4. Conclusions

It is until now that the spherical pressure hull is the most extensively used structure for the deep manned submersible. However, low buckling resistance, difficult interior arrangement and poor hydrodynamics are found with this type of pressure hull. In this study, investigations on egg-shaped pressure hulls are performed to improve these problems possessed by the spherical pressure hull.

As shown in the above research, shape and size of the geometry imperfections have a big effect on the buckling load of pressure hulls. For shell structures with densely spaced eigenvalues, higher rather than the first eigenmode imperfection is often the worst equivalent buckling mode which might lead to the lowest buckling load. The more densely spaced eigenvalues exists, the more geometry imperfection sensitivity is the shell with. Egg-shaped pressure hulls are less sensitive to the geometry imperfections compared with the spherical pressure hull.

Finally, it is found that safety, buoyancy reserve, and space efficiency of egg-shaped pressure hulls could be optimally coordinated, which perform better than spherical pressure hull. This research work offers a new concept of pressure hull designs for future development of the deep-sea manned submersible.

Acknowledgments

This work was supported by a grant from the Natural Science Foundation of Jiangsu Province (BK20150469). The authors would like to thank Prof. Tao Liu for his excellent technical supports and Prof. Wenwei Wu for critically reviewing results.

(4) 实例4

Buckling of Egg-shaped Shells Subjected to External Pressure

5. Conclusions

This paper proposes a family of egg-shaped shells that have a constant capacity and mass from a bionic perspective. To determine the SI of the egg-shaped shell, the minor and major axes of 333 goose eggs were carefully measured. According to the experimental results, eight SIs in the 0.65-0.72 range were selected for creating the egg-shaped shell. Besides, to extend the SI range, six shells with SIs of 0.4, 0.5, 0.6, 0.8, 0.9 and 1.0 were also proposed. In addition, the meridians, volumes, and surface areas of 50 goose eggs were obtained experimentally to confirm the egg-shaped equation proposed by Narushin and the volumes and surface area functions proposed by Mohsein. Close agreement was obtained between Narushin's and Mohsein's predictions and the experimental data.

The results of the numerical and analytical analyses of the buckling behavior of fourteen egg-shaped shells are provided. The numerical linear buckling loads of the egg-shaped shells increase monotonically in conjunction with increases in the SI; this agrees with the analytical results. The linear buckling shape of the egg-shaped shells has the form of several circumferential waves and one meridional half-wave. This is typical for shells of revolution with positive Gaussian curvature. The imperfection sensitivity increases as the shapes become more spherical. The equilibrium path of all of the shells has an unstable characteristic.

The critical buckling shape is identical to the linear buckling shape. The postbuckling mode at the end of the paths has the form of local dents; this finding is consistent with results obtained in previous studies. Based on our research, this is the first study to investigate the effect of SI on the buckling and postbuckling behavior of egg-shaped shells. Our study presents a new design concept: non-typical shells of revolution that are based on biological properties. The proposed configuration has potential in fields such as underwater pressure hulls, underground pressure vessels, and underpressure tanks. Our results are encouraging and should be further explored using a series of laboratory scale tests; the results can be compared with those obtained for other non-typical shells such as the barreled shells proposed by Blachut and Jasion. The effect of openings on the load carrying capacity should be determined to ensure that the application of egg-shaped shells in engineering is viable.

Acknowledgments

This work was supported by two grants from the Natural Science Foundation of Jiangsu Province, China (BK20140512, and BK20150469). The authors would like to express their thanks and appreciation to the anonymous reviewers whose constructive comments significantly improved the paper.

第 6 章 图表处理

6.1 图表概述

6.1.1 使用图表的原因

一位审稿人曾经这样写道:"我审稿时看稿件的顺序是题目、摘要、图表、前言、参考文献和正文。"由此可见,在论文投稿时,论文中的图表对论文的质量来说十分重要,有时甚至会决定一篇论文能否发表。所以如果投稿人希望在高质量期刊上面尤其是 SCI 期刊上面发表论文,图表的处理至关重要。

那么,论文中为什么要插入图表呢?首先,图表用于形象地表达正文所述结果。换言之,它们是表达正文结果最有效的方式。每一篇科技论文尤其是 SCI 科技论文都应该有一点创新的东西,这一点创新的东西就是这篇论文的质。论文的质对他人来讲都是新东西,都含有专业性很强的新知识或新方法。因此,作者要花大量的文字语言,来详细介绍和描述这一新东西以让他人明白。读者需要再完全理解和重新想象这些文字语言,才能明白作者的原意。但是由于文字语言本身的局限性,作者的原意有时可能被误解了、被曲解了。

再者,由于英文对我们来说是外语,我们撰写的英文文字一般都带有中文文字的结构和文化。不会读或写中文论文的读者,有时很难理解我们撰写的英文文字,更难通过我们撰写的英文文字,来重新想象我们的创新原意。

因此,处理好论文中的图表,对于投稿人来说十分重要。此外,所有期刊都对图表有自己期刊的具体要求,这些在投稿指南中可以查到。本章将从图表分类,组成结构和制图实例三个方面来进行阐述,组织结构如图 6-1 所示。

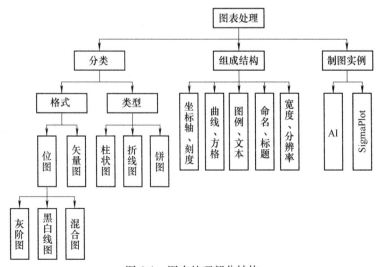

图 6-1 图表处理部分结构

6.1.2 处理图表的通用原则

这里总结了投稿中处理图表的一些共通性原则：

1）确保一篇论文中所有图表使用统一的字体和字号

2）图表里的字体和正文里的字体统一起来（字号尽量也和正文相统一，但是考虑到图形中的一些其他因素可以略微放大或缩小）

3）将插图按照它们在图中出现的顺序进行编号（通常使用（a）、（b）、（c）、…进行编号）

4）使用合理的命名习惯对图片进行命名

5）按出版社的要求处理图片的大小（宽度、分辨率）

6）每个图都给出一个单独的标题描述

7）投稿时图文根据期刊要求是否要分开，如果是，那么每个图片都要作为一个单独的文件给出（投稿时，正文和图片）

6.2 图表的分类

论文中的图表种类繁多，在不同场合适用的图表不尽相同，为了在论文写作中更加熟练使用各种图表，首先要认识各类图表，了解期刊对不同图表的要求。下面将按照不同方法对图表进行分类以更加深入了解论文中的不同类型图表。

6.2.1 按照图表格式对图表进行分类

图表按照格式分类可以分为矢量图和位图两大类。

所谓矢量图是根据几何特性来绘制图形，是用线段和曲线描述图像。矢量可以是一个点或一条线，矢量图只能靠软件生成，矢量图文件占用内存空间较小，因为这种类型的图像文件包含独立的分离图像，可以自由无限制地重新组合。

所谓位图图像也称为点阵图像，位图使用我们称为像素的一格一格的小点来描述图像。

二者最大的区别在于矢量图形与分辨率无关，可以将它缩放到任意大小和以任意分辨率在输出设备上打印出来，都不会影响清晰度，而位图是由一个一个像素点产生，当放大图像时，像素点也放大了，但每个像素点表示的颜色是单一的，所以在位图放大后就会出现咱们平时所见到的马赛克状。

同样源数据制作好的位图和矢量图效果如图 6-2 所示，而将两种图表放大到一定倍数后得到的效果图如图 6-3 所示。

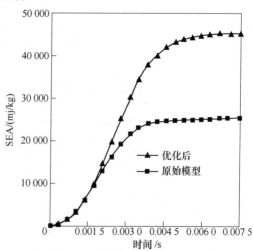

图 6-2 同一源数据制作的位图和矢量图

 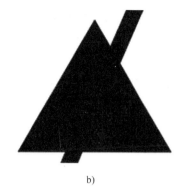

a) b)

图 6-3 位图和矢量图放大到一定倍数后的差异
a）位图格式 b）矢量图格式

位图的文件类型很多，如 bmp、pcx、gif、jpg、tif、photoshop 的 psd 等；一般期刊要求的位图图片格式为 TIFF 和 JPEG 格式，一般处理图片的软件都可以处理位图。

矢量图形格式也很多，如 Adobe Illustrator 的 AI、EPS；SVG、AutoCAD 的 dwg；dxfCorel DRAW 的 cdr 等。一般期刊要求的矢量图图片格式为 EPS 格式，获得矢量图需要通过特殊的矢量图处理软件如 AI、SigmaPlot 等进行处理。

期刊对位图和矢量图的通用要求如下：

（1）位图图表

根据灰阶度的不同，位图又可以分为如下几类：

1）灰阶图又称灰度图（Gray Scale Image）

把白色与黑色之间按对数关系分为若干等级，称为灰度，一般分为 256 阶。用灰度表示的图像称作灰阶图，如图 6-4 所示。要求保存为 TIFF 格式或者 JPEG 格式，分辨率一般情况下不得低于 300dpi（具体参照投稿期刊要求）。

图片要满足以下要求：

1）图表模式为灰度模式

2）图表分辨率不得低于 300dpi

3）线条在图片中的位置要紧实

4）如果可以，使用杂志推荐的字体给图表命名

5）保存为 TIFF 格式

2）黑白线图（Bitmapped line drawings）

这种图主要用于折线图、散点图等线图，如图 6-2 所示，主要的特点就是图片中只有纯黑、纯白两种颜色组成的线条。

图 6-4 蛋型球壳灰阶图

图表要满足以下要求：

1）图表中仅有黑白两种颜色且为线图

2）图表分辨率不得低于 1000dpi，如果有特别细的线不得低于 1200dpi

3）线条在图片中的位置要紧实

4）如果杂志有规定，使用杂志推荐的字体给图片命名

5) 保存为 TIFF 或者 JPEG 格式

3) 线图和其他颜色（彩色图、灰阶图）的混合图（combination artwork）

如图 6-5 所示，线图和灰阶图混合；如图 6-6 所示，线图和彩色图混合。图 6-5、图 6-6 所采用的案例源于同一源数据，但是图 6-5 采用不同数据标记点，而图 6-6 采用不同颜色来区分不同线型。分辨率一般不得低于 500dpi。

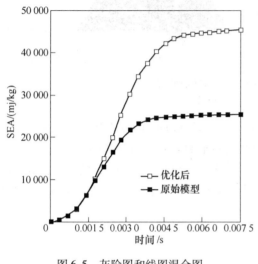

图 6-5　灰阶图和线图混合图

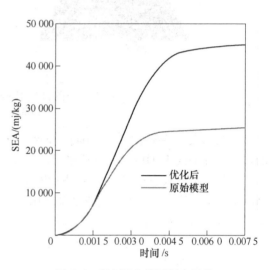

图 6-6　彩色图和线图混合图片

图表要满足以下要求：

1）图表中彩色图和线图混合用 RGB 模式，灰阶图和线图混合采用灰度模式

2）线条在图片中的位置要紧实

3）如果杂志有规定，使用杂志推荐的字体给图片命名

4）保存为 TIFF 或者 JPEG 格式

（2）矢量图图表

矢量图形格式是光栅图形（即位图，例如照片）的补充。如果期刊投稿过程中用到了矢量图，正常情况下期刊的投稿指南中会要求矢量图格式为 EPS 矢量格式，可以由 AI 和 SigmaPlot 软件制作生成。

混合矢量图是指通过软件在位图中加入文本注释、线条和箭头等，然后另存为 EPS 格式，这样生成的图片为混合矢量图。

图表要满足的要求：

1）嵌入的字体使用期刊要求的字体，以具体期刊为准

2）线宽从 0.1~1.5 磅之间变化

3）如果是混合矢量图，要设置为 RGB 模式

6.2.2　按照图表类型对图表进行分类

为了达到不同的效果，论文写作中会用到不同类型的图表，每种图表根据其本身的特点都有特定的使用场合和使用标准。下面根据图标的类型对图表进行分类。

(1) 柱状图

如图 6-7 所示，柱状图能够使人们一眼看出各个数据的大小，易于比较数据之间的差别，能清楚地表示出数量的多少，但是并不是所有场合都适用柱状图。

在使用柱状图时要注意以下几点：

1) 用纯黑纯白表示不同柱图不可取，用不同灰度表示要更好些，如图 **6-7** 所示

2) 当前面一组数据对后面一组数据有影响的时候不能用柱状图

3) 柱状图主要是表示不同类型数据之间的差异

4) 图中整个柱身的宽度要大于柱与柱之间的距离

5) 图表中尽量减少不必要的曲线，当数据类型较多尽量使用线图

6) 在柱图中，每组最多也就两到三个"柱"

(2) 折线图

如图 6-8 所示，折线统计图能够显示数据的变化趋势，反映事物的变化情况。绘制折线图时应该注意以下几点：

1) 折线图用于显示研究结果随时间变化的规律

2) 制作折线图时要满足期刊对图表的分辨率要求

3) 可以通过线段类型、线段颜色、数据标记点形状或者数据标记点颜色其中之一对线图曲线进行标记区别

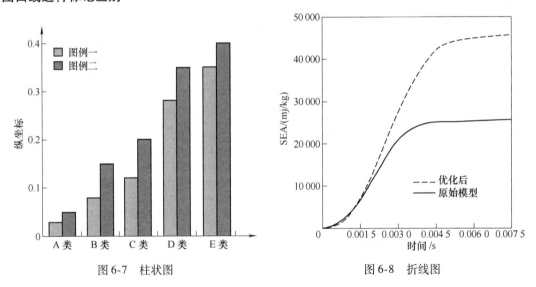

图 6-7　柱状图　　　　　图 6-8　折线图

(3) 饼状图

在科技论文中，饼状图一般被认为是最浪费版面但又不能说明规律的一种图表，所以在科技论文投稿时，尽量不要使用饼状图。

6.2.3　总结

为了获得清晰的图表，需要对图表进行处理，但是期刊也制定了以下规定：图像中的特点不能被增强、遮蔽、移动、移除；但是调整亮度、对比度或颜色平衡这些是可以接受的，只要它们不掩盖或消除原文中的任何信息；对特点的非线性调整是不允许的。

6.3 图表的格式

6.3.1 期刊推荐的图表格式

一般期刊建议 EPS、PDF、TIFF 或 JPEG 的文件格式用于电子稿。如果是 Microsoft Office 文件（Word，Excel 和 PowerPoint）也接受。进一步详细信息参考投稿准则。

EPS（封装的 PostScrip）是矢量图形（图表，图形，技术图纸，注释图像）的首选格式。

Adobe Acrobat PDF 格式（PDF）主要用于发行打印文件，是一个越来越常见的文件格式，这种格式可用于提交任何类型的图表作品。

TIFF（标记图像文件格式）是推荐的位图文件格式，灰阶图、彩色图、混合模式图像都适合。

JPEG 文件用于彩色图、混合图像（照片等）。

Microsoft Office 文件（Word，Excel 和 PowerPoint）能够制作一系列不同类型的文件，比如文字文档、表格、演示文档和数据库等。

6.3.2 其他软件的图表

基本上所有其他常用软件都允许用户以各种格式导出图表。通常情况下，用户可以通过"另存为"或者"导出图表为"的方式选择一个恰当的格式，一般为 EPS 或者 TIFF 格式。

EPS 格式的图表要求选择附件的形式（选择最高水平显示），包括其中的字体（选择嵌入所有字体）。某些图片软件没有这些功能，但是可以输出为 PDF 格式。

对于 TIFF 格式有分辨率的要求，那么就选择可选项中的最高分辨率，或者选择图片分辨率为 1000dpi、其他分辨率为 500dpi。

如果上述两种格式都不能实现，就直接将其以图片形式插入 Microsoft Word 软件里。

6.4 图表的结构组成

由于曲线图为论文中最为常见、最重要的一类图，就以曲线图为例分析图表的一般结构。

在绘制曲线图之前，要明确曲线图的几个要素：坐标轴、坐标轴名称、刻度、刻度值、曲线、方格曲线、数据标记点、图例、文本、宽度、颜色。

6.4.1 坐标轴、坐标轴名称、刻度、刻度值

横坐标起点和终点要和数据的起点和终点相适应，虽然坐标轴一般从 0 刻度开始，但是如果数据起始点和 0 值相差很远，起始点也可以从非零点开始。一个坐标轴的刻度一般不得少于 5 个，但是不得多于 10 个（包括起始刻度）。

为了使读者在读图时获得直观的数据效果，期刊会要求作者尽量绘制 4 轴图表，这样读者就可以方便地在图表上面绘制曲线，而不用标尺。将右侧 Y 轴放在 X 轴的一个精准坐标位置处，将上侧的 X 轴放在 Y 轴的某一个精准坐标位置（右、上侧的坐标轴应该在下、左

侧坐标轴的一个刻度处）。X、Y 轴可以使用不同的刻度。

刻度线要使用粗的大线条，尽量将刻度线放在折线图的内部，这样视觉效果更好。

如果 X 轴的上下两轴的刻度相同，那么上侧 X 轴就不需要标注数值；这种规律也适用于 Y 轴的左右两轴。

坐标轴名称由制图软件生成或者写入，字体和字号应满足期刊的规定要求。

如图 6-9a 所示，横纵坐标轴均为 6 个刻度，并且为 4 轴图表，上、右两坐标轴均和下、左整刻度对齐，且上、右两坐标轴分别和下、左刻度相同，所以不需要标注数值。

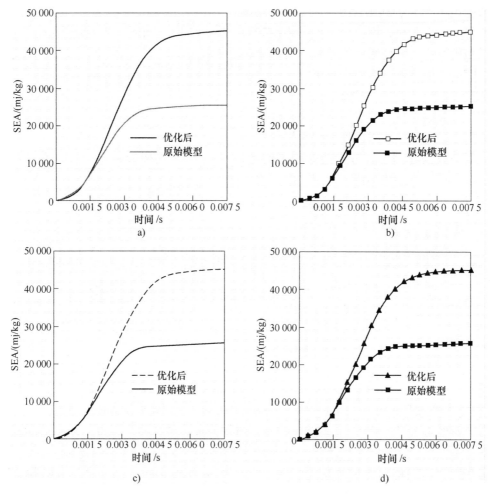

图 6-9　同一源数据得到的四种曲线图

6.4.2　曲线、方格曲线

尽量不要在图片中插入方格线，哪怕它们是虚线、点划线也不行，如果非加不可，需改为灰阶图，而且方格线线条要尽量细，要使数据曲线尽量明显，区别于其他曲线。

对曲线尤其是点划线来说，如果不对它们进行线宽设置，线型会太细，所以要对坐标轴、刻度线、曲线进行线宽设置。

在一幅图里的不同曲线，可以用实线、虚线、点划线等不同特征进行区分。但是曲线的特征之间要有明显区别,不能混淆。

数据标记点用以区分不同数据代表的曲线,甚至也可以仅用一些数据标记点而不用曲线来表达数据的趋势。在使用数据标记点时可以用不同形状的数据标记点来表达不同曲线,如圆形、三角形、矩形等;也可以用不同颜色来表达不同曲线,即使所投期刊采用黑白色发表,不同颜色在转换为灰阶图时,因为颜色不同会有不同的灰度。

如图6-10所示,此图为图6-9c添加方格线之后所得,可以看出,即使添加的方格线和数据曲线相比很细,但是依然使整幅图看起来很混乱,图例看不清晰。再如图6-9中a、b、c、d四幅图,全部源于同一组数据分别采用曲线颜色不同、数据点标记颜色不同、曲线线型不同、数据标记点形状不同四种方法来制作的图表。这四种方法在用于区分曲线时均可使用,但一幅图只需一种方法即可,切忌一幅图用多种方法。

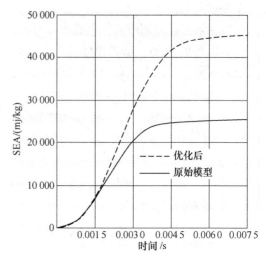

图6-10 带有方格线的曲线图

6.4.3 图例、文本

图表,尤其是通过软件生成的各类曲线图,图片里的字体类型要和正文相同。由于英文期刊正文一般要求的文字格式为:

Arial

Courier

Symbol

Times(or Times New Roman)

所以图片上面的标注信息字体也要是上面的字体,和正文保持一致(以具体期刊为准);字体大小也要和正文一致,但为了尽量做到美观,可以略微增大或者缩小。

在图表里插入的文本要尽量地少而简洁,可用简称代替全称,例如:Temperature(℃)可以换为T(℃),$2\mu m$可以代替$2\times10^{-6}m$。

图6-9中四幅图,纵坐标使用简称SEA,横坐标用Time,而非T,用以和常用的Temperature区分,图中添加图例。字体Arial,字号为8磅,和正文字号一样。

6.4.4 图表的命名、标题

(1) 命名

有时候期刊会要求所投论文正文和图表分开投稿,为了可以轻松识别作者的源文件,请确保图表的编号、类型和格式反映在文件名中。一些例子如下:

FIG1. TIF   <=>   图1以TIFF格式

SC4. EPS   <=>   表4以EPS格式

PL2. TIF   <=>   插图2以TIFF格式

为了迅速识别文件，确保文件存在扩展名。

（2）标题

图表的标题由一个简短的小标题和对图片的一个简短的描述两部分组成；图表的标题应该独立于图表之外（不要用 Photoshop 等软件将标题插入图表，将标题变成图片的一部分）。

同时，图表标题中用于解释图表的文字要尽量简洁，但也要能表达出图表含义（具体标题格式以投稿期刊为参考：例如是 figure.1 还是 Fig.1 等）。

在图表命名时，名称要有规律，文本内容要精少，用尽量少的字数表达精确的信息，字体信息要根据具体期刊规定而设置。

6.4.5 图表的宽度要求

图表的物理尺寸：正常情况下，期刊只对投稿图表的宽度做出了要求，而对其高度不作要求。期刊的出版纸张为 A4 大小，正常情况分为两栏；写作之前要确定插入图表的宽度，即确定预期的图表大小为 1 栏、1.5 栏、还是 2 栏。

如图 6-11 所示，根据经验 1 栏的图表宽度为 9cm，1.5 栏图表约 14cm 左右，2 栏图表约为 19cm 左右，具体制作图表时可略微变化，以期刊要求为准。

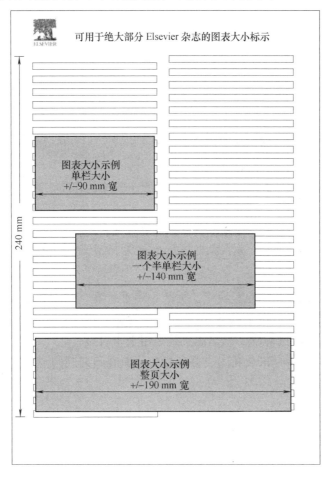

图 6-11　论文中图表的宽度要求

本章中图 6-2、图 6-10 图表物理宽度均为 8.5cm，在所投论文中占用空间 1 栏。

6.4.6 图表的分辨率

图像分辨率，像素和打印尺寸相关，像素 = 像素分辨率（dpi）×打印尺寸（英寸）。

图表的分辨率指的是像素的密度，即每英寸像素的个数，500dpi 即为 1 英寸宽度的图片里面有 500 个像素点。以 1.5 栏宽度的图片为例：

期刊要求宽度 140mm，分辨率为 500dpi，已知 1cm = 0.3937in，那么 1.5 栏宽度的图片在宽度方向上的像素点总数为

$$14 \times 0.3937 \times 500 = 2756$$

此期刊在宽度上的要求即为 2756 像素。表 6-1 列举了一些常用图像大小的像素。

表 6-1 图片像素

目标尺寸	图像宽度	300dpi	500dpi	1000dpi
最小尺寸	30mm（85 磅）	354	592	1181
1 栏	90mm（255 磅）	1063	1172	3543
1.5 栏	140mm（397 磅）	1654	2756	5512
2 栏	190mm（539 磅）	2244	3740	7480

6.5 一些总结

一般情况下对于矢量图和位图期刊分别要求的格式为 EPS 格式和 TIFF 或者 JPEG 格式，但是推荐 EPS 和 TIFF。不要将截图直接得到的图片插入文档。

图表的分辨率为图表生成时的分辨率，对于低分辨率的作品，通过软件修改分辨率是没有意义的。

对于彩色图片的颜色模式：要根据具体期刊要求来，期刊分为电子出版和纸质出版两种方式，对于在网上出版的期刊，彩色图片投稿模式为 RGB 模式，对于纸质出版的期刊，彩色图片投稿模式为 CMYK 模式。

RGB 色彩模式是最基础的色彩模式，所以 RGB 色彩模式是一个重要的模式。只要在电脑屏幕上显示的图像，就一定是以 RGB 模式。因为显示器的物理结构就是遵循 RGB 模式的。CMYK 也称作印刷色彩模式，顾名思义就是用来印刷的。

有些期刊要求在投稿时正文和图表分开投稿，而有些期刊则要求图片插入正文一起投稿，视具体期刊而定。

6.6 软件制图实例

在制作图表之前，一定要细读投稿指南（guide for authors），明确期刊对要处理图表的要求：图表的尺寸要求、所投图表格式的分辨率要求、所投图表字体字号要求（一般和正

文一样)、所投图表命名的要求;同时自己要准备:绘制图表所需数据、明确横纵坐标名称、是否需要添加图例等。

此例为以上章节处理的图表,目标宽度为 8.5cm,高度期刊不做要求;目标格式类型 TIFF;目标图表类型纯黑白线图;期刊要求分辨率不得低于 500dpi。

6.6.1 Adobe Illustrator (AI) 制作图表

步骤一:新建文档

打开 AI 软件,在菜单栏中,选择"文件"→"新建",打开如图 6-12 所示对话框。在名称一栏按照期刊的规定对制作的图表进行命名,宽度方面设定为 85mm,高度不作要求,设置为 80mm。单击"确定",软件中间区域出现空白画布。

图 6-12 新建文档

步骤二:创建散点图

如图 6-13 左图所示,在 AI 软件左侧的工具栏中,双击"柱形图工具",出现如图 6-13 右图所示的对话框。

类型选项框中选择"散点图"图标;数值轴选择"位于两侧";选项中选取"标记数据点""连接数据点""绘制填充线";线宽设置为 0.25pt。

设置图表纵坐标刻度。在图 6-13 右图左上角"图表选项"的下拉三角选项中选择"数值轴",这里"数值轴"即为纵坐标,打开如图 6-14 所示对话框。选择"忽略计算出的值",最大值/最小值即为目标纵坐标的最大值与最小值,此例的纵坐标数值范围设置为: 0~50000,分为 5 段。设置之后如图 6-14 所示。

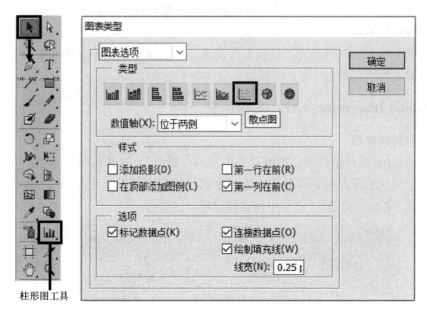

图 6-13 图表选项设置

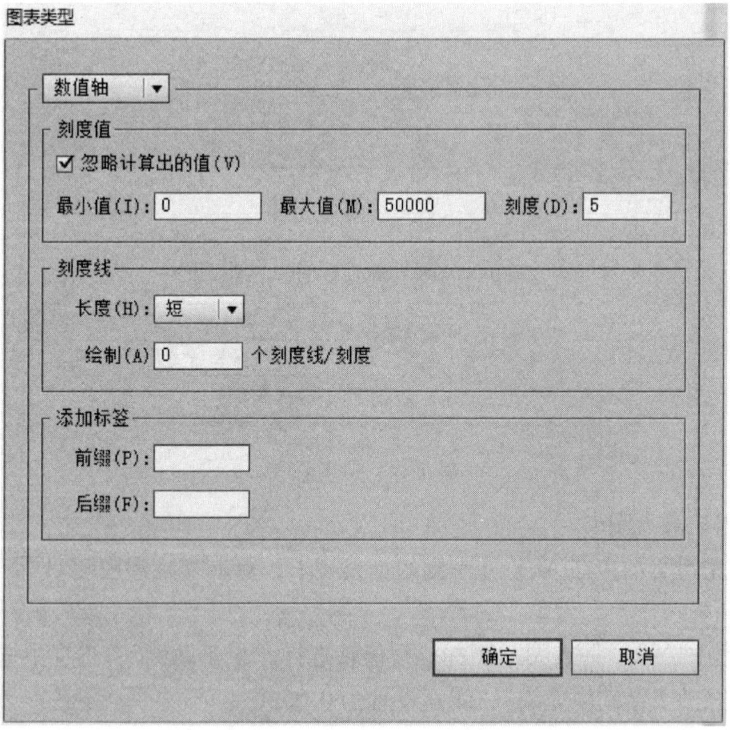

图 6-14 纵坐标选项设置

设置图表横坐标刻度。在图 6-13 右图左上角"图表选项"的下拉三角选项中选择"下侧轴",这里"下侧轴"即为横坐标,打开如图 6-15 所示对话框。选择"忽略计算出的值",最大值/最小值即为目标纵坐标的最大值与最小值,此例的横坐标数值范围设置为:0~0.0075,分为5段。设置之后如图6-15所示。

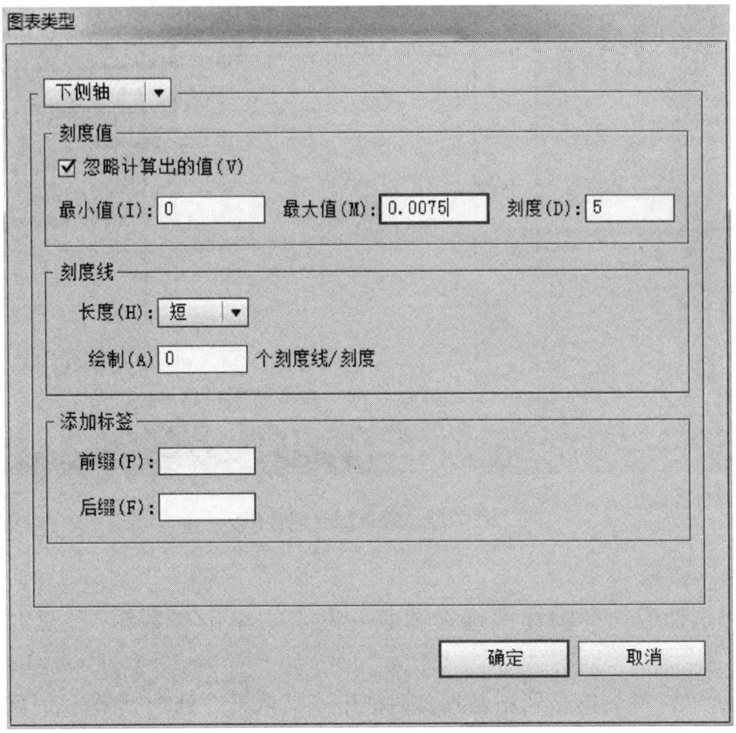

图 6-15 横坐标选项设置

单击确定按钮,此刻鼠标变为十字光标,在画布左上角处单击一下,出现如图6-16所示的对话框,设置散点图的宽度和高度。目标图表的整体宽度为85mm,故将散点图的大小设置如下

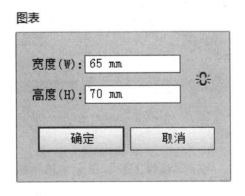

图 6-16 设置散点图的宽度和高度

单击确定按钮,出现如图6-17所示界面。单击左侧工具栏的"选择工具"图标,选择散点图将其移动至画布中心,但注意不要将其移出画布;单击"选择工具",选中右侧、上侧刻度值,将其设置为无色。效果如图6-17所示。

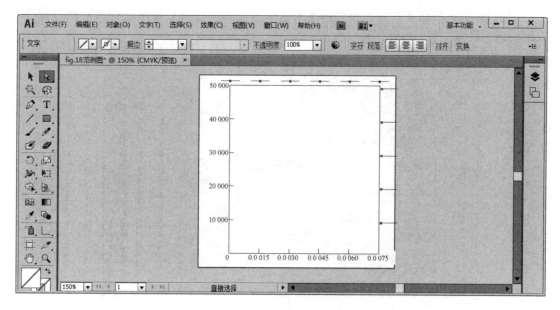

图 6-17 散点图界面效果

步骤三：导入数据

通过单击"选择工具"图标→选择图表→右击→单击"数据"，调出待输入数据对话框。

如图 6-18 所示，将数据整列粘贴到对话框中。默认第一列为纵坐标，第二列为横坐标，第二组数据以此类推。若原始数据按"行"排列，可通过单击"换位行/列"按钮变更数据排列顺序。单击"应用"按钮，生成的折线图如图 6-19 所示。

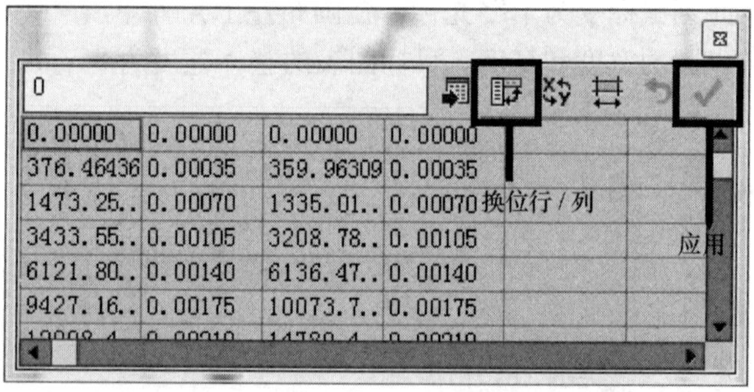

图 6-18 导入数据

步骤四：标记数据点

如果不需要标记数据点，单击"选择工具"图标→选择图表→右击→单击"类型"，"标记数据点"选项取消打钩。

如果需要调节数据点标记的大小，单击"选择工具"→选择图表→右击→单击"变换"→"缩放"，得到如图 6-20 所示对话框。

选择"等比"缩放，以中间数据点为例，选择 50% 缩放比例，单击"确定"，得到效果图如图 6-21 所示。

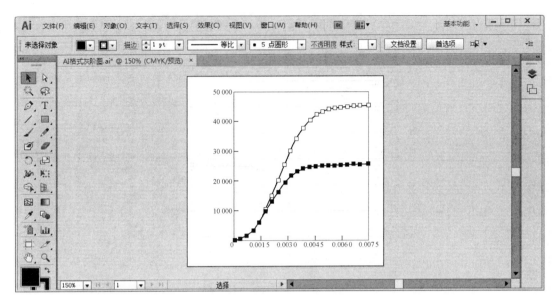

图 6-19　生成折线图

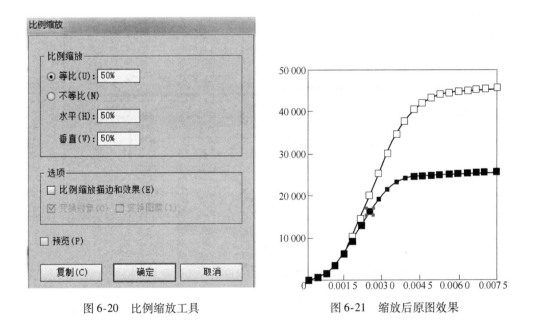

图 6-20　比例缩放工具　　　　图 6-21　缩放后原图效果

步骤五：增加注释

图表的横纵坐标和图例都需要添加注释，在左侧工具栏中选择"文字工具"，单击画布任意位置输入所需文字。单击"选择工具"选择文档，并将其移动至合适位置。

如果文本需要纵向放置，单击"选择工具"→选择文本→右击→单击"变换"→"旋转"，输入旋转角度 90°，单击确定。

使用工具栏"直线段工具"，添加图例并附上说明文字，最终效果如图 6-22 所示。

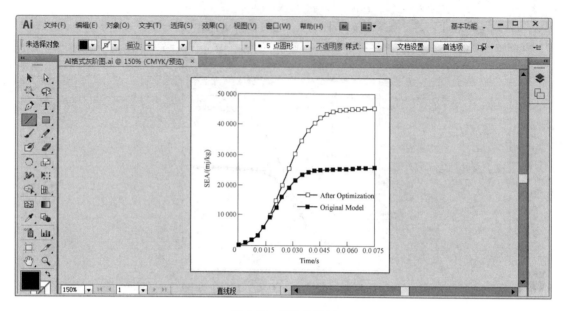

图 6-22　最终效果图

步骤六：调整字体字号

应用"选择工具"分别单击注释和图例，菜单栏下侧会出现调整文本字体和字号的工具栏，如图 6-23 所示，分别设置字体为 Arial，字号为 8pt。

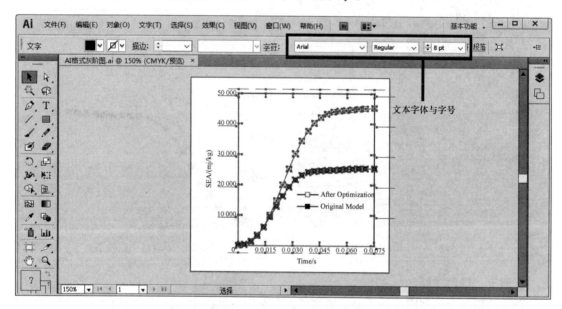

图 6-23　调节图表字体字号

步骤七：转为 TIFF 格式

AI 默认格式为 AI 格式，此时图表即为矢量图格式，放大后不会出现像素点。单击左侧工具栏"缩放工具"，选择缩放区域，放大 16 倍后如图 6-24 所示。

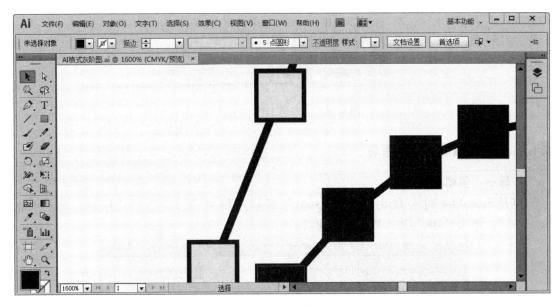

图 6-24　放大 16 倍效果图

如果目标图表要求为矢量图：将图表存为期刊要求的矢量图格式 EPS 格式，"文件"→"存储为"，选择 EPS 格式，单击"确定"。

如果目标图表要求为位图：将图表保存为默认的 AI 格式，然后用 Photoshop 软件打开以 AI 格式保存的图表。如图 6-25 所示，右侧界面"裁剪到"选项框选择"媒体框"，分辨率 500dpi，"模式"为"RGB 颜色"（或者根据期刊要求选择 CMYK），单击"确定"。

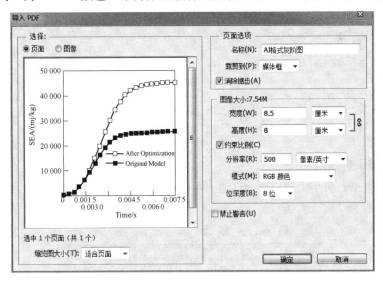

图 6-25　Photoshop 打开 AI 格式图表设置

随后，"文件"→"另存为"，选择 TIFF 格式，单击"确定"。出现如图 6-26 所示对话框，选择"扔掉图层并存储拷贝"，单击"确定"，即可得到能用一般软件打开的 TIFF 格式图片。

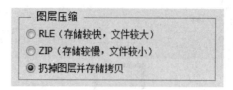

图 6-26 另存为 TIFF 格式选项

6.6.2 SigmaPlot 制作图表

步骤一：创建文档

打开 SigmaPlot 时会跳出"Quick start"窗口（图 6-27），选择"Create new blank notebook"，单击"OK"进入数据输入窗口。

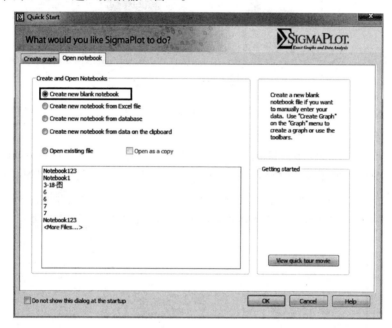

图 6-27 新建文档

步骤二：创建折线图

如图 6-28 所示，将原始数据导入至 SigmaPlot。其中第 1 列作为横坐标 Times(s)，第 2、3 列作为两组纵坐标 SEA(mj/kg)。

	1	2	3
1	0.0000	0.0000	0.0000
2	3.5123e-4	376.4644	359.9631
3	7.0163e-4	1473.2527	1335.0186
4	1.0500e-3	3433.5594	3208.7805
5	1.4004e-3	6121.8099	6136.4740
6	1.7508e-3	9427.1663	10073.7671

图 6-28 导入原始数据

如图6-29所示，单击"Create Graph"→"Line/Scatter"→单击"Multiple Straight Lines & Scatter"；弹出对话框，选择"X Many Y"→单击"下一步"；默认第1列为横坐标，第2、3列为纵坐标，也可根据实际需要调整横坐标和纵坐标数据，单击"完成"生成折线图如图6-30所示。

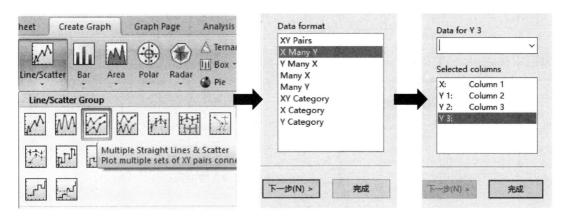

图6-29 生成折线图步骤

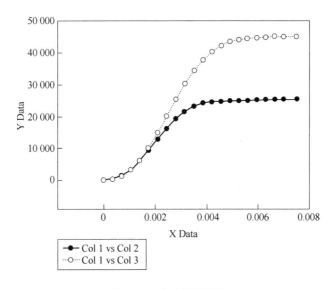

图6-30 生成的折线图

步骤三：对折线图进行修改

（1）对坐标轴进行修改

1）以横坐标为例，双击横坐标弹出对话框（图6-31）。将起始点的值改为0，终止点的值改为0.0075。

2）单击左侧边栏"Axis/Lines"，将线宽按要求设置为1.0mm（图6-32）。

3）如图6-33左图所示，单击"Axis/Major Tick Labels"。手动调节刻度值中小数点显示，位数改为4位。

4）如图 6-33 右图所示，单击"Axis/Major Ticks"。在"Tick intervals"中将间距设置为手动，间距大小为 0.0015；将"Bottom"与"Top"设置为刻度线朝内；刻度线的长度设置为 2.0mm，厚度设置为 1.0mm。

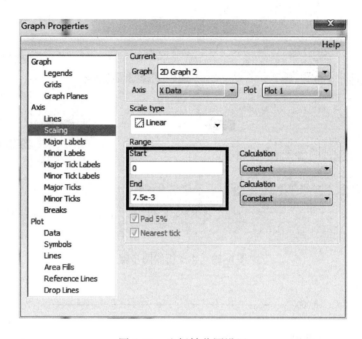

图 6-31　坐标轴范围设置

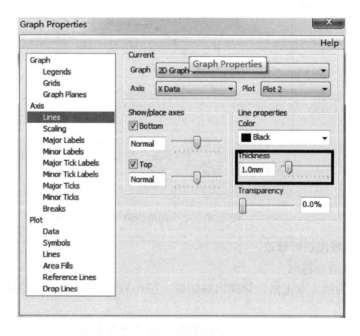

图 6-32　坐标轴线宽设置

5）对纵坐标轴进行上述 1）—4）重复操作。

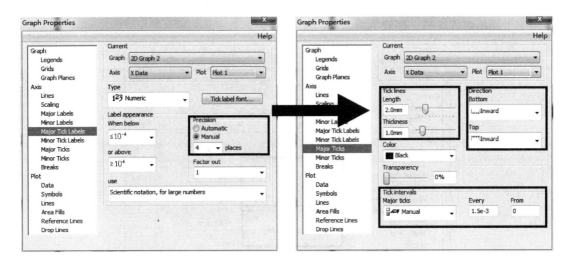

图 6-33 坐标轴刻度设置

6)修改坐标轴名称。将"X Data"与"Y Data"分别修改为"Time/s"与"SEA/(mj/kg)";字体设置为 Arial,字号 12pt。

最终坐标轴修改完成后如图 6-34 所示。

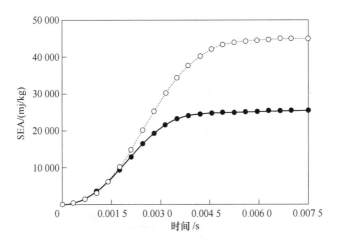

图 6-34 修改坐标轴后效果

(2)对折线进行修改

1)双击折线,选择"Plot/Lines"选项。如图 6-35 所示,在"Type"属性中选择"Solid(实线)",线宽改为 0.5mm;在"Shape"属性中选择"Smoothed(光滑)"。

2)如图 6-36 所示,选择"Plot/Symbol"选项,将数据点的形状改为正方形,设置尺寸为 4.5mm。

步骤四:添加图例

双击图表,选择"Graph/Legends"选项(图 6-37)。在"For legend symbol"勾选需要

的选项，在下方添加相应的图例注释，字体设置为 Arial，字号为 9pt；取消勾选图例边框；左键单击图例附件区域，拖放至恰当的位置。

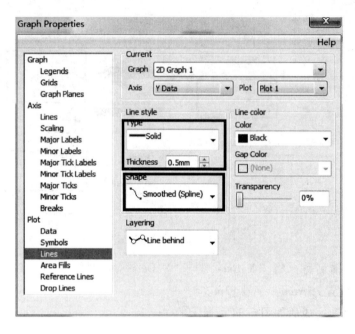

图 6-35　折线线型设置

图 6-36　标记点设置

SigmaPlot 作图为矢量图，放大后不见像素点，放大 5.5 倍后如图 6-38 所示。

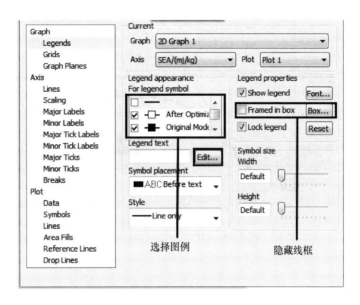

图 6-37 图例编辑设置

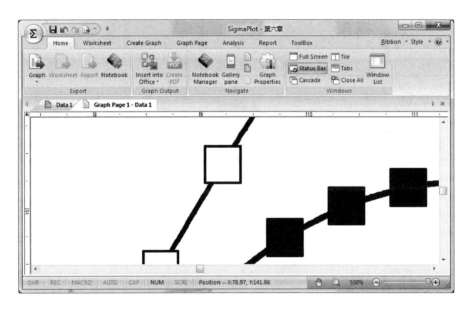

图 6-38 放大效果图

步骤五：转为 TIFF 格式

在菜单栏中选择"Graph Page"，单击"Select All"图标，选中全部内容；在菜单栏中的"Home"中，单击"Graph"倒三角形选项框，在下拉列表中选择"Export"；跳出"另存为"界面，保存为 TIFF 格式；跳出图像大小界面，根据要求，设置宽度为 85mm，高度因期刊不要求可按比例自动生成，分辨率设为 500dpi。如效果不佳，可导入 Photoshop 进行修改。最终 TIFF 格式效果图如图 6-39 所示。

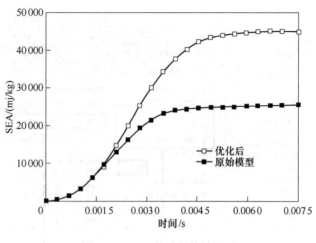

图 6-39　TIFF 格式最终效果图

6.7　实例练习

（1）章节 6.6 软件制图实例中的原始数据见表 6-2，运用 AI 软件分别制作图 6-9a、c、d 中的图表类型。要求目标宽度为 8.5cm，高度不做要求；目标格式类型 TIFF；期刊要求分辨率不得低于 500dpi。

表 6-2　图表原始数据

时间/s	SEA/(mj/kg)	
	原始模型	优化后
0	0	0
0.00035123	376.4644	359.9631
0.00070163	1473.253	1335.019
0.00105000	3433.559	3208.781
0.00140040	6121.81	6136.474
0.00175080	9427.166	10073.77
0.00210120	12908.44	14780.45
0.00245150	16276.11	20021.74
0.00280190	19282.26	25291.3
0.00315030	21607.12	30196.62
0.00350080	23214.29	34378.27
0.00385100	24154.01	37669.48
0.00420140	24517.21	40247.82
0.00455170	24678.08	42130.3
0.00490010	24805.08	43295.21
0.00525050	24926.26	43978.42
0.00560090	25031.43	44294.28

（续）

时间/s	SEA/(mj/kg)	
	原始模型	优化后
0.00595130	25175.95	44459.98
0.00630170	25311.45	44701.05
0.00665010	25420.73	44999.85
0.00700000	25420.73	44999.85
0.00750000	25420.73	44999.85

（2）根据表6-2中的原始数据，运用SigmaPlot软件分别制作图6-9a、c、d中的图表类型。要求目标宽度为8.5cm，高度不做要求；目标格式类型TIFF；期刊要求分辨率不得低于500dpi。

第 7 章 文献检索、管理与引用

7.1 概述

信息时代,信息无所不在,信息检索也无所不在,内容无所不包。海量的信息资源如何有序组织,如何利用检索工具在需要时迅速查找等,是信息时代和经济时代面临的核心问题。

文献资源在科研工作中占有很大比重。据美国自然科学基金会统计,一个科研人员花费在查找和消化科技资料上的时间需占全部科研时间的51%,计划思考占8%,实验研究占32%,书面总结占9%。由上述统计数字可以看出,科研人员花费在科技出版物上的时间为全部科研时间的60%。无疑科技人员要查找与课题有关的资料,信息检索是基本功。

在信息化社会中,我们不能一方面被淹没在数据和信息的海洋里,一方面却忍受着知识的饥渴。不能以信息取代知识,更不能以知识取代能力。我们需要发展将有效数据和可靠信息内化为有用知识的能力,即在不同的情景中应用、完善和传输知识的能力,提高我们的信息素养。信息素质包括有效地查找、评估和利用信息的能力,信息意识和信息道德等,已经被广泛认为是当代社会有效参与的基本能力。因此,在全面推行研究生信息素质教育的今天,加强研究生信息检索方面的教育与培养显得尤为迫切。

所谓文献检索是指将信息按一定的方式组织和存储起来,并根据用户的需要找出有关信息的过程。文献管理是指把自己所收集的文献进行分类,使其在需要时能够被快速找到。如果能提高大学生在这方面的能力,在以后的科研工作中就能起到事半功倍的效果。本章主要介绍如何实现 Mendeley 的各项功能,其组织结构如图 7-1 所示。

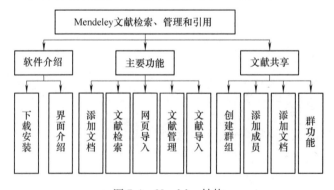

图 7-1 Mendeley 结构

7.2 Mendeley 基本情况

7.2.1 背景介绍

Mendeley 是由三位德国哲学博士研发出来的文献管理软件,名字源于遗传学家孟德尔

（Gregor Mendel）和化学家门捷列夫（Dmitri Mendeleyev）。Mendeley 一问世就凭借其超前的理念和强大的产品功能被用户们青睐。2013 年，Mendeley 被老牌科技出版巨头爱思唯尔（Elsevier）收购，使其能够整合 Elsevier 庞大的线上内容资源，并保持其开放的特性。

7.2.2 Mendeley 的介绍及其优点

Mendeley 是一款免费的跨平台文献管理软件，同时也是一个在线的学术社交网络平台，可一键抓取网页上的文献信息添加到个人的数据库中，还可安装 MS Word 和 Open Office 插件，方便在文字编辑器中插入和管理参考文献。参考文献格式与 Zotero 一样使用各种期刊格式的 CLS 文件。

Mendeley 支持多种平台，从网页版、桌面版到移动端，一应俱全。移动端同时包含 iOS 和安卓（Andriod）两种版本。有如此强大的平台支撑，你的所有文献都可以云端存储。Mendeley 免费提供 2GB 的文献存储和 100MB 的共享空间，可以随时随地从手机端文献库中便捷地找到所需文献。

Mendeley 跟 EndNote、Papers 等文献管理软件相比，其优势见表 7-1。

表 7-1 Mendeley 的优势

软件功能		Mendeley	EndNote	Papers
参考文献及文档的管理	PDF 及其他文件格式	√	√	√
	文字的引用插件	√	√	√
	引用插件 LibreOffice 等	√	√	√
	PDF 文件的注释	√	√	√
	各平台的同步性	×	×	×
文献的检索	免费开放的大型数据库	√	×	×
	个人论文推荐	√	×	×
	社区标记与阅读量统计	√	×	×
	开放的网页 API	√	×	×
	个人文献的全搜索	√	√	√
	外部数据的搜索	√	√	√
协作群体	私人团体	√	√	×
	公共团体	√	×	×
	社会团体	√	×	√
	新闻合作社	√	×	×

7.2.3 软件的下载与安装

1）首先注册一个账户。这个账户很有用，它用于网络与本地的数据库同步。也就是，不管使用哪台计算机，登录后直接同步即可。（下载后登录时即可注册）

2）去官网进行下载，网站地址：http://www.mendeley.com。

3）单击官网右上角的"Download"按钮，选择合适的操作系统即可自动下载（桌面版现支持 Windows 7 及后续版本、Mac OS 和 Linux）。

Mac 等其他系统可以参照网站（http://www.mendeley.com）介绍安装，选择相应的系统自行进行下载（图7-2）。

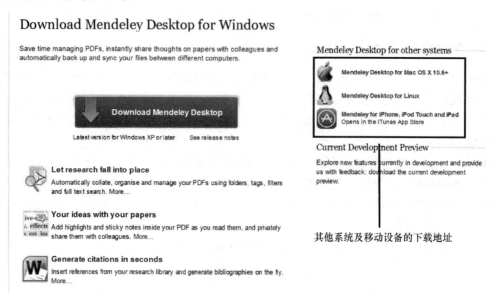

图 7-2　Mendeley 的下载界面

7.3　Mendeley 操作界面介绍

如图 7-3 所示，Mendeley 的操作界面大体可分为 5 个区，分别是：

图 7-3　Mendeley 的操作界面

1）菜单区：进行文献的添加、新建文件夹、同步上传等。
2）搜索框：进行文献的搜索。
3）文献分组区：分类管理文献。
4）文献显示区：文献内容的浏览。
5）笔记记录和文献编辑区：对文献进行标注与编辑。

7.4 Mendeley 的主要功能

1. 添加文档

Mendeley 的文档添加有三种方式。

1）可以通过最左边的"Add Files"按钮添加 PDF 文档到 Mendeley。
2）直接把 PDF 文档拖入 Mendeley 的文献显示区（图 7-4）。
3）从其他文献管理软件导入到 Mendeley。

例如从 Endnote 中将文档导入 Mendeley 中，需要改变其格式。只需要变更为 XML 格式的文档即可导入到 Mendeley 中。

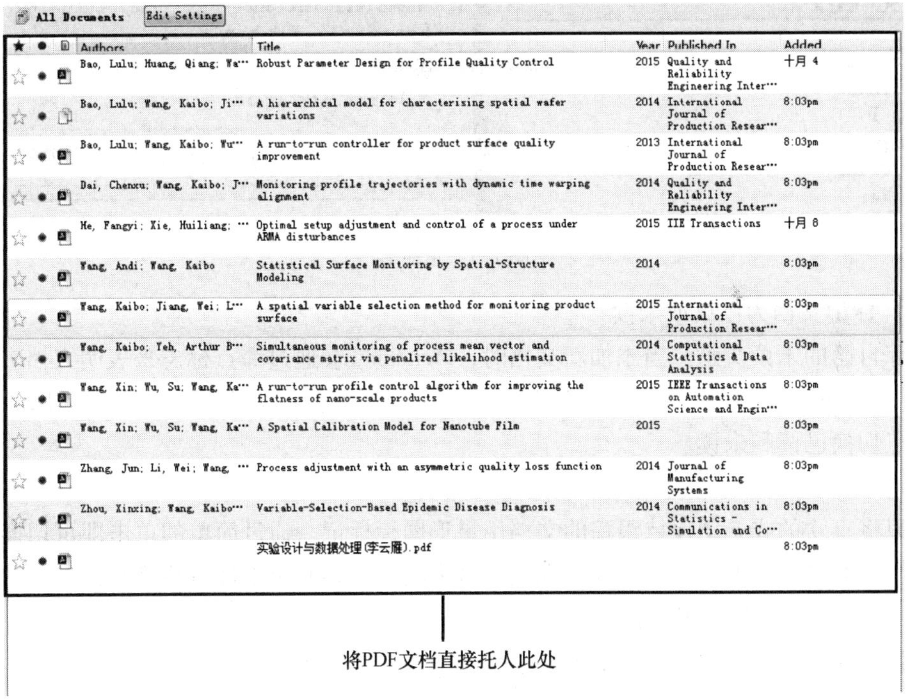

图 7-4　文档拖放界面

无论哪种方式，Mendeley 都会自动检测文档的详细信息，如果信息缺失，Mendeley 会提示用户人工核对补充，或者单击搜索后通过自动搜索补全文档信息。

2. 文献检索功能

Mendeley 的文献搜索一般有三种途径：

1）借助 PubMed 进行关键词搜索，即根据课题方向搜索关键词。网址：http://

www.pubmed.cn。

2）直接搜索（Literature search），即利用 Mendeley 内自带的检索功能进行文献检索，一般用于参考文献的检索。

3）借助 Google 进行文献标题搜索，在阅读文献过程中，发现进一步需要了解的文献。

3. 一键式网页导入

选择"Tools"→"Install Web Importer"在 Web 网页上安装，即可从 ACM Portal 等服务中导入文献资料。

4. 文献管理功能

（1）重命名

在"Filter by Authors"过滤器窗格中，可以将重复或不正确的名称拖放到正确的名称上进行重命名（图 7-5）。

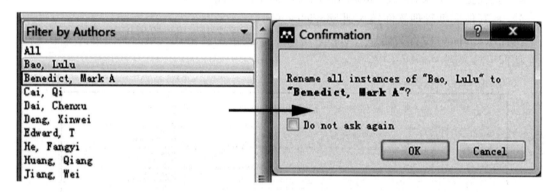

图 7-5　重命名

（2）标记文档为已读或未读

跟踪自己的未读文献。当添加新文档时，Mendeley 会通过绿点标志来表明文档未读。如果使用 Mendeley 内置的 PDF 阅读器打开它们，文档便被标记为已读。或者也可以通过直接单击绿点切换已读和未读。

（3）收藏夹

可以将喜欢的或希望保持跟踪的文档用星形图标标记。通过简单的单击即可切换标记和未标记。所有被标记的文档会自动出现在收藏夹内，需要时单击即可找到它们。

（4）为 PDF 文档添加注释

可以在 Mendeley 中为文档中的内容添加高亮显示或注释（图 7-6）。

1）在中央窗格中双击 PDF 文档就可以在 Mendeley 里的 PDF 浏览器中打开文档。

2）单击菜单栏中的"Text High Light Text"或"Add Note"按钮实现高亮显示文字，并给其添加注释。

（5）即时搜索

文档中的智能搜索可以在输入文字的同时高亮显示词组，以便快速查找。只需在搜索框中输入所需要的文字，就能看到 Mendeley 在文档中找到的匹配结果。例如，在搜索框中输入"wafer"，即会在文中显示该词相应的位置（图 7-7）。

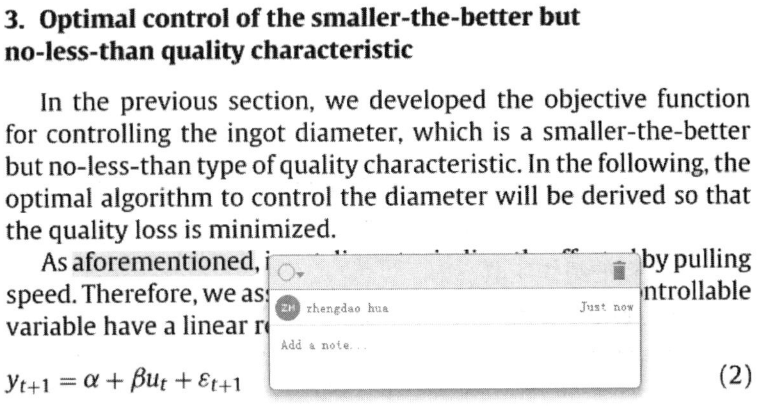

3. Optimal control of the smaller-the-better but no-less-than quality characteristic
In the previous section, we developed the objective function for controlling the ingot diameter, which is a smaller-the-better but no-less-than type of quality characteristic. In the following, the optimal algorithm to control the diameter will be derived so that the quality loss is minimized.
As aforementioned,
by pulling
speed. Therefore, we as
ntrollable
variable have a linear r
zhengdao hua
Just now
Add a note...
$y_{t+1} = \alpha + \beta u_t + \varepsilon_{t+1}$
(2)

图 7-6　为 PDF 添加注释

wafer
mechanical polishing [4–6], photolithography [7] and ploy silicon gate etching [8]. Card et al. [9] studied a plasma etch process for 8-in. silicon wafers by maintaining targeted values of post-etch metrology variables. Sachs et al. [10] combined the Statistical Process Control (SPC) and the feedback control. Bode et al. [11]

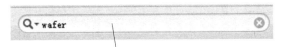

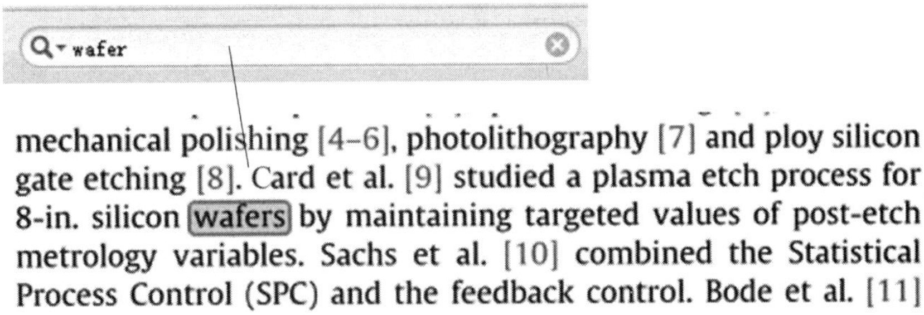

图 7-7　即时搜索界面

（6）文档信息修改的多重撤消

用户可以撤销最近对文档信息或注释的修改。在“Edit”下拉菜单中选择“Undo”或使用快捷键〈Ctrl + Z〉。需要注意的是只能在已经添加注释的情况下，才能使用 Undo 功能。

（7）同时对多个文档进行编辑或添加标签（图 7-8）

Authors
Title
Details
Notes
Contents
12 documents selected
Edits will affect all selected documents.
Merge Documents
Type: Journal Article
Title
Authors: Authors
Journal:
Year:
Volume:
Issue:
Pages:
Abstract:
Tags:
Author Keywords:
类型
标签或注释

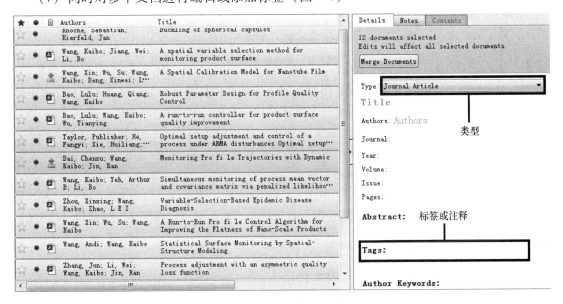

图 7-8　为多个文档添加标签界面

1）通过〈Ctrl〉+左键单击选择多个想要编辑的文献。
2）编辑多个文献的类型。
3）输入自己想要的标签、注释或者其他信息。
（8）文档管理工具

Mendeley 的文档管理工具，可以自动重命名用户的 PDF 文档并将它们归入具有清晰结构的文件夹当中，方便在 Mendeley 之外对文档进行查找。可以通过"Tools"→"Options"→"File Organizer"找到文档的组织工具。

可在 File Organizer 选项卡（图 7-9）中选择如下复选框：

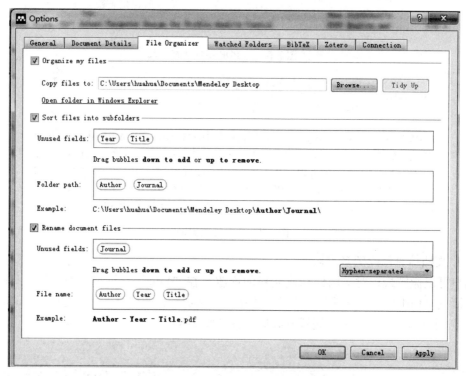

图 7-9 文档管理界面

1）Organize my files：将所有添加到 Mendeley 中的文档复制到一个想要放入的文件夹中。
2）Sort files into subfolders：创建一个所选文档信息的文件夹组织结构。
3）Rename document files：将无意义的 PDF 文档名改为有作者、年份等信息的文档名。

最后，如果文档已经添加到 Mendeley，就可以轻松地在 Word 中引用它们了。
（9）利用 Mendeley 的网络账号进行同步。

在图 7-9 所示的"All Documents"单击"Edit Settings"编辑自己想要上传的文件。编辑后按"Sync"即可以利用自己的 Mendeley 账号进行同步，然后就可以在网络上浏览自己的文档。

7.4.5 导入参考文献

（1）使用 Word 插件进行导入（图 7-10）

1）Word 插件的安装。首先要将 Mendeley 的 Word 插件安装到文字处理软件中。安装时，只需在"Tools"下拉菜单中选择要使用的文字处理软件。

2) Word 插件的使用（图 7-10）

安装完插件，文字处理软件中会出现相应的工具栏按钮，方便引用文献、生成题录或手动编辑其他条目。

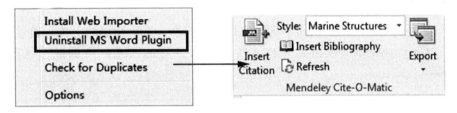

图 7-10　Word 插件导入文献

①如果论文想引用 Mendeley 中的文献，只需单击 Word "引用"中 Mendeley 工具栏中的 "Insert Citation"。目前 Mendeley 只能安装在 Word 中且不支持 64 位的版本。

②此时会弹出一个对话框，可以通过作者姓名、文档标题或发表年份搜索文献。

③找到想引用的文献后，只要单击"OK"按钮即可。如果需要同时引用多篇文献，可用逗号将其分开。

（2）使用 Mendeley 进行文献导入（图 7-11）。

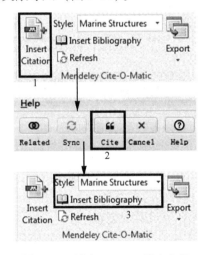

图 7-11　利用 Mendeley 导入文献

单击 Word "引用"中 Mendeley 工具栏中的"Insert Citation"选项，然后选择"go to Mendeley"，在 Mendeley 中选择文献后回到 Word，选择自己需要的文献格式，然后单击 "Send Citation to MS Word"即可。也可以通过〈Ctrl〉+ 单击各文献，选择想要引用的多篇文献。

（3）可从 Mendeley 中将文档直接拉入 Word 中，它会自动生成参考文献格式。

（4）在 Google 文档和其他文字编辑软件中引用文献。

也可以在其他文字编辑软件中引用文献，例如 Google 文档。只需在 Mendeley 中选择欲引用的文献，单击"Edit"→"Copy Citation"，然后将其粘贴到所编辑的文档中；或者也可以从 Mendeley 中拖放文献到所编辑的文档中，题录便会以当前引文格式添加到文档中。

7.5 文档与参考文献的共享

7.5.1 创建群（图7-12）

创建一个可以与你的同学或同事进行文档分享的群，进行文档的上传。通过单击左边窗格中的"Create Group"按钮创建群，然后根据自身的需求，给群赋予详细的信息（图7-12）。

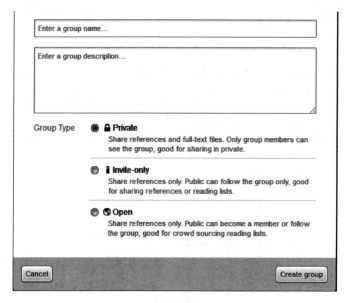

图7-12 创建群的界面

1）在"Enter a group name"中为群起一个名字。
2）在"Enter a group description"中添加群的描述内容。
3）在"Group Type"中选择群的隐私类型。
4）单击"Create Group"按钮完成群的创建。

7.5.2 添加成员和文档

完成群的创建后，可以向群里添加成员，添加或下载文档（图7-13）。

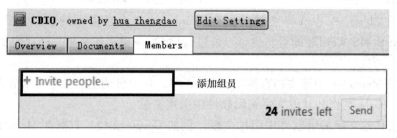

图7-13 添加小组成员

1. 添加成员

可以单击"Members"选项卡邀请成员加入群,也可以通过单击"Add"添加已在 Mendeley 中的联系人,或者单击"Invite People…"邀请其他人加入 Mendeley。

2. 添加或下载文档

单击"Documents"选项卡,浏览群内文档。

添加文档时,可以通过单击上部工具栏中的"Add documents"添加文档,也可以从 Mendeley 的文件夹或本地计算机上拖放文档到群里。

下载群中其他成员的 PDF 文档时,可以在"Edit Settings"中选中"Download attached files to group",单击"确定"下载(图7-14)。

图 7-14 下载其他成员的文档

7.5.3 群功能的使用

在"Overview"选项卡里显示了所在群的最新动态,包括新入群成员、成员的新言论、成员的新文档。可以在"Overview"里发表自己的动态,也可以通过"comment"对您感兴趣的内容进行讨论。

7.6 实例练习

1)搜索自己导师近 5 年来的 SCI/EI 论文,并将其导入到 Mendeley 中。
2)撰写自己导师近 5 年来研究工作的总结报告,并在相应的位置插入文献。
3)以班级为单位创建 Mendeley 群组,并下载其中一位成员的文献文档。

第 8 章 评审与答复

8.1 论文评审的概念与分类

8.1.1 什么是论文评审

论文评审是论文发表的一条必经之路,可以将它看成产品出售前的质检工序。论文评审又被称为同行评审,因为它通常由一群与你相同研究领域的专家、同行来对你的论文进行评审,判断论文是否达到期刊的发表要求并提出整改意见。

论文评审就像手稿和出版物之间的一道质量过滤器,如果通过了,那么恭喜你!你长久以来的努力终于得到回报,科研成果就能付梓成册;如果不幸没有通过这道过滤器,那么你还需加倍努力,根据专家、同行们的意见提升自己的论文,争取早日修成正果。

论文评审在 1665 年由伦敦皇家协会首次使用(图 8-1),从此以后同研究领域专家以审稿人的身份成为论文评审的主体,并与作者一起成为科研论文发表的核心。审稿人通过验证和批注进行编辑工作,并以此来保证学术交流的质量。可以这么说,没有审稿人对学术论文进行严格的评审工作,就没有我们今天发展如此迅速的科学研究。

作者们经常视论文评审为畏途,视审稿人为拦路虎(图 8-2)。然而,平心而论,大部分科学工作者还是认可论文评审的,认为他们的论文通过论文评审这道关卡后都得到了显著的升华。作为作者,我们应该放正心态,视论文为棋盘,意见和修改为棋子,将整个论文评审过程看作一场与审稿人相互提高的围棋博弈,而编辑则作为裁判站在旁观者的角度公正地评判整个过程(图 8-3)。

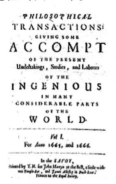

图 8-1　皇家学会期刊封面

图 8-2　稿件评审漫画

本章将从论文评审的分类出发,讨论如何阅读和撰写评审报告,最后根据不同的评审意见有针对性地探讨如何应对并答复。本章的组织结构如图 8-4 所示。

图 8-3　论文评审理想状态

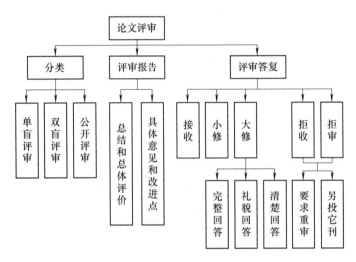

图 8-4　论文评审部分结构

8.1.2　论文评审分类

现在主流的评审类型可以大致分为三类：单盲评审，双盲评审以及公开评审。

单盲评审指的是审稿人知道作者信息，而作者对审稿人毫不知情。这是目前学术界最常见的论文评审模式，它免除了审稿人害怕作者记恨的顾虑，能够公正地、带有批判眼光地评审论文。不过反过来看，单盲评审缺乏问责机制，让不道德的审稿人可以无所顾忌地提出不恰当的负面评论，延迟他人论文出版过程，甚至存在窃取他人研究思想和成果的情况。

双盲评审，顾名思义就是作者和审稿人双方都互不知情，多用于人文社科类的论文评审。相比于单盲评审，它减少了可能存在的学术偏见，因为审稿人不知道作者是谁，在什么机构工作，能够单纯依靠论文自身的水平来确定评审意见。不过现实中通常无法实现真正的双盲评审，审稿人往往能够猜出作者是谁（特别是当作者大量引用自己论文时）。

最后就是公开评审，所有作者和审稿人的信息都是公开的。通常审稿人的信息和评审意见也会出现在最后的出版物上，所有评审过程中的意见和修改也都公开可见。公开评审这一机制会带给审稿人更大的责任感和减少他们不恰当行为的可能性,并接受公众对他们评审工作的监督。正因如此,那些潜在的审稿人更趋向于拒绝审稿,因为他们身份的公开可能会导致作者对他们的敌意,破坏彼此之间的关系,影响以后的工作,甚至于升职和项目申请的机会。

8.2 论文评审报告

8.2.1 评审报告意义

正所谓知己知彼,百战不殆。想要了解审稿人的心思,妥帖地回答审稿人的每一个疑问,最好的方法就是站在审稿人的角度来看待自己的论文。那么首先就从撰写论文评审报告开始,以一个审稿人的角色来评审他人或者自己的论文,从而发现论文写作中的共性问题,提升自己的论文写作和学术研究水平。科研工作者通常存在一种"文人相轻"的思想,认为他人的研究不值一提而自己的研究具有划时代意义,通过评审他人论文也帮助作者客观地看待他人和自己的研究成果。

正如前文所说,审稿人和编辑们为论文评审设置了一道质量门槛。如果这道门槛太低,那么这个研究领域就会被很多"垃圾"出版物所充斥,严重影响研究生态;反之,如果这道门槛过高,那么一些能够撬动行业巨大发展的"微小"工作就有可能被忽视掉。在我们正式进行论文评审报告撰写前,我们首先要回答以下一些问题,并以此来反问我们自己的论文:

- Does the paper fit the standards and scope of the journal it is being considered for?
- Is the research question clear?
- Was the approach appropriate?
- Is the study design, methods and analysis appropriate to the question being studied?
- Is the study innovative or original?
- Does the study challenge existing paradigms or add to existing knowledge?
- Does it develop novel concepts?
- Does it matter?
- Are the methods described clearly enough for other researchers to replicate?
- Are the methods of statistical analysis and level of significance appropriate?
- Could presentation of the results be improved and do they answer the question?
- If humans, human tissues or animals are involved, was ethics approval gained and was the study ethical?
- Are the conclusions appropriate?

8.2.2 评审报告清单

通常来说,一个好的评审报告可以分为以下两个主要部分:总结和总体评价、具体意见和改进点。

关于总结和总体评价,一般首先由论文的一个简短概括开始,通过审稿人组织的几句话来描述这篇论文的主要成果。这样能够帮助你明确这篇论文是否属于期刊发表范围。随后，审稿人应该对包括这篇论文的整体印象，论文的整体质量做一个评价。举例来说，这篇论文合理吗？这篇论文内容的整体可取吗？

其次关于具体意见和改进点，审稿人一般从论文的整体和各个章节主要的评审意见和建议开始，再到更具体、更细致的改进点（如拼写、语法等等）。最后，审稿人会检查一下论文的引用文献，但是不能利用自己的评审权利来促使作者引用自己的出版论文。

总而言之，作为审稿人应该清楚自己的评审意见并且在评审报告中明确地指出。一篇成功的评审报告就是对整个论文写作流程的一次重新审视，是对我们前面所学的各个章节的一个整体梳理，大家可以根据如下的清单进行逐条核对：

(1) **First impressions**
- Is the research original, novel and important to the field?
- Has the appropriate structure and language been used?

(2) **Abstract**
- Is it really a summary?
- Does it include key findings?
- Is it an appropriate length?

(3) **Introduction**
- Is it effective, clear and well organized?
- Does it really introduce and put into perspective what follows?
- Suggest changes in organization and point authors to appropriate citations
- Be specific-don't write 'the authors have done a poor job'

(4) **Methodology**
- Can a colleague reproduce the experiments and gets the same outcomes?
- Did the authors include proper references to previously published methodology?
- Is the description of new methodology accurate?
- Could or should the authors have included supplementary material?

(5) **Results and discussion**
- Suggest improvements in the way data is shown
- Comment on general logic and on justification of interpretations and conclusions
- Comment on the number of figures, tables and schemes
- Write concisely and precisely which changes you recommend
- List separately suggested changes in style, grammar and other small changes
- Suggest additional experiments or analyses
- Make clear the need for changes/updates
- Ask yourself whether the manuscript should be published at all

(6) **Conclusion**
- Comment on importance, validity and generality of conclusions
- Request toning down of unjustified claims and generalizations
- Request removal of redundancies and summaries

- The abstract, not the conclusion, summarizes the study

(7) References, tables and figures
- Check accuracy, number and readability
- Assess completeness of legends, headers and axis labels
- Check presentation consistency
- Comment on color in figures

8.2.3 经典范文分析

(1) 范文1

这是一篇本书作者论文的评审报告,该论文现已发表在 IEEE Transactions on Automation Science and Engineering 期刊。这篇一审评审报告共有 3 名审稿人,评审意见为 CONDITIONALLY ACCEPTED,介于小修和大修之间。论文原文可查看:Yun Chen and Hui Yang, Sparse Modeling and Recursive Prediction of Space-time Dynamics in Stochastic Sensor Network, IEEE Transactions on Automation Science and Engineering, 2016, 13(1):215-226 (SCI:000374443300022)

以下是评审报告原文:

T-ASE-2015-218

Associate Editor

Comments to the Author: (编辑意见)

This paper is decent and interesting. However, all the comments raised by all the reviewers need to be addressed before it may be considered for publication.

Reviewer's comments to author:

Reviewer: 1(第一位审稿人意见)

This paper presents an approach to characterize the spatiotemporal dynamics by considering the uncertainties existing in stochastic sensor networks. Although a lot efforts have been done on design and optimization on sensor networks recently, this paper raises an interesting topic from healthcare service as it is believed as a frontier study on stochastic sensor network of physiologic signals. This paper is well organized and written, however, I have a few comments regarding this work. (总结和总体评价)

1) In PART V. B, the authors borrow KF in the comparison. However, the authors state that 'spatiotemporal data from DSN are highly nonlinear and non-stationary', so it seems not very appropriate to use KF as a benchmark because KF always fails in this case. It is suggested that author may try other tools which are suitable to non-stationary and non-Gaussian cases to demonstrate the superiority of the sparse particle filtering. (比较的方法是否合理)

2) Fig. 18 shows that those NLPCA-based methods are always superior to those PCA-based methods, whereas the performance among PF, KF and ARMA are quite close. It seems that NLPCA here is dominant. Please justify the efficacy of using particle filtering rather than other nonlinear filters. (实验数据是否合理)

3) The introduction part is a little bit cumbersome. Since literature [1] has provided the comprehensive explanations of sensor failure and malfunction, it is not necessary to spend a paragraph to give those examples. (论文组织意见)

4) In Equation 1, I believe that f' means the transpose of the function. However, it may cause misunderstanding to the first order derivative off. (公式的准确性)

5) In Fig. 3, what is the relationship between sparse particle filtering and optimal kernel placement while using an arrowhead to connect each other. (图表组织合理性)

6) In Equation 2, is there any reason to choose the Gaussian kernel as the weighting kernel? Please justify it. (方法的合理性)

7) In practice, it is critical to choose the number of kernel components. In Part V, the authors use RPE as an index to find the appropriate number of kernels. Is there any guidance for practitioners to initiate the number of kernels? (同行如何设置此方法的参数)

8) In page 4 line 45, does sigma(1) means the standard deviation of x? Same case for sigma(2). If so, please keep consistent as stated in mu(x) and mu(y). (公式的准确性)

Reviewer: 2(第二位审稿人意见)

The paper is well written and organized. A few comments are: (总体评价)

1) Please define the "stochastic sensor network" when it is first used in Introduction. (定义原创名词)

2) It is said that very little work exists on resilient sensor network. I guess this means there are some work. Please discuss them and explain why your work is the first-of-its-kind. (是否恰当引用前人工作)

3) Please provide the website address of PhysioNet in the text where it is mentioned in Section IV. (是否恰当引用前人工作)

Reviewer: 3(第三位审稿人意见)

Overall, the manuscript presented a decent method. However, the unique ontributions should be emphasized and made clear. Below are some detailed comments. (总体评价)

1) The title of this paper is a little bit misleading. In the paper the term "sparse" is used to describe both the kernel-weighted regression model and the particle filters. Using "sparse particle filtering" gives readers an impression that this paper has developed a new particle filtering algorithm, and this PF is the main part of this paper. To me, the spatiotemporal modeling (kernel-weighted regression, NLPCA for beta) and estimation (optimal kernel placement, particle filtering) are both important parts for this paper. Using "sparse" to describe the kernel-weighted regression looks more appropriate. (题目是否合理)

2) Is the spatial model in Eq. (1) a new model? (方法是否创新)

3) In the optimal kernel placement (Eq. 6), is the MAP estimate of $\boldsymbol{\beta}_t$ used in Eq. 6? If so, you may state it in that part. (表达是否清楚、准确)

4) What is ω_t in Eq. 14? (表达不完整)

5) Z_{t-1+1} should be $Z_{t-\tau+1}$ in the equation below Eq. 14. (表达不准确)

6) Is there any randomness in $\boldsymbol{Z}_{t+1}$ given $\boldsymbol{Z}_{1:t}$, $\boldsymbol{\theta}$, ω_t? Is ω_t the Gaussian noise? (表达不完整)

7) The θ in Eq 6 and Eq. 14 denotes different parameters. I suggest you to use different symbols to avoid confusion.（表达的一致性）

（2）范文2

这是一篇本书作者作为审稿人的评审报告，投稿期刊是 IEEE Journal of Biomedical and Health Informatics。本次评审为单盲评审，本书作者给出的评审意见是拒收，编辑给出的最终意见为大修。为保护论文作者版权和隐私，故不显示论文原文。

Review on JBHI-00689-2014 "Noninvasive Multi-blood Flow Parameter Monitoring System for Traumatic Brain Injury"

This paper developed a wireless non-invasive multi-blood flow parameter monitoring system that is design based on the technique of biomedical optics and is capable of monitoring the blood flow rate and hemoglobin parameters simultaneously. The proposed system is compared with a commercial laser Doppler flowmetry. The experimental results show that hemoglobin parameters and blood flow rate suddenly changed at the impact point, and the impact also caused the post-FPI apnea which cause the distortion of the cerebral vasculature and the cerebral hypoxia.（总结）

Some comments are listed as follows:

1) Experimental design: It is important to report all details of the experimental design, such as the number of subjects used in the experiments, control group, tests of statistical significance. In the current version, it is not clear how many rats are used, statistical comparison with LDF as well as the confidence interval on the impact strengths and their pertinence to the parameters. Without these information, it is hard to justify the accuracy of instrumentation.（实验方法、细节缺失，不具有可重复性）

2) Parameter derivation: based on the manuscript, it appears that [20-24] dominates the derivation of parameters in the section II. B-C. Many of the terms are not explicitly defined before the use. It will be better if the authors can provide more details for the technical terms. In addition, because most of equations are from[20-24], it is not clear about the innovation of this work.（公式符号不明确，不具有原创性）

3) References are well-organized, but most of them lack the issue number.（文献引用不完整）

4) Why use the log scale for the x-axis in Fig. 4 and Fig. 5? Both figs show the impact is induced in less than 1 minute. The change is very rapid in a short time interval. For FPI, why not delay the impact? In addition, are the results from multiple subjects? What about the statistics on the response to FPI?（图表信息不明确，实验结果不清楚，缺少统计分析）

5) This engineering work is well done. Can the authors show a baseline measurement without the impact? This will give a straightforward comparison with the impact group.（缺少比较实验）

Overall, this work is interesting. The authors may strengthen this work by a better designed experiment, and more details explanation of parameter derivation process.（总体评价）

8.3 论文评审答复

8.3.1 评审意见分类

最终的评审意见相当于一篇论文的"生死簿"。一般而言，可以分为以下五种情况：接收、小修、大修、拒收、拒审。接收：很好理解，就是论文一审通过直接接收。小修：论文存在细小错误，经过修改一般就能被接收。大修：论文存在明显漏洞，需要按照评审意见仔细修改，论文的命运取决于作者的修改质量。拒收：经过同行专家评审过后，论文没有达到出版要求被拒绝。拒审：编辑直接拒绝，没有送审同行专家，一般是因为论文质量太差或者内容与期刊范围严重不符。论文如若接收则皆大欢喜，之前所有的磨难和付出都得到了应有的回报。我们下面主要讲讲如何面对其他四种情况。

8.3.2 评审意见处理方法

如果幸运的话，评审意见是小修，那么最好的处理方式就是根据意见做简单修改而不涉及太多争辩。如果你能很快地修改好并且发送到编辑手中，那么他可能还对你的文章保留新鲜的记忆，很大可能你的论文能够很快被接收。总而言之，根据意见做简单修改并尽快送还编辑处。

然而绝大多数的情况是有 2 到 3 名同行专家的评审意见，并且其中几位的意见是大修。那么作者就需要依次认真阅读和回复每一位审稿人的意见，并遵循以下 3 条"黄金"准则——完整回答；礼貌回答；清楚回答。只要意见是公正合理的，一般还是建议重新修改并送审同一期刊，即使需要花费大量时间来回复这些意见。以下列举了一些需要遵循的回复准则，这些可以帮助大家在答复评审意见时做到不亢不卑，有理有据。

- Do not use aggressive or defensive tone
- Never use one reviewer's response against another
- Say things like "we agree" or "this is an excellent point" if you are going to change your manuscript as suggested
- Thank reviewers for good suggestions
- Pick your battles! If you can make some changes easily, for ahead. Then, if you refuse other suggestions, it looks like you are compromising with the reviewer instead of fighting them
- Number the response. Use a new set of numbers for each reviewer
- Restate the reviewer's question or concern OR quote the reviewer's comment
- Write each response so it can be ready by itself. Never refer to other responses (do no say "see the response to Reviewer 2")
- Try to acknowledge something that can be improved. For example:
  - Say your text may have been unclear or that you could provide more detail
  - Say that the suggestion is valid but would belong in another paper

如果你确定要另投其他期刊，你可以向新的期刊展示你的论文在经过之前的评审后得到了哪些提升，有些编辑会非常欣赏这一点。总而言之，论文评审答复就是做到两点：明白审稿人的疑惑是什么，他们想要知道什么；明确你的答复能够让审稿人知道你的本意。

如果你的论文不幸被拒，要么是你的研究内容不适合这个期刊，要么就是审稿人提出了你方法论中无法挽救、致命的逻辑错误。到了这一步你还有两种选择。一种是如果你坚信审稿人的意见不公正、不正确，那么你可以写信给编辑要求换人重审。另一种就是停止哭诉，选择一个适合你的期刊重新投稿。当然你需要审视那些导致你论文被拒的审稿意见，以免悲剧再次发生。

8.3.3 经典范文实例

（1）范文1

We would like to thank editor and reviewers for the comments and suggestions. After careful considerations, we have revised the paper and prepared this detailed response. We hope to produce a stronger body of work based on the feedback. (**Note**: *Revisions are highlighted in blue color in the manuscript*)

Point-to-point response to associate editor's comments:

This paper is decent and interesting. However, all the comments raised by all the reviewers need to be addressed before it may be considered for publication.

Ans: Thank the editor for the generous comments. After careful considerations, we have addressed all the reviewer points and prepared the detailed responses to each question in this letter. We hope to produce a stronger body of work based on the feedbacks.

Point-by-point response to Reviewer #1's comments:

1) In PART V. B, the authors borrow KF in the comparison. However, the authors state that 'spatiotemporal data from DSN are highly nonlinear and non-stationary', so it seems not very appropriate to use KF as a benchmark because KF always fails in this case. It is suggested that author may try other tools which are suitable to non-stationary and non-Gaussian cases to demonstrate the superiority of the sparse particle filtering.

Ans: Thank you for the comment. Actually very little work has been done to estimate nonlinear and non-stationary data. Our proposed sparse particle filtering is the first-of-its-kind to deal with such problem.

- It is not appropriate to use KF as benchmark since its performances always not good in this case. However, we cannot say it fails in estimating non-stationary and non-Gaussian cases, it is a commonly used estimation method and still provides approximated estimation of this case.
- We do try other tools to benchmark our proposed sparse particle filtering method as shown in Fig. 18. For examples, linear PCA with PF, KF and ARMA model, nonlinear PCA with KF and ARMA model.

2) Fig. 18 shows that those NLPCA-based methods are always superior to those PCA-based methods, whereas the performance among PF, KF and ARMA are quite close. It seems that NLPCA here is dominant. Please justify the efficacy of using particle filtering

rather than other nonlinear filters.

Ans: Thank you for the comment.

- First, Fig. 18 shows that NLPCA is the dominant effect for performances by comparing with PCA-based methods. This is because linear PCA combined with traditional estimate methods, e. g. , PF, KF and ARMA, are not able to deal with the nonlinearity inherent in the dataset.
- Second, as shown in Fig. 18, the performance among PF, KF and ARMA are quite close because the relative prediction error (RPE) is too small to see the differences between different methods. However, if we zoom in Fig. 18 in the following figure, we can find out that PF outperformances KF and ARMA model very well.

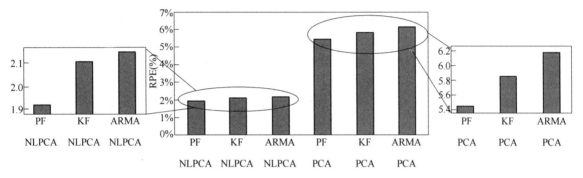

- Third, when we look at the prediction performances of the first 10 PCs in Fig. 17, we find out that PF results are shown to outperform KF and ARMA models for each PCs.

3) The introduction part is a little bit cumbersome. Since literature [1] has provided the comprehensive explanations of sensor failure and malfunction, it is not necessary to spend a paragraph to give those examples.

Ans: Thank you for the comment. We have deleted those examples and revise the first paragraph of introduction part as follows:

"Distributed sensing provides an unprecedented opportunity to monitor space-time dynamics of complex systems and to improve the quality and integrity of operation and services. For examples, environmental sensor networks are often distributed in a spatial region to monitor and forecast space-time climatic variations, thereby mitigating catastrophic effects of extreme weather conditions. In addition, the deployment of distributed sensor networks in rapidly changing battlefields is critical for monitoring terrain situations, gathering action information, and optimizing the strategic decision making."

4) In Equation 1, I believe that f' means the transpose of the function. However, it may cause misunderstanding to the first order derivative of f.

Ans: Thank you for the suggestion. The f' in Equation 1 does mean the transpose of the function. We have revised the equation as:

$$Y(s) = M(s;\boldsymbol{\beta}) + \varepsilon(s) = \sum_{i=1}^{N} w_i(s) \boldsymbol{f}_i^T(s) \boldsymbol{\beta}_i + \varepsilon(s)$$

Moreover, we revised other transpose expressions in the manuscript in case of misunderstanding.

5) In Fig. 3, what is the relationship between sparse particle filtering and optimal kernel placement while using an arrowhead to connect each other.

Ans: Thank you for the comment. As shown in Fig. 13, the two parts sparse particle filtering and optimal kernel placement are combined together to support our proposed spatiotemporal model.

- First, the backward arrow means that the optimal kernel placement algorithm is developed to optimize the compactness of spatiotemporal model. Which determines kernel parameters used in the sparse particle filtering model.
- Second, the forward arrow means that the sparse particle filtering model is developed to reduce the dimensionality of model parameters arising from optimal kernel placement algorithm. Moreover, model parameters are sequentially update when new observations are available at the next time point.

In summary, these two parts work together to sequentially estimate and update our spatiotemporal model.

6) In Equation 2, is there any reason to choose the Gaussian kernel as the weighting kernel? Please justify it.

Ans: Thank you for the comment. Actually, the form of the weighting kernel is not limited to be Gaussian kernel in the spatial model. There are two reasons why we choose the Gaussian kernel as the weighting kernel in Equation 2:

- First, the Gaussian kernel is the most widely used kernel function. Without loss of generality, we choose Gaussian kernel as the kernel function in the spatial model to show the effectiveness of our developed spatiotemporal model.
- Second, we found that the Gaussian kernel matched the pattern of real-world ECG potential mapping data very well. As shown in the following figure (Fig. 14b in the manuscript), combination of two Gaussian kernels can capture the majority pattern of the surface.

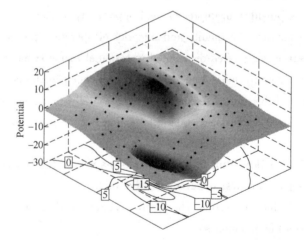

- Third, the performances shown in the result part indicated the chosen Gaussian kernel performed very well in our case.

Therefore, we choose Gaussian kernel as the weighting kernel in Equation 2. It may be noted that the weighting kernel is not limited to be Gaussian kernel, people can choose their own preference based on their own dataset.

7) In practice, it is critical to choose the number of kernel components. In Part V, the authors use RPE as an index to find the appropriate number of kernels. Is there any guidance for practitioners to initiate the number of kernels?

Ans: Thank you for the comment. There are two dominant effects relate to decide the number of kernels:

- First, the spatiotemporal dataset. Since the first few kernels capture the majority pattern of the spatiotemporal data. If the residual still has large variations, perhaps we need more kernels to capture the remaining patterns in order to have a good modeling performance. Otherwise, a few of kernels are enough to model the spatiotemporal data.
- Second, the desired criteria of model performances. As shown in Fig. 14, we can see that the more kernels we placed, the better model performances we achieved. Therefore, if the desired criteria asks for high model performances, then we need to place more kernels, otherwise, a small number of kernels is enough.

In summary, the initial number of kernels depends on your own spatiotemporal dataset. In our real-world ECG mapping data, we suggest to choose 20 kernels for a good model performance, and 60 kernels for a high model performance.

8) In page 4 line 45, does sigma(1) means the standard deviation of x? Same case for sigma(2). If so, please keep consistent as stated in mu(x) and mu(y).

Ans: Thank you for the comment. σ_1 does mean the standard deviation of x, and σ_2 means the standard deviation of y. We have revised all "σ_1" as "σ_x", and "σ_2" as "σ_y" in the manuscript.

Point-by-point response to Reviewer #2's comments:

1) Please define the "stochastic sensor network" when it is first used in Introduction.

Ans: Thank you for the comment. We define the "stochastic sensor network" when it is first used in Introduction as

"Maintaining strict skin contacts for hundreds of sensors is not only challenging but also greatly deteriorates the wearability of ECG sensor networks. Therefore, we propose a novel strategy named as "stochastic sensor network" in this present investigation. The stochastic sensor network means that the sensor network is functioning stochastically, in other words, allow a subset of sensors at varying locations within the network to transmit dynamic information intermittently. Notably, the new strategy of stochastic sensor networks is generally applicable in many other domains."

2) It is said that very little work exist on resilient sensor network. I guess this means there are some work. Please discuss them and explain why your work is the first-of-its-kind.

Ans: Thank you for the comment. There are some work exist on resilient sensor network.

- For example, a multipath routing design is used to study energy-efficient recoveryfrom node failure in resilient sensor network [Ref].
- D. Ganesan, R. Govindan, S. Shenker and D. Estrin, "Highly-resilient, energy-

effiecientmultipath routing in wireless sensor networks," *ACM SIGMOBILE Mobile Computing and Communication Review*, Vol. 5, pp. 11-25, 2001.

However, our work is the first-of-its-kind to study ECG sensor network on both aspects, i. e. , hardware and mathematical methodology development.

- First, in the hardware aspect. Existing smart shirts have twolimitations: poor resolution and wearability. Poor resolution is because current smart shirts use a limited number of leads ($\leqslant 3$). Wearability is because current smart shirts require rigid contact with the outer skin. However, our proposed stochastic sensor network provides the opportunity to capture multiple leads ($\geqslant 120$) leads simultaneously and release the requirement of sensor-skin contact.
- Second, in the mathematical methodology development aspect. Previous analytical methods consider eitherspatially-varying time series model or temporally-varying spatial model. However, our proposed approach not only considers spatial and temporal information, but also captures space-time correlations.

In summary, our proposed stochastic sensor network is the first-of-its-kind to not only lower thehardware requirements of ECGI systems but also develop new mathematical methodology development to support this stochastic design.

3) Please provide the website address of PhysioNet in the text where it is mentioned in Section IV.

Ans: Thank you for the suggestion. We have added the website address of PhysioNet in the text as follows:

"The proposed methodology is evaluated and validated using real-world ECG potential mapping data, available in the PhysioNet database (http://www.physionet.org/) [29]."

Point-by-point response to Reviewer #3's comments:

1) The title of this paper is a little bit misleading. In the paper the term "sparse" is used to describe both the kernel-weighted regression model and the particle filters. Using "sparse particle filtering" gives readers an impression that this paper has developed a new particle filtering algorithm, and this PF is the main part of this paper. To me, the spatiotemporal modeling (kernel-weighted regression, NLPCA for beta) and estimation (optimal kernel placement, particle filtering) are both important parts for this paper. Using "sparse" to describe the kernel-weighted regression looks more appropriate.

Ans: Thank you for the comment. We revised the title from "Sparse Particle Filtering for Modeling Space-Time Dynamics in Stochastic Sensor Networks" to "Sparse Design for Modeling and Estimating Space-Time Dynamics in Stochastic Sensor Network".

2) Is the spatial model in Eq. (1) a new model?

Ans: Thank you for the comment. The spatial model in Eq. (1) is a widely used model. However, we extended this equation in both spatial and temporal aspects.

- First, we extend this one location spatial model to be a multiple location spatial model. We consider observations $Y = (Y(s_1), \cdots, Y(s_K))^T$ at multiple locations $s_1, \cdots, s_K$ and rewrite it in a matrix form as shown in Equation 3:

$$Y = \begin{bmatrix} Y(s_1) \\ \vdots \\ Y(s_K) \end{bmatrix} = \Psi \beta + \varepsilon$$

$$= \begin{bmatrix} w_1 f_{11} \mid s_1 & \cdots & w_1 f_{1p} \mid s_1 & \cdots & w_N f_{N1} \mid s_1 & \cdots & w_N f_{Np} \mid s_1 \\ w_1 f_{11} \mid s_2 & & w_1 f_{1p} \mid s_2 & & w_N f_{N1} \mid s_2 & & w_N f_{Np} \mid s_2 \\ \vdots & & \vdots & & \vdots & & \vdots \\ & & & \ddots & & & \\ w_1 f_{11} \mid s_K & \cdots & w_1 f_{1p} \mid s_K & \cdots & w_N f_{N1} \mid s_K & \cdots & w_N f_{Np} \mid s_K \end{bmatrix} \begin{bmatrix} \beta_{11} \\ \beta_{12} \\ \beta_{13} \\ \vdots \\ \beta_{Np} \end{bmatrix} + \varepsilon$$

- Second, we further consider time evolution in the model. The modelparameters β_t are sequentially estimated and updated over time as shown in Equation 4:

$$\beta_t = g_t(\beta_{t-1}, \gamma)$$

- Finally, we integrate these models together and formed our proposed spatiotemporal model:

$$Y_t = \Psi_t \beta_t + \varepsilon$$
$$\beta_t = g_t(\beta_{t-1}, \gamma)$$

3) **In the optimal kernel placement (Eq. 6), is the MAP estimate of β_t used in Eq. 6? If so, you may state it in that part.**

Ans: Thank you for the comment. The MAP estimate of β_t is used in Eq. 6. We revised the sentence ahead Fig. 7 as:

"After the estimation step, the maximum posteriori probability (*MAP*) *estim*ate of β_t is obtained. It may be noted that the *MAP estim*ate of β_t is used in Eq. 6 to identify a compact set of kernels. Then, nonlinear PCA transforms the high-dimensional β_t to the low-dimensional latent variables Z by $Z = \Phi(\beta)$."

4) **What is ω_t in Eq. 14?**

Ans: Thank you for the comment. ω_t is white noise. We revise the sentence where ω_t is first introduced in section III. C as:

"Further, model structure $h_t(\cdot)$ and model parameters θ need to be determined and estimated in the nonlinear state space equation $Z_{t+1} = h_t(Z_{1:t}, \theta, \omega_t)$, where ω_t is white noise. As aforementioned, spatiotemporal data from distributed sensor network are highly nonlinear and nonstationary."

5) **Z_{t-l+1} should be $Z_{t-\tau+1}$ in the equation below Eq. 14.**

Ans: Thank you for the comment. We have revised it in the manuscript.

6) **Is there any randomness in Z_{t+1} given $Z_{1:t}, \theta, \omega_t$? Is ω_t the Gaussian noise?**

Ans: Thank you for the comment.

- There is randomness in Z_{t+1} given $Z_{1:t}, \theta, \omega_t$. Since the state space model $Z_{t+1} = h_t(Z_{1:t}, \theta, \omega_t)$ needs to be determined and estimated. We use the logistic model to model the nonlinear relationships of the hidden states as shown in Equation 14. Then the sequential Monte Carlo method and Kernel smoothing approach are used to simultaneously estimate model states Z_{t+1} and model parameters θ. This is based on an approximation of complex probability density function rather than an exactly analytical representation. Then the accuracy of the approximation will depend upon the number of samples used in the Monte Carlo process.

- Also, ω_t is white noise, not needs to be Gaussian. Because particle filtering can deal with noise distribution with any form.

7) The θ in Eq 6 and Eq. 14 denotes different parameters. I suggest you to use different symbols to avoid confusion.

Ans: Thank you for the comment. We have revised all "θ"s referring to Eq. 14 as "φ" in the manuscript.

(2) 范文 2

Author's replies to the comments of reviewer:

[Comment 1]

Experimental design: It is important to report all details of the experimental design, such as the number of subjects used in the experiments, control group, tests of statistical significance. In the current version, it is not clear how many rats are used, statistical comparison with LDF as well as the confidence interval on the impact strengths and their pertinence to the parameters. Without these information, it is hard to justify the accuracy of instrumentation.

Answer:

Many thanks for the reviewer's comments. According to the reviewer's comments, the description for the detail of the experimental design, including the number of the rat, the control group, and the statistical significance have been added and modified in the section II. D, III, and IV of the revised manuscript. Moreover, the error bars and significances have also been added in Fig. 4, Fig. 5, and Fig. 6.

[Comment 2]

Parameter derivation: based on the manuscript, it appears that [20-24] dominates the derivation of parameters in the section II. B-C. Many of the terms are not explicitly defined before the use. It will be better if the authors can provide more details for the technical terms. In addition, because most of equations are from [20-24], it is not clear about the innovation of this work.

Answer:

Many thanks for the reviewer's comments. The description for the terms in Section II has been added and modified in the revised manuscript.

[Comment 3]

References are well-organized, but most of them lack the issue number.

Answer:

Many thanks for the reviewer's comments. The issue number of the references have been added in the revised manuscript.

[Comment 4]

Why use the log scale for the x-axis in Fig. 4 and Fig. 5? Both figs show the impact is induced in less than 1 minute. The change is very rapid in a short time interval. For FPI, why not delay the impact? In addition, are the results from multiple subjects? What about the statistics on the response to FPI?

Answer:

Many thanks for the reviewer's comments. After the impact, the rat has to be treated immediately to ensure its patent airway to avoid the death by suffocation. The higher impact strength easily results in a dysfunctional or absent respiratory response. Therefore, the longer impact time may easily cause the death of the rat. Moreover, the FPI equipment used in this experiment can only provide a short impact time, because the impact is generated from the fluid wave generated by the struck of the pendulum. The above description has been added in the revised manuscript.

Because the change of blood flow parameters at the impact point is very short and they became stable after respiration treatment, the log scale for the x-axis in Fig. 4 and Fig. 5 is used to clearly present the detail information of the blood flow parameters at the impact point and after respiration treatment. Moreover, according the reviewer's comments, the statistic information, including error bar and significance, has been added in Fig. 4, Fig. 5, and Fig. 6 of the revised manuscript.

[Comment 5]

This engineering work is well done. Can the authors show a baseline measurement without the impact? This will give a straightforward comparison with the impact group.

Answer:

Many thanks for the reviewer's comments. The experimental results for the sham group (without impact) have been added in Fig. 4 and Fig. 5 of the revised manuscript.

8.4　实例练习

1. 阅读章节 9.1.2 中中文论文原始稿，并撰写评审意见报告。
2. 阅读章节 9.2.2 中英文论文原始稿，并撰写评审意见报告。
3. 阅读章节 9.1.3 中编辑与专家意见，并撰写评审意见答复。
4. 阅读章节 9.2.3 中编辑与专家意见，并撰写评审意见答复。

第 9 章　写作与发表实例

9.1　中文论文实例

9.1.1　《中国造船》投稿指南

《中国造船》稿件版面质量要求

（附论文样稿，供书写）

科技论文书写和科技期刊出版应符合国家标准及规范。关于科技论文撰写，有 CY/T 35—2001《科技文献的章节编号方法》、GB/T 7714—2015《文后参考文献著录规则》等国标。依据这些标准，结合《中国造船》编辑工作经验，对稿件的版面质量提出一些具体要求。稿件用 word 文档格式书写，以黑白印刷的形式出版。

作者在投稿前请阅读本文，了解和掌握基本书写格式，使稿件符合版面质量要求。

1. 体例

（1）按下列顺序**完整书写论文**：

    题目
    作者
    单位
    摘要及关键词
    正文
    参考文献
    英文摘要（包括英文题目、作者、单位、内容摘要、关键词）
    作者简介

（2）正文的章节编号从 0 开始连续编排。书写格式如下例所示：

    0　引言
    1　海洋平台试验模型设计
    2　模型试验方案
    3　……
    ……
    5　结论（这是正文最后一节。一般编号为 3~7，较多的是 4~5。）

首节"引言"和末节"结论"（或"结语"）是必不可少的。

除"引言"和"结论"这两节外，其他章节还可再设最多两层子节，如：

    1　……
    1.1　……
    ……
    1.2.1　……

　　　　　……
　　　1.2.2　……
　　　　　……
　　　2　……
　　　　　……

在各章节或子节中还可用（1），（2），（3），…，对文字段落编号。继而可用①，②，③，…，对词句或小段落编号。

为避免文章条理过于繁琐而影响可读性，**不支持更细的分层编号**。

2. 题目

论文的题目应简明扼要，准确反映研究主题。**字数一般不超过 20 字**。

一般情况下，不支持设立副标题。

为保持学术研究的氛围，在题目中慎用"浅谈""初探"等词。不恰当的使用，易于误认为是科普类或浅层次综述类文章。

3. 作者和单位

多个作者在同一单位的书写格式，如下例所示：

　　　　　王磊，杨申申，徐鹏飞，谢俊元
　　　　　（中国船舶科学研究中心，无锡，214082）

多个作者不全在一个单位的书写格式，如下例所示：

　　　　　程　龙[1]，刘新宝[1]，姚　坤[2]
　　（1. 中海油能源发展股份有限公司监督监理技术公司，天津 300452；
　　　2. 中海油天津分公司 QHD32-6 作业公司，天津 300452）

4. 摘要

不少作者对摘要的书写不够重视，比较随意和潦草。摘要是论文的窗口，应予以重视和着力提高写作水平。

书写摘要时，要围绕研究的目的、方法、结果和结论等方面来展开。着重说明研究取得的进展、突破和创新之处，以及工程应用意义等。文句简明流畅，不使用令人费解的长句。不宜在摘要中介绍研究背景、罗列空洞的结果或者没有根据的推测。更不能将没有进行的工作写入摘要。

摘要的书写不能过于简略，以不少于 150 字为宜。

5. 参考文献著录

（1）按照正文中被引用的先后顺序，对参考文献编号。参考文献目录中的每一篇文献都必须在正文中被引用。

（2）每一篇文献都要有一个表示文献类型的标志代码，置于题名后的方括号中。例：

［5］姚熊亮，郭君，许维军. 船舶结构远场爆炸冲击动响应的数值试验方法［J］. 中国造船，2006，47(2)：24-34.

普通的（纸质印刷）文献类型标志代码主要有：

　　　M（书，论文集等）
　　　J（期刊）
　　　N（报纸）
　　　C（会议）

D（学位论文）
R（报告）
S（标准）
P（专利）

从非连续出版物（会议，多作者的著作汇编等）中析出的文献，要在带方括号的文献标志代码后添加双斜线"//"，再列出相应的会议、著作等。例：

SUPACHAWAROTE C, GEORGENES S. Inclined pull-out capacity of suction caissons[C]//The Fourteenth (2004) International Offshore and Polar Engineering Conference Toulon, France, May, 2004: 23-28.

（注意：[C]和//之间没有"."号。）

电子文献除以上的各种文献类型外还有 DB（数据库）、CP（计算程序）和 EB（电子公告）这三种类型。

电子文献不仅要有文献类型标志代码，还要写出载体类型。目前常见的载体类型有 CD（光盘）和 OL（联机网络）。书写格式是[文献类型/载体类型]。例如[EB/OL]、[M/CD]等。

对于载体类型是 OL 的电子文献，在著录时还须写上（上网）引用日期和访问路径（网址）。引用日期写在方括号内。例：

[2] 绿地公司. 荒漠植被方法：中国，01129210 [P/OL]. 2001-10-24 [2002-05-28]. http://211.152.9.47/sipoasp/zlijs/hyis-new.asp? recid=011299210.5&leixin.

（3）英文文献中，作者是外国人时，姓放在前面，所有字母大写；名在后，缩略为单个大写字母，且不加缩写点"."。例：

作者	文献著录中的书写法
Albert Einstein	EINSTEIN A
Tom Frank Brown, Jr.	BROWN T F, Jr.

作者是中国人且使用汉语拼音表示姓名时，著录中不能使用缩写，应写出全部汉语拼音。双名之间不使用连字符。这和正文中的书写方法是一致的。例：

作者	文献著录中的书写法
Zhou Yuan（周元）	ZHOU Yuan
Zhu Dajing（朱大进）	ZHU Dajing

若责任者（作者）是机关团体，它的名称须由上至下分级著录（与文本中的书写顺序相反）。例：

作为责任者的机关团体	文献著录中的书写法
Department of civil engineering, Stanford University	Stanford University, Department of civil engineering

（4）文献是期刊类型的，须要书写出版年、卷和期；或者只书写年和期。注意：不是书写出版的年和月。

若是书写出版年、卷和期，在年和卷之间加逗号，期数放在圆括号中。例：

中国造船，2009, 50 (3): 32-39.

若只书写年和期，在年和期之间无需加逗号。例：

中国造船, 2009 (3): 32-39.

(5) 每一条文献的末尾统一加上点号"."，表示这条文献著录完毕。

注：**参考文献中的标点符号按西文书写格式**，即：英文、半角、键盘单键输入符号。

(6) 参考文献在正文中的标注

在正义中引述某论文或该论文作者的观点时，引述到的参考文献有两种标注方式：

以上角的形式标注。例：

为了快速应急响应，需要有应对初稳性高为负时的合理的抗沉措施。国内在此方面的研究不是很多[1,2]。

Sheng Meiping[4]和 Mace 等[5]用统计能量法对机械系统的振动功率流进行了计算评估。宋济平等[6]采用结构导纳分析法，研究了复杂机械系统的动态传递特性。

注：在这种标注方式的引述中，不直接出现"文献"二字。

② "文献[x]"作为主词，直接放在行文中。例：

文献[2]给出了静稳性曲线的计算方法，但是只研究了破损后初稳性高为负状态下对称进水时应采取的抗沉决策。

在正文中某一处同时引用多篇文献时，应将这些文献的编号放在一个方括号中，其中，不连续的序号之间用逗号分隔；对2个或2个以上的连续序号，只写起、讫号，之间插入连字符。例：

张杨[1]指出„„，李大飞[2-3]认为„„，形成了多种数学模型[7, 9, 11-13]。

(7) 鉴于有些作者对文献的检索和阅读还不够重视，编辑部要求每一篇论文中**参考文献的引用量不少于4篇**。

着重关注《中国造船》近年来刊登的论文将相关的文献，补充到文后的"参考文献"中来。

6. 正文中的物理量（变量，参数）

1) 量符号一般为单个拉丁字母或希腊字母。只有少数准则数使用2个字母构成。如 Eu（欧拉数）、Re 雷诺数等。

对常用的物理量，应尽量采用国家标准中规定的（也是通常使用的）符号，不要随意更改。除工程上已习惯使用的一些由多字母组成的量符号，如 NPSH（净正吸上高度）等，不提倡作者编造多字母符号。可**在单字母上加下标或上标等**方式，来形成新的表示量的符号。

例如，阻力系数（Drag Coefficient）的符号宜用 C_d，而不是使用 DC 或 COD 之类的多字母符号。

2) **向量和矩阵符号一律使用黑斜体**。不再使用字母上面加箭号或字母外面加大括号等表示方式。更不可和普通的变量混同，使用白斜体。这是因为向量和矩阵的运算法则特殊，若不和普通表示数值的量明显加以区别，势必引起运算上的混乱或矛盾。

3) 物理量单位应使用法定计量单位。英制单位（如英尺、磅）等虽然在某些工程领域还在使用，但它们不是我国的法定计量单位。在科技论文中应换算为相应的法定计量单位。

7. 图的处理

1) 平面图、流程图、曲线图等须由使用绘图软件制作，**处于可编辑修改的状态**，一般应在指定的版面尺寸下制作，**颜色模态为黑白**。图中的字符大小统一为六号。中文字符使用仿宋体，西文字符和数字使用 Times New Roman 字体。

慎用那些将大图过分缩小制成的图片。若出现线条模糊，字符太小、难以识读等情况，应按实际版面重新制作。

2）在当前黑白印刷条件下,应尽量避免使用彩色图(个别实物照片除外)。彩色云图在黑白印刷后的表现效果很差,须将这类图形想要表示的内容用其他方式表示。

对于那些经过修改仍未达到要求的图,要予以删除,以免影响版面质量。

3）论文中常用坐标曲线来表示物理量之间的关系。在横坐标和纵坐标上应标明相应的物理量符号(斜体书写)和物理量单位的符号(正体书写),书写格式为:

物理量符号(斜体)/物理量单位(正体)

图例如图 9-1 所示。

若是无量纲的量则不须列单位。若物理量具有组合单位应将组合单位置于小括号中。例如:$a/(m/s^2)$,a 表示加速度。

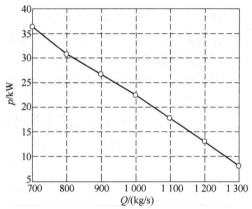

图 9-1 功率-流量曲线

4）论文中的图按出现顺序统一编号。每一张图都要有图号和图名,置于图的下方。图中的说明作为图的组成部分来处理,如图 9-2 所示。

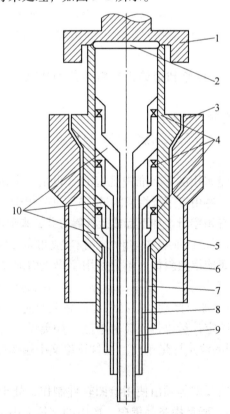

图 9-2 浮式钻井平台典型钻井结构与泥线悬挂系统
1—液压连接器 2—AX 密封环 3—套管头(井口头) 4—套管密封
5—导管 6—表层套管 7—技术套管1 8—技术套管2 9—生产套管 10—套管挂

5）若一张图包含了若干分图，则分图以（a），（b），（c），…，等编号，每一张分图亦应有图名。在文字段落中引用分图时称图1（a）、图3（d）等。分图示例如图9-3所示。

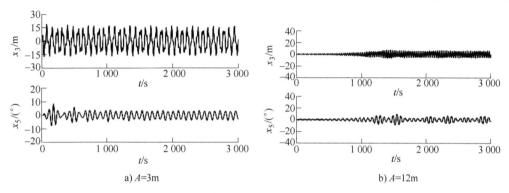

a) $A=3m$ b) $A=12m$

图9-3　垂荡、纵摇时历曲线比较（$T=80s$）

8. 表格

对于大部分形式不复杂的表格，应使用三线表的形式，它的表达方式最为简洁。示例如下：

（1）例1

表1　$L/D=4$，$S_u=1kPa$ 的吸力锚的极限承载力

L/m	D/m	S_u/kPa	$\theta/(°)$	H/kN	V/kN
20	5	1	0	14000	0
20	5	1	15	15590	4177
20	5	1	30	16246	9380
20	5	1	45	10691	10691
20	5	1	60	6350	10998

复杂的表格，可在表头添加辅助横线。示例如下：

（2）例2

表2　几种供氧技术优缺点分析

| 效能 | 超氧化物 | 物理供氧 | | 电解水 | | 氧烛 |
		气体供氧	液氧	碱性电解质	固态聚合物	
耗能	低	低	高	高	较高	低
装置体积	小	较大	大	大	较大	小
二次污染	无	无	无	大量氢气	大量氢气	微量氯气
产氧速度	较快	较快	较快	快	快	快
安装位置	舱内	舱内外均可，但深海时受制约	舱内外均可，但深海时受制约	舱内	舱内	舱内
是否可循环使用	否	否，但可再次填充	否，但可再次填充	是	是	否
温度影响	无	无	大	无	无	无
湿度影响	大	无	无	无	无	较小
效率	低	高	高	高	高	较高
使用成本	低	较低	高	高	较高	较低

9. 英文摘要

英文题名、摘要内容、选用的关键词与中文基本一致。**英文摘要中的作者（包括排序）和单位应和中文一致**。尤其是在修改稿件时，若需调整作者，应将中、英文作者名、作者单位，还有中文作者简介，同步调整。

英文作者名使用汉字的拼音书写，确认每个字的拼音正确无误。

科技专业词汇应尽可能源自西文权威书刊，不宜随意编造。

一般情况下，建议主要使用现在时、被动语态书写。

10. 作者简介

按姓名、性别、出生年份、学历、主要工作的顺序对论文所有作者按原有排序逐一介绍，使用相同格式。示例如下：

王圣强　男，1981年生，硕士。主要从事海洋平台陆地建造及海上安装工作。

李　飒　女，1970年生，博士，副教授。主要从事海洋结构物的研究。

舒仕勇　男，1983年生，硕士，助理工程师。主要从事企业资产管理、投资管理、装备管理等工作。

9.1.2　投稿信与原始稿

以《深海球形耐压壳力学特性研究》一文的投稿信和原始稿为例。

（1）投稿信

尊敬的编辑同志，您好！

现将论文《深海球形耐压壳力学特性研究》投于贵刊《中国造船》，该论文是本人在702所做博士后课题的研究成果（合作导师：王纬波/吴文伟研究员），请查收！

祝：工作顺利，万事如意！

张建

2015.6.1

邮编：212003

联系人：张建

电话：15896387748

邮箱：zhjian127@163.com

地址：江苏省镇江市梦溪路2号 江苏科技大学机械工程学院

（2）原始稿

深海球形耐压壳力学特性研究

张建[1,2]，高杰[1]，王纬波[2]，唐文献[1]，周通[1]

（1. 江苏科技大学，江苏 镇江 212003；2. 中国船舶科学研究中心，江苏 无锡 214082）

摘　要

系统研究了球形耐压壳理论和数值分析方法。分别建立了球形耐压壳薄壳力学模型、厚

收稿日期：　　　　修改稿收稿日期：

基金项目：国家自然科学基金项目（51205173）

壳力学模型、浮力系数求解公式以及6km水深球形耐压壳的壳单元、体单元数值模型，对比分析1-6km球形耐压壳强度、稳定性、储备浮力特性，并研究网格划分形式、单元类型、密度对数值结果的影响规律。结果表明，采用厚壳理论、体单元数值分析进行深海球形耐压壳设计与评估更为合理；强度是厚球壳设计的主要影响因素，建议先根据内表面应力公式确定耐压壳厚度，再运用厚壳屈曲理论或数值分析校核其稳定性。

关键词：球形耐压壳；强度；稳定性；厚壳理论
中图分类号：U661.4，TE58　**文献标识码**：A

0 引言

根据《中国制造2025》文件，国家将大力推动海洋工程装备突破发展，深海潜水器是大洋勘查与深海科学研究的重要海洋工程装备。作为潜水器的重要组成部分，耐压壳起着保障下潜过程中内部设备正常工作和人员健康安全的作用，其重量占潜水器总重的1/4-1/2[1]。

目前球形耐压壳的设计与分析均基于薄壳理论，并被各国船级社规范认同。潘彬彬等对比分析了现有深水球形耐压壳的设计规范，表明薄壳理论是这些规范的共性理论基础，认为现有规范计算存在缺陷，需要修订[2]；在此基础上，通过原型试验和非线性有限元分析，建立了预测深海钛合金球形壳极限强度的经验公式。马永前等参考中厚板壳稳定性理论研究厚球壳屈曲问题，指出由于厚度方向的剪切效应，厚球壳的实际临界屈曲载荷低于薄壳理论（Zolley公式）结果[3]。王自力、刘涛等认为，随着水深增加，耐压壳分析从薄壳问题转化为中厚壳问题，现有的潜水器规范不适用于深海耐压壳分析，对于厚球壳可直接根据有限元计算确定其极限强度[4-5]。然而，在有限元建模过程中，模型简化、单元类型、网格密度、划分形式、边界条件、求解方法等对球形壳结果影响很大，致使不同人员对同一问题的分析结果存在差异，且由于缺少试验验证和厚壳理论支撑，数值解的可信度有待商榷。

为此，本文分别从理论和数值2个方面，系统研究球形耐压壳的强度、稳定性、储备浮力等性能。首先，建立球形耐压壳薄壳力学模型、厚壳力学模型、浮力系数求解公式，以1-6km水深耐压壳为对象，从薄壳理论和厚壳理论角度，对比其强度、稳定性特性，并分析经验法和解析法求解浮力系数的结果差异；其次，建立6km水深球形耐压壳的壳单元数值模型，研究划分形式、单元类型、网格密度对其强度、稳定的影响规律；最后，建立同比条件下体单元数值模型，研究单元类型、网格密度对耐压壳强度、稳定的影响规律，并与壳单元数值模型、理论模型结果作对比分析。研究成果可为深海球形耐压设计提供理论指导。

1 问题描述

以直径为2m球形耐压壳为对象，研究其强度和稳定性规律，计算载荷根据式1确定。假设球形耐压壳的材料为Ti-6Al-4V（TC4），其基本力学参数：屈服强度为$\sigma_b = 830Mpa$，密度$\rho_{ph} = 4.5g/cm^3$，弹性模量$G = 110Gpa$，泊松比$\mu = 0.3$。由于本文目的在于探讨厚球壳的设计方法，故忽略其他因素（如材料物理非线性修正系数、制造效应系数等）的影响，假设许用应力$[\sigma]$等于材料的屈服强度，得到计算载荷P_S。

$$P_S = K\rho_w gh/0.9 \tag{1}$$

其中，K为安全系数取1.5，ρ_w为海水密度取1g/cm3，g为重力加速度取9.8/s2，h为水深取0-6km。

2 理论模型
2.1 薄壳力学模型

根据薄壳强度理论,球形耐压壳中面应力 σ_{mid} 计算公式 2 所示,该公式为船级社球形耐压壳强度校核的共性理论基础。

$$\sigma_{mid} = \frac{P_S R}{2t} \tag{2}$$

假设 $\sigma_{mid} = [\sigma]$,根据式 2 可推出极限强度载荷 $P_{\sigma 1}$ 与 t/R(厚度半径比)的关系:

$$P_{\sigma 1} = 2[\sigma]\frac{t}{R} \tag{3}$$

根据薄壳屈曲理论,球形耐压壳屈曲临界载荷 P_{cr1} 采用 Zolley 公式[6]表述,该公式为船级社球形耐压壳稳定性设计规范的共性理论基础,即:

$$P_{cr1} = \frac{2Et^2}{R^2}\sqrt{\frac{1}{3(1-\mu^2)}} \tag{4}$$

2.2 厚壳力学模型

随着工作水深增加,耐压壳厚度随之增大,其强度和稳定性计算从薄壳问题变为厚壳问题,采用薄壳理论研究厚壳问题偏于危险。对于承受静水压力的厚球壳结构,内表面应力 σ_{inner} 最大,外表面应力 σ_{outer} 最小,分别如式 5、6 所示,中面应力根据式 2 确定。

$$\sigma_{inner} = \frac{3P_S\left(2+\frac{t}{R}\right)^3}{2\left[\left(2+\frac{t}{R}\right)^3 - \left(2-\frac{t}{R}\right)^3\right]} \tag{5}$$

$$\sigma_{outer} = \frac{3P_S\left(2-\frac{t}{R}\right)^3}{2\left[\left(2+\frac{t}{R}\right)^3 - \left(2-\frac{t}{R}\right)^3\right]} \tag{6}$$

根据式 2、式 5,可得出薄壳强度理论评价厚壳应力的偏差 Δ_σ,即:

$$\Delta_\sigma = \frac{|\sigma_{inner} - \sigma_{mid}|}{\sigma_{inner}} \times 100\% = \left\{1 - \left[1 - \left(\frac{2-\frac{t}{R}}{2+\frac{t}{R}}\right)^3\right] \times \frac{3}{\frac{t}{R}}\right\} \times 100\% \tag{7}$$

假设 $\sigma_{inner} = [\sigma]$,据式 5 可推出极限强度载荷 $P_{\sigma 2}$ 与 t/R 的关系:

$$P_{\sigma 2} = \frac{2[\sigma]\left[\left(2+\frac{t}{R}\right)^3 - \left(2-\frac{t}{R}\right)^3\right]}{3\left(2+\frac{t}{R}\right)^3} \tag{8}$$

深水球形耐压壳屈曲临界载荷采用式 9 表述[7],该公式采用勒让德函数求解球形壳屈曲控制方程[8],推导出厚球壳稳定性问题的解析解 P_{cr2}:

$$P_{cr2} = \frac{2Et}{R(1-\mu^2)}\left(\sqrt{\frac{(1-\mu^2)}{3}}\frac{t}{R} - \frac{\mu t^2}{2R^2}\right) \tag{9}$$

将式 3 代入式 9 可得:

$$P_{cr2} = \left(1 - \frac{\sqrt{3}}{2}\frac{\mu}{\sqrt{1-\mu^2}}\frac{t}{R}\right)P_{cr1} \tag{10}$$

则：

$$P_{cr2} = \left(1 - f\left(\frac{t}{R}\right)\right)P_{cr1} \quad 其中, \quad f\left(\frac{t}{R}\right) = \frac{\sqrt{3}}{2}\frac{\mu}{\sqrt{1-\mu^2}}\frac{t}{R} \tag{11}$$

根据式3、式11，可得出经典Zolley公式在计算厚壳屈曲临界载荷的误差为：

$$\Delta_{cr} = \frac{|P_{cr1} - P_{cr2}|}{P_{cr2}} \times 100\% = \frac{f\left(\frac{t}{R}\right)}{1 - f\left(\frac{t}{R}\right)} \times 100\% \tag{12}$$

2.3 球形耐压壳浮力系数

耐压壳浮力系数定义为耐压壳体重量与其排水量比值 δ：

$$\delta = \frac{\rho_{ph}V_{ph}}{\rho_w V_w} \tag{13}$$

式中，V_{ph} 为耐压壳材料体积，V_w 为排水量体积。

在现有设计中，耐压壳材料体积可采用其中面面积与厚度乘积确定，耐压壳的排水体积可近似为中面围成区域的体积，因此，可得出球形耐压壳经验法浮力系数 δ_1：

$$\delta_1 = \frac{3\rho_{ph}}{\rho_w}\frac{t}{R} \tag{14}$$

实际上，球形耐压壳材料体积应为外表面所谓围成区域的体积减去内表面所围成区域的体积，耐压壳的排水体积则为外表面所谓围成区域的体积，即解析法浮力系数 δ_2：

$$\delta_2 = \frac{\rho_{ph}\left[\left(2+\frac{t}{R}\right)^3 - \left(2-\frac{t}{R}\right)^3\right]}{\rho_w\left(2+\frac{t}{R}\right)^3} \tag{15}$$

根据式14、式15，可得出经验法计算球形耐压壳浮力系数的误差，即：

$$\Delta_\delta = \frac{|\delta_1 - \delta_2|}{\delta_2} = \left(\frac{3\frac{t}{R}}{1-\left(\frac{2-\frac{t}{R}}{2+\frac{t}{R}}\right)^3} - 1\right) \times 100\% \tag{16}$$

3 球形耐压壳数值模型

以6km水深球形耐压壳为对象，研究其强度、稳定性数值分析方法，设计厚度为75mm。

3.1 壳单元模型

采用Pro/E软件，进行三维CAD建模，并抽取中面，采用ANSA前处理软件，进行网格划分；计算载荷以均布压力形式施加在耐压壳表面；理论上耐压壳是不受任何约束，为了消除模型的刚性位移，选择三个点限制其六个方向位移。所求得各约束反力接近0，说明所施加的约束为虚约束，仅限制了模型的刚体位移。定义2种工况进行分析：1）线性准静态分析；2）线性屈曲分析。采用ABAQUS/Standard对该模型进行求解计算，最后，运用

ABAQUS/Viewer 进行后处理。采用单因素控制变量法分别建立不同网格划分形式、单元类型、单元密度下的数值模型，进行分析计算。

采用随机划分、钱币划分、网球划分三者的划分形式，分别对应于模型1、模型2、模型3，如图1所示，单元类型为4节点完全积分线性壳单元（S4），网格单元数量约为6500。对于单元类型，采用4节点完全积分线性壳单元（S4）、4节点减缩积分壳单元（S4R）、每个节点5个自由度的4节点减缩积分壳单元（S4R5）、8节点双曲厚壳单元（S8R）、每节点5个自由度的8节点双曲厚壳单元（S8R5），分别对应于模型3、模型4、模型5、模型6、模型7，这些模型均采用网球划分的形式，单元数、节点数与模型3一致。对于数值模型，需要进行网格的收敛性检查来验证模型结果的正确性。故分别采用平均尺寸为200mm、120mm、100mm、70mm、60mm、45mm、35mm、20mm的网格进行分析，分别对应于模型8、模型9、模型10、模型11、模型3、模型12、模型13、模型14，单元类型均为S4，均采用网球划分。

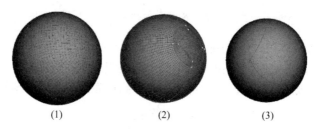

图1　球形耐压壳网格模型
（1）随机划分　（2）钱币划分　（3）网球划分

3.2　体单元模型

体单元网格模型可以通过壳单元网格沿厚度方向偏移4层单元得到，其中载荷、边界、工况与壳单元一致。首先，根据模型3的网格，建立体单元模型，单元类型设定为三维8节点体单元（C3D8）、三维8节点减缩积分体单元（C3D8R）、三维8节点非协调模式体单元（C3D8I）、三维20节点体单元（C3D20）、三维20节点减缩积分体单元（C3D20R），分别对应于模型15、模型16、模型17、模型18、模型19。此外，分别采用周向平均尺寸为200mm、120mm、100mm、70mm、60mm、45mm、35mm、20mm的网格进行分析，分别对应于模型20、模型21、模型22、模型23、模型24、模型25、模型26、模型27，这些模型的网格分别由模型8、模型9、模型10、模型11、模型3、模型12、模型13、模型14的网格沿厚度方向偏移所得，单元类型均为C3D20R。

4　结果分析与讨论

4.1　球形耐压壳力学特性分析

根据式2、式4、式5、式9，绘制出薄壳力学模型和厚壳力学模型在不同t/R下的极限强度载荷和屈曲临界载荷的分布曲线，如图2（1）所示。可见，当t/R小于0.013时，屈曲临界载荷小于极限强度载荷，稳定性为耐压壳安全评估的主要影响因素；当t/R大于0.013时，屈曲临界载荷大于极限强度载荷，强度为耐压壳安全评估的主要影响因素，且随着水深的增加，强度因素的影响越来越大，而屈曲因素的影响越来越小。

由图2（1）可知，经典Zolley公式所得出屈曲临界载荷偏于保守，其误差曲线如图2（2）所示，随着厚度半径比的逐渐增加，Zolley公式误差不断增大，与t/R成线性关系，当

t/R 为 0.075 时,误差最大,约为 2.1%;由此可以认为,Zolley 公式在计算厚壳的临界屈曲载荷时,误差较小,可用于厚球壳的稳定性初步评估。马永前也研究厚球壳稳定性问题,基于板壳理论建立了厚球壳屈曲临界载荷的修正公式,指出 Zolley 公式所得出屈曲临界载荷偏于保守,但该方法依赖拟合有限元分析结果得到相关修正系数,不具备通用性,且不是厚球壳屈曲临界载荷解析解。

由图 2(1)还可以发现,随着厚度半径比的增加,球形耐压壳中面应力与内表面应力差值随着 t/R 增加逐渐增大,差值曲线如图 2(3)所示,当 t/R 增加到 0.075 时,中面应力与内表面应力差值达到最大的 10.4%,即使 t/R 为 1/20(厚壳、薄壳分界线)时,两种差值也达到了 7.1%,此时薄壳强度理论(式 2)进行球形耐压壳强度校核时,结果比较危险;当 t/R 小于 0.015 时,误差在 2% 以内,在这种情况下,薄壳强度理论可适用于球形耐压壳强度的初步评估。

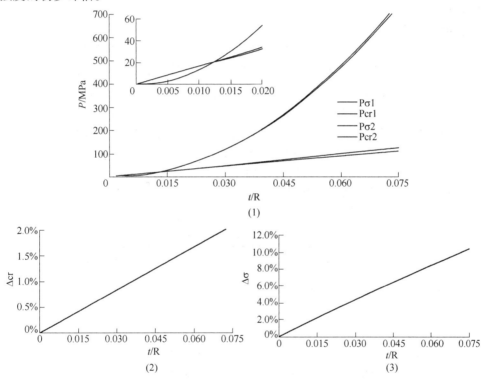

图 2 薄壳厚壳理论模型公式及相对误差曲线
(1)薄壳、厚壳力学模型计算结果 (2)屈曲误差 (3)应力偏差

4.2 球形耐压壳浮力系数分析

两种方法所得的浮力系数曲线如图 3(1)所示。可见,两种计算方法得到的浮力系数均与 t/R 成近似的线性递增关系,但是经验法得到的浮力系数要比解析法高。且随着 t/R 的逐渐增大,经验法所得的浮力系数误差越来越大,如图 3(2)所示;当 t/R 达到 0.075 时,误差值达到的 10.1%,即使 t/R 为 1/20(厚壳、薄壳分界线)时,两种差值也达到了 6.8%,故在进行中厚球壳浮力系数评估时,经验法不在适用;当 t/R 小于 0.015 时,经验法误差在 2% 以内,在这种情况下,经验法可适用于球形耐压壳浮力系数的初步评估。刘涛[9]关于球形耐压壳的浮力系数的研究也有相近的结论,说明采用经验法在进行深海耐压

壳设计时偏于保守。

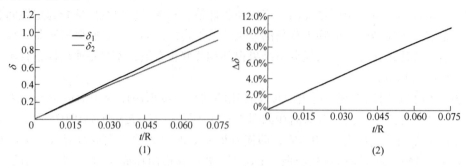

图 3 浮力系数求解结果
(1) 两种方法所得浮力系数曲线 (2) 经验法浮力系数误差

4.3 数值结果分析
4.3.1 壳单元数值结果

根据式 2、式 9 求出 6km 球形耐压壳的中面应力和临界屈曲载荷分别为 653.33MPa、733.67MPa。第 3 节所建立的 14 种壳单元数值模型的计算结果及误差如表 1 所示。由模型 1、模型 2、模型 3 的结果可知，在强度方面，随机形式的平均应力结果与理论值最为接近，钱币划分和网球划分形式的平均应力与理论值相差也较小，不足 0.1%；但随机划分的最大最小应力相差太大，出现明显应力集中，网球划分和钱币划分的最大最小应力相差很小，较为吻合球形耐压壳的等强度特性。在稳定性方面，网球划分的临界屈曲载荷与理论值相差最小，为 0.049%，而随机划分和钱币划分的临界屈曲载荷与理论值相差较大，分别为 1.782%、0.167%。因此，从强度和稳定性两方面考虑，采用网球划分为球形耐压壳建模的最佳选择。

表 1 壳单元数值模型结果

模型	σ_{max}	σ_{min}	$\sigma_{max} - \sigma_{min}$	$\sigma_{平均}$	P_{cr}	$\dfrac{\sigma - \sigma_t}{\sigma_t} \times 100\%$	$\dfrac{P_{cr} - P_{cr_t}}{P_{cr_t}} \times 100\%$
模型 1	664.511	634.967	29.544	653.332	746.7404	0.00%	1.782%
模型 2	655.075	651.919	3.156	652.871	734.8922	0.07%	0.167%
模型 3	653.825	648.554	5.271	652.885	734.0298	0.07%	0.049%
模型 4	653.942	651.251	2.691	652.889	732.4422	0.07%	0.167%
模型 5	653.946	651.253	2.693	652.889	692.4974	0.07%	5.612%
模型 6	654.926	648.65	6.276	652.803	690.4688	0.08%	5.888%
模型 7	654.768	648.686	6.082	652.805	691.978	0.08%	5.683%
模型 8	665.638	580.459	85.179	640.219	831.0596	2.01%	13.274%
模型 9	659.112	613.638	45.474	647.367	772.0832	0.91%	5.236%
模型 10	657.445	624.145	33.3	649.313	756.315	0.62%	3.087%
模型 11	654.145	646.268	7.877	652.612	735.6762	0.11%	0.273%
模型 12	653.559	650.934	2.625	653.13	733.0596	0.03%	0.083%
模型 13	653.478	651.703	1.775	653.202	732.3442	0.02%	0.181%
模型 14	653.417	652.348	1.069	653.259	731.7366	0.01%	0.264%

由模型 3、模型 4、模型 5、模型 6、模型 7 结果可知，在强度方面，无论是否采用减缩积分单元，得到的平均应力结果与理论值相差都非常小，几乎可以忽略不计；而从最大最小应力差值考虑，减缩积分单元 S4R 和 S4R5 较为理想，陆蓓、潘彬彬等在进行球形耐压壳数值分析时，也采用了 S4R 和 S4R5 单元。在稳定性方面，S4 计算精度最高。因此，从强度和稳定性两方面考虑，4 节点完全积分线性壳单元（S4）为球形耐压壳建模的最佳选择。

网格疏密对数值模拟的准确度影响很大，因此先进行网格无关性检验，只有当网格数的增加对计算结果影响不大时，这时的仿真结果才具有意义。单元密度的选取要综合考虑计算时间和结果精度[10]。由表 1 中的模型 8、模型 9、模型 10、模型 11、模型 3、模型 12、模型 13、模型 14 结果，绘制应力误差曲线、屈曲临界载荷误差曲线，分别如图 4（1）、（2）所示。图 4（1）为球形耐压壳中面上最大应力，最小应力和平均应力与理论强度应力 σ_{mid} 的比值曲线，可见，单元平均尺寸与球形耐压壳半径比为 0.07 时，数值模型得到的结果就开始收敛，且网格尺寸越小，数值模型的平均应力越趋近于理论值，而最大最小值的差值也越来越小，趋于解析解。

一般认为，网格尺寸的选取应该使屈曲临界载荷的相对浮动量小于等于 1%，结果趋于收敛[12]。由图 4（2）可知，当单元平均尺寸与球形耐压壳半径比达到 0.07 时，屈曲临界载荷的相对浮动量小于等于 1%，数值模型得到的屈曲结果就开始收敛逼近于 1，网格尺寸继续减小时得到的屈曲应力全部逼近于 1。因此，从强度和稳定性两方面考虑，单元尺寸和半径比为 0.07 为球形耐压壳建模的最佳选择。

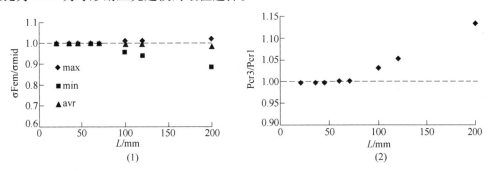

图 4　壳单元数值模型网格收敛性曲线
（1）壳单元数值模型强度应力收敛曲线　（2）壳单元数值模型屈曲应力收敛曲线

图 5 为模型 3 计算所得的中面应力云图、内外表面应力云图、1 阶屈曲振形图，显然，采用壳单元进行数值模拟时，中面和内外层面的应力相差仅仅不到 1%，这与理论结果相差甚远，说明采用壳单元进行厚球壳强度分析是不合理的。

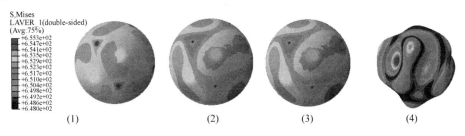

图 5　S4 壳单元模型应力与屈曲云图
（1）内层面　（2）中层面　（3）外层面　（4）1 阶屈曲云图

4.3.2 体单元数值模型分析

根据式2、式5、式6、式9求出球形耐压壳的中面应力、内表面应力、外表面应力和临界屈曲载荷分别为653.33MPa、729.28MPa、582.28MPa、733.67MPa。第3节所建立的5种体单元数值模型的计算结果、及数值解误差如表2所示。由模型15、模型16、模型17、模型18、模型19的结果可知,在强度方面,采用减缩积分单元C3D20R,内中外三个面得到的平均应力结果与理论值最为接近,采用C3D8I单元和C3D20单元得到的三个表面应力与理论值相差相差都较小;而采用C3D8单元和C3D8R单元,三个面应力的最大最小值或者平均值都与理论值相差太大。在稳定性方面,采用C3D8I单元的临界屈曲载荷与理论值相差最小,为0.59%,而采用C3D20单元和C3D20R单元的临界屈曲载荷计算误差也较小,分别为0.89%、0.88%。因此,从强度和稳定性两方面考虑,采用C3D20R体单元为球形耐压壳建模的最佳选择。

表2 不同单元类型体单元数值模型结果

Type		C3D8	C3D8R	C3D8I	C3D20	C3D20R
Inner Stress /MPa	max	717.218	710.689	725.026	732.098	732.857
	min	714.201	707.792	720.358	726.644	727.796
	max - min	3.017	2.897	4.668	5.454	5.061
	average	715.124	708.128	720.811	728.604	729.603
	theory	729.282	729.282	729.282	729.282	729.282
	error	1.94%	2.90%	1.16%	0.09%	0.04%
Middle Stress /MPa	max	650.569	650.612	650.151	649.874	651.006
	min	649.183	649.359	648.706	648.992	649.546
	max - min	1.386	1.253	1.445	0.882	1.46
	average	650.181	650.313	649.865	649.419	650.334
	theory	653.333	653.333	653.333	653.333	653.333
	error	0.48%	0.46%	0.53%	0.60%	0.46%
Outer Stress /MPa	max	593.558	598.606	588.551	583.102	583.875
	min	589.119	593.97	582.256	578.027	578.584
	max - min	4.439	4.636	6.295	5.075	5.291
	average	592.594	598.007	587.841	581.395	582.127
	theory	582.282	582.282	582.282	582.282	582.282
	error	1.77%	2.70%	0.95%	0.15%	0.03%
Buckling Load /MPa	PCr	760.8916	721.476	737.9694	740.194	740.1646
	theory	733.69	733.69	733.69	733.69	733.69
	error	3.71%	1.66%	0.58%	0.89%	0.88%

由模型20、模型21、模型22、模型23、模型24、模型25、模型26结果,绘制应力误

差曲线、屈曲临界载荷误差曲线,分别如图6(1)、(2)、(3)、(4)所示。图6(1)、(2)、(3)分别为球形耐压壳内表面、中面、外表面上最大应力,最小应力和平均应力与理论强度应力 σmid 的比值曲线,可见,体单元的单元平均尺寸与球形耐压壳半径比也为0.07时,数值模型得到的结果同样开始收敛,且网格尺寸越小,数值模型的平均应力越趋近于理论值,而最大最小值的差值越小,趋于解析解。由图6(4)可知,当单元平均尺寸与球形耐压壳半径比达到0.07时,屈曲临界载荷的相对浮动量小于等于1%,数值模型得到的屈曲结果就开始收敛逼近于1,网格尺寸继续减小时得到的屈曲应力全部逼近于1。因此,从强度和稳定性两方面考虑,体单元的单元尺寸和半径比为0.07为球形耐压壳建模的最佳选择。

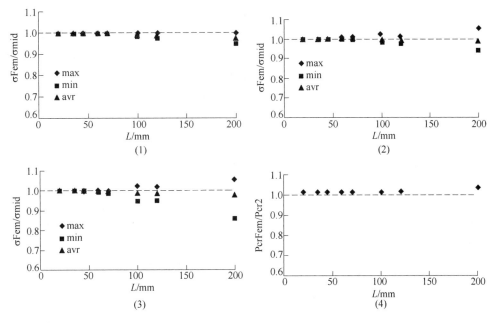

图6 体单元数值模型网格收敛性曲线
(1) 内面应力 (2) 中面应力 (3) 外面应力 (4) 临界屈曲载荷

图7为模型24计算所得的中面应力云图、内外表面应力云图、1阶屈曲振形图,可见,采用体单元进行数值模拟时,内表面和外表面的应力相差与与理论结果较为吻合,说明采用体单元进行厚球壳强度分析是合理的;而图5(4)所示的壳单元数值模型的1阶屈曲振形与图7所示体单元的1阶屈曲振形基本一致,结果相互佐证。

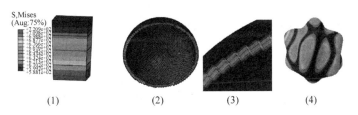

图7 C3D20体单元模型应力与屈曲云图
(1) 厚度方向 (2) 剖面方向 (3) 局部方向 (4) 1阶屈曲云图

5 结论

（1）强度是厚球壳设计主要影响因素，中面应力与内表面应力差值随着 t/R 增加而逐渐增大，当 t/R 增加到 0.075 时，两者差值达到最大为 10.4%，即使 t/R 为 1/20 时，两者差值也达到了 7.1%，建议以内表面应力为基准设计和评估深海球形耐压壳。Zolley 公式误差随着 t/R 增加而逐渐增大，当 t/R 为 0.075 时，两者差值达到最大为 2.1%，薄壳理论可用于厚球壳稳定性初步评估。经验法求解球形耐压壳浮力系数偏于保守，其误差随着 t/R 增加而逐渐增大，当 t/R 达到 0.075 时，误差达到 10.1%，即使 t/R 为 1/20 时，误差也高达 6.8%，建议采用解析法评估深海球形耐压壳的浮力系数。

（2）综合考虑计算精度和效率，建议采用网球划分、4 节点完全积分线性壳单元、单元平均尺寸 $0.07R$，建立球形耐压壳的壳单元数值模型；建议采用网球划分、三维 20 节点减缩积分体单元、周向单元平均尺寸 $0.07R$、厚度方向 4 层单元，建立球形耐压壳的体单元数值模型。壳单元数值模型、薄壳理论模型可用于浅海耐压壳设计与评估，体单元数值模型、厚球壳理论模型可用于深海耐压壳设计与评估，建议船级社在进行深海耐压壳设计规范修订时，采用内表面应力、厚壳临界屈曲载荷作为评价指标。

参考文献

[1] Zhang J, Zuo X L, Wang W B, Tang W X. Overviews of Investigation on Submersible Pressure Hulls[J]. Advances in Natural Science, 2014, 7(4): 54-61.
[2] Pan B B, Cui W C. A Comparison of Different Rules for the Spherical PressureHull of Deep Manned Submersibles[J]. Journal of Ship Mechanics, 2011, 15(3): 276-285.
[3] Ma Y Q, Wang C M, Ang K K. Buckling of super ellipsoidal shells under uniform pressure[J]. Thin-Walled Structures, 2008, 46(6): 584-591.
[4] 王自力, 王仁华, 俞铭华, 李良碧. 初始缺陷对不同深度载人潜水器耐压球壳极限承载力的影响[J]. 中国造船, 2007, 02: 45-50.
[5] 陆蓓, 刘涛, 崔维成. 深海载人潜水器耐压球壳极限强度研究[J]. 船舶力学, 2004, 01: 51-58.
[6] Pan B B, Cui W C. An overview of buckling and ultimate strength of spherical pressure hull under external pressure[J]. Marine Structures, 2010, 23(3): 227-240.
[7] Wang C M, Wang C Y, Reddy J N. Exact Solutions for Buckling of Structural Members[M]. CRC Press, 2004.
[8] Timoshenko S P, Gere J M. Theory of Elastic Stability[M]. Dover Publications, 1961.
[9] 刘涛. 大深度潜水器结构分析与设计研究[D]. 中国船舶科学研究中心. 2001, 3.
[10] Tomas A, Tovar J P. The influence of initial geometric imperfections on the buckling load of single and double curvature concrete shells[J]. Computers & Structures. 2012, 96(97): 34-45.

Investigation on Mechanical Properties of Deep Sea Spherical Pressure Hull

ZHANG Jian[1,2], GAO Jie[1], WANG Weibo[2], TANG Wenxian[1], ZHOU Tong[1]

(1. Jiangsu University of Science and Technology, Jiangsu Zhenjiang 212003, China
2. Chinese Ship Scientific Research Center, Jiangsu Wuxi 214082, China;)

Abstract

Theoretical and numerical analysis methods of the spherical pressure hull were systematically investigated. Mechanical models based on thin shell and thick shell, buoyancy factor equations for the hull were presented, respectively. Numerical models based on shell elements and solid elements for the hull with the water depth of 6 km were proposed as well. Strength, stability and buoyancy reserve capacity of the spherical hull with the water depth of 1-6 km were analyzed. Furthermore, effects of meshing, element type and density on the numerical results were studied. The results showed that, it is suitable to design and assess the deep sea spherical pressure hull using theory of thick shell and numerical models based on solid elements. Strength is the main influence factor during the thick spherical shell design process. Therefore, it is suggested to determine the thickness of the pressure hull based on the inner stress equation firstly. Then, the stability of the hull could be verified using buckling theory of thick shell and numerical analysis method.

Key words: spherical pressure hull; strength; stability; theory of thick shell

作者简介：
张　建　男，1984年生，博士，讲师。研究方向：深海耐压装备现代设计理论与方法。
高　杰　男，1992年生，硕士研究生。研究方向：深海耐压壳CAE技术研究。
王纬波　男，1969年生，博士，研究院。研究方向：舰船复合材料结构设计。
唐文献　男，1963年生，博士，教授。研究方向：海洋工程结构设计与研究。
周　通　男，1991年生，硕士研究生。研究方向：深海耐压壳CAE技术研究。

9.1.3　一通意见答复与修改稿

（1）编辑与专家意见

1）专家邮件意见

张建：您好！

编辑部对您的稿件进行了初步审读。稿件存在的问题较多。

（1）论文的目的不明确。是发展理论？研究计算方法？探讨设计规范？作者只能选择一个主题，深入下去。不能面面俱到，泛泛而谈。

（2）论文结构松散，章节编排不合理。第1节应删去，部分内容并入第3节。第4节撤销，其中的4.1，4.2节归并到第2节；4.3节归并到第3节。建议增加一节，对理论公式和有限元计算结果比较和分析。

（3）第3节数值计算写得很乱，可读性差。

首先要对数值试验方案进行论证。（建议把这节中的"模型"改为"方案"，比较确切。）这和物理模型的试验一样，要说明为什么要选这些方案，想要达到什么目的。

对选用的方案用列表的方式表达，更简洁和有条理性。避免使用繁琐的长段文字叙述。

对计算结果的讨论要有明确的目的，着重于对今后的计算有何借鉴作用。

稿件修改时请按照《中国造船》关于稿件质量的要求书写。

前3页正文的具体修改意见参看附件。

《中国造船》编辑部　张编辑

2）专家纸质意见

深海球形耐压壳力学特性研究

张建[1,2]，高杰[1]，王纬波[2]，唐文献[1]，周通[1]

(1. 江苏科技大学，江苏 镇江 212003；2. 中国船舶科学研究中心，江苏 无锡 214082)

摘 要

系统研究了球形耐压壳理论和数值分析方法。分别建立了球形耐压薄壳力学模型、厚壳力学模型、浮力系数求解公式以及6km水深球形耐压壳的壳单元、体单元数值模型，对比分析1-6km球形耐压壳强度、稳定性、储备浮力特性，并研究网格划分形式、单元类型、密度对数值结果的影响规律。结果表明，采用厚壳理论、体单元数值分析进行深海球形耐压壳设计与评估更为合理；强度是厚球壳设计的主要影响因素，建议先根据内表面应力公式确定耐压壳厚度，再运用厚壳屈曲理论或数值分析校核其稳定性。

关键词： 球形耐压壳；强度；稳定性；厚壳理论

中图分类号： U661.4, TE58 **文献标识码：** A

0 引言

根据《中国制造2025》文件，国家将大力推动海洋工程装备突破发展。深海潜水器是大洋勘查与深海科学研究的重要海洋工程装备。作为潜水器的重要组成部分，耐压壳起着保障下潜过程中内部设备正常工作和人员健康安全的作用，其重量占潜水器总重的1/4到1/2[1]。

民用球形耐压壳的设计与分析均基于薄壳理论，并被各国船舶社规范认同。潘彬彬等对比分析了现有深水球形耐压壳的设计规范，表明薄壳理论是这些规范的共性理论基础，认为现有规范计算存在缺陷，需要修订[2]；在此基础上，通过原型试验和非线性有限元分析，建立了预测深海钛合金球形壳极限强度的经验公式。马永前等参考中厚板壳稳定性理论研究厚球壳屈曲问题，指出由于厚度方向的剪切效应，厚球壳的实际临界屈曲载荷低于薄壳理论(Zolley公式)结果[3]。王自力、刘涛等认为，随着水深增加，耐压壳分析从薄壳问题转化为中厚壳问题，现有的潜水器规范不适用于深海耐压壳分析，对于厚球壳可直接根据有限元计算确定其极限强度[4,5]。然而，在有限元建模过程中，模型简化、单元类型、网格密度、划分形式、边界条件、求解方法等对球形壳结果影响很大，致使不同人员对同一问题的分析结果存在差异[6]。由于缺少试验验证和厚壳理论支撑，数值解的可信度有待商榷。

为此，本文分别从理论和数值两方面，系统研究球形耐压壳的强度、稳定性、储备浮力等性能。首先，建立球形耐压壳薄壳力学模型、厚壳力学模型、浮力系数求解公式，以1-6km水深壳为对象，从薄壳理论和厚壳理论角度对比强度、稳定性特性，并分析经验法和解析法求解浮力系数结果差异；其次，建立6km水深球形耐压壳的壳单元数值模型，研究划分形式、单元类型、网格密度对强度、稳定的影响规律；最后，建立同比条件下体单元数值模型，研究单元类型、网格密度对耐压壳强度、稳定的影响规律，并与壳单元数值模型、理论模型结果作对比分析。研究成果可为深海球形耐压设计提供理论指导。

1 问题描述

以直径为2m球形耐压壳为对象，研究其强度和稳定性规律，计算载荷根据式(1)确定。假设球形耐压壳的材料为Ti-6Al-4V(TC4)，其基本力学参数：屈服强度为σ_s=830MPa，密度ρ_{ph}=4.5g/cm³，弹性模量G=110GPa，泊松比μ=0.3。由于本文目的在于探讨厚球壳的设计方法，故忽略其它因素（如材料物理非线性修正系数、制造效应系数等）的影响，假设许用

收稿日期：2015-06-01；修改稿收稿日期：
基金项目：国家自然科学基金项目（51205173）

应力$[\sigma]$等于材料的屈服强度,得到计算载荷P_s。

$$P_s = K\rho_w gh/0.9 \tag{1}$$

其中,K 为安全系数取 1.5,ρ_w 为海水密度取 $1g/cm^3$,g 为重力加速度取 $9.8/s^2$,h 为水深取 0-6km。

2 理论模型

2.1 薄壳力学模型

根据薄壳强度理论,球形耐压壳中面应力 σ_{mid} 计算公式(2)所示,该公式为船级社球形耐压壳强度校核的线性理论基础。

$$\sigma_{mid} = \frac{P_s R}{2t} \tag{2}$$

假设 $\sigma_{mid} = [\sigma]$,根据式 2 可推出极限强度载荷 P_{01} 与 t/R(厚度半径比)的关系。

$$P_{01} = 2[\sigma]\frac{t}{R} \tag{3}$$

根据薄壳屈曲理论,球形耐压壳屈曲临界载荷 P_{cr1} 用 Zolley 公式表述,该公式为船级社球形耐压壳稳定性设计规范的线性理论基础,即:

$$P_{cr1} = \frac{2Et^2}{R^2}\sqrt{\frac{1}{3(1-\mu^2)}} \tag{4}$$

2.2 厚壳力学模型

随着工作水深增加,耐压壳厚度随之增大,其强度和稳定性计算从薄壳问题变为厚壳,采用薄壳理论研究厚壳问题偏于危险。对于承受静水压力的厚球壳结构,内表面应力 σ_{inner} 最大,外表面应力 σ_{outer} 最小,分别如式(5)(6)所示,中面应力根据式(2)确定。

$$\sigma_{inner} = \frac{3P_s(2+\frac{t}{R})^3}{2\left[(2+\frac{t}{R})^3 - (2-\frac{t}{R})^3\right]} \tag{5}$$

$$\sigma_{outer} = \frac{3P_s(2-\frac{t}{R})^3}{2\left[(2+\frac{t}{R})^3 - (2-\frac{t}{R})^3\right]} \tag{6}$$

根据式(2)、式(5),可得出薄壳强度理论评价厚壳应力的偏差,即:

$$\Delta_\sigma = \frac{|\sigma_{inner} - \sigma_{mid}|}{\sigma_{inner}} \times 100\% = \left\{1 - \left[1 - \left(\frac{2-\frac{t}{R}}{2+\frac{t}{R}}\right)^3\right] \times \frac{3}{\frac{t}{R}}\right\} \times 100\% \tag{7}$$

假设 $\sigma_{inner} = [\sigma]$，根据式5可推出极限强度载荷 P_{o2} 与 t/R 的关系：

$$P_{o2} = \frac{2[\sigma\left[(2+\frac{t}{R})^3 - (2-\frac{t}{R})^3\right]}{(2+\frac{t}{R})^3} \quad (8)$$

求球形耐压壳屈曲临界载荷采用式9表达[6]，该公式采用勒让德函数求解球形壳屈曲控制方程[8]，推导出厚球壳稳定性问题的解析解 P_{cr2}：

$$P_{cr2} = \frac{2Et}{R(1-\mu^2)}\left(\sqrt{\frac{(1-\mu^2)}{3}}\frac{t}{R} - \frac{\mu^2}{2R^2}\right) \quad (9)$$

将式(3)代入式(9)可得：

$$P_{cr2} = (1 - \frac{\sqrt{3}}{2}\frac{\mu}{\sqrt{1-\mu^2}}\frac{t}{R})P_{cr1} \quad (10)$$

则有：

$$P_{cr2} = (1 - f(\frac{t}{R}))P_{cr1}, \quad 其中，f(\frac{t}{R}) = \frac{\sqrt{3}}{2}\frac{\mu}{\sqrt{1-\mu^2}}\frac{t}{R} \quad (11)$$

根据式(3)和式(11)，可得出经典Zolley公式在计算厚壳屈曲临界载荷的误差为：

$$\sigma_{cr} = \frac{|P_{cr1} - P_{cr2}|}{P_{cr2}} \times 100\% = \frac{f(\frac{t}{R})}{1 - f(\frac{t}{R})} \times 100\% \quad (12)$$

2.3 球形耐压壳浮力系数

耐压壳浮力系数定义为耐压壳体重量与其排水量比值 δ：

$$\delta = \frac{\rho_{ph} V_{ph}}{\rho_w V_w} \quad (13)$$

式中 V_{ph} 为耐压壳材料体积，V_w 为排水量体积。

在现有设计中，耐压壳材料体积可采用其中面面积与厚度乘积确定，耐压壳的排水体积可近似为中面围成区域的体积，因此，可得出球形耐压壳经验法浮力系数 δ_1：

$$\delta_1 = \frac{3\rho_{ph}}{\rho_w}\frac{t}{R} \quad (14)$$

实际上，球形耐压壳材料体积应为外表面所谓围成区域的体积减去内表面所围成区域的体积，耐压壳的排水体积则为外表面所谓围成区域的体积，即解析法浮力系数 δ_2：

$$\delta_2 = \frac{\rho_{ph}\left[\left(2+\frac{t}{R}\right)^3 - \left(2-\frac{t}{R}\right)^3\right]}{\rho_w(2+\frac{t}{R})^3} \quad (15)$$

（2）专家意见答复及修改说明

专家意见邮件答复：

尊敬的编辑同志，您好！

　　非常感谢您为本论文付出了大量劳动、感谢审稿专家为本论文提出了大量建设性的修改意见。针对专家意见，作者对论文作了全面修改，请见附件"修改稿"。此外，作者对专家意见作了逐一答复，并附上相应的修改说明，具体请见附件"专家意见答复及修改说明"。请您及专家对本论文作进一步考察。

祝：工作顺利，万事如意！

张建

2015.9.13
　　联系人：张建
　　手机：15896387748
　　邮箱：zhjian127@163.com

专家意见答复及修改说明

　　意见之一：论文的目的不明确。是发展理论？研究计算方法？探讨设计规范？作者只能选择一个主题，深入下去。不能面面俱到，泛泛而谈。

　　答：论文的目的在于研究一种深海球形耐压壳计算方法，在归纳总结现有的理论和规范的基础之上，系统性研究球形耐压壳数值计算的影响因素、对比薄壳理论和厚壳理论的结果差异。具体修改内容见修改稿摘要的第一句。

　　意见之二：论文结构松散，章节编排不合理。第1节应删去，部分内容并入第3节。

　　答：重新编排了文章的总体结构，具体修改如下：

　　原始稿中第1节关于数值方案建立的参数计算内容已经删去，部分内容归纳总结并入了原始稿中第3节，即修改稿中的1.4节。

　　第4节撤销，其中的4.1，4.2节归并到第2节；4.3节归并到第3节。

　　答：已将原始稿中第4节全部删去，其中第4.1、4.2节归并到修改稿中的第1节，见修改稿中1.4节、1.5节；原始稿中4.3节已归并到修改稿中的第2节，见修改稿中第2.3.1节、第2.3.2节。

　　建议增加一节，对理论公式和有限元计算结果比较和分析。

　　答：修改稿表3和表4中将数值结果和理论公式结果进行比较，并且在修改稿中第2.3.1节第1段，2.3.2节第1段中增加了详细分析两种不同数值方案得出的数值结果与经典理论公式的偏差百分比和精度。

　　意见之三：第3节数值计算写得很乱，可读性差。

　　首先要对数值试验方案进行论证。（建议把这节中的"模型"改为"方案"，比较确切。）这和物理模型的试验一样，要说明为什么要选这些方案，想要达到什么目的。

答：已将原始稿第 3 节、即修改稿中第 2 节中的"模型"改为"方案"，并在修改稿中第 2 节第一段增加说明了选择这种方案的目的在于"目前对球形耐压壳数值计算研究并未系统性考虑网格划分形式、单元类型和单元密度等因素对球形耐压壳数值分析的影响，本文为了系统研究这几种影响因素的影响规律，分别建立了多种数值方案来进行探讨这几种影响因素对球形耐压壳的数值计算分析的影响规律。"

对选用的方案用列表的方式表达，更简洁和有条理性。避免使用繁琐的长段文字叙述。
答：精简了对方案的说明内容，并且将所有的 26 种方案总结归纳为列表的形式来表达，增加的方案列表，见修改稿中第 2 节表 1、表 2。

对计算结果的讨论要有明确的目的，着重于对今后的计算有何借鉴作用。
答：修改稿中第 3 节结论中归纳总结得到结论，即综合考虑精度和计算效率，对于球形耐压壳进行数值计算，如果采用网球划分形式的体单元进行计算，其数值结果与理论值更为相符，尤其球形耐压壳为厚壳时内外表面应力相差较大，不宜采用壳单元和薄壳理论计算，并对深海球形耐压壳的数值计算应该采用何种网格类型，划分形式等等内容以及壳体理论选取给出了具体说明，见修改稿中第 3 节。

其他——专家纸面意见修改
根据专家在论文前三页的详细修改意见，如语句表述、部分词汇、标点符号、章节调整等，均在修改稿中作了仔细、严格修改。具体内容见修改稿。

此外，章节编号、图表编号均作了相应调整，具体内容见修改稿。

（3）附件：修改稿

深海球形耐压壳力学特性研究

张建[1,2]，高杰[1]，王纬波[2]，唐文献[1]，周通[1]

(1. 江苏科技大学，江苏 镇江 212003；2. 中国船舶科学研究中心，江苏 无锡 214082)

摘 要

本文系统研究了深海球形耐压壳计算方法。分别建立了球形耐压壳薄壳和厚壳的力学模型、浮力系数求解公式以及 6km 水深球形耐压壳的壳单元、体单元数值模型，对比分析 1～6km 球形耐压壳强度、稳定性、储备浮力特性，并研究网格划分形式、单元类型、密度对数值结果的影响规律。结果表明，采用厚壳理论、体单元数值分析进行深海球形耐压壳设计与评估更为合理；强度是厚球壳设计的主要影响因素，建议先根据内表面应力公式确定耐压壳厚度，再运用厚壳屈曲理论或数值分析校核其稳定性。

关键词：球形耐压壳；强度；稳定性；厚壳理论
中图分类号：U661.4，TE58　**文献标识码**：A

收稿日期：　　　修改稿收稿日期：
基金项目：国家自然科学基金项目（51205173）

0 引言

根据《中国制造 2025》文件，国家将大力推动海洋工程装备突破发展。深海潜水器是大洋勘查与深海科学研究的重要海洋工程装备。作为潜水器的重要组成部分，在下潜过程中，耐压壳起着保障内部设备正常工作和人员健康安全的作用，其重量占潜水器总重的 $1/4 \sim 1/2$[1]。

现有的球形耐压壳的设计与分析基于薄壳理论，并被各国船级社规范认同。潘彬彬等对比分析了现有深水球形耐压壳的设计规范，表明薄壳理论是这些规范的共性理论基础，但现有规范计算存在缺陷，需要修订[2]。然后通过原型试验和非线性有限元分析，建立了预测深海钛合金球形壳极限强度的经验公式。马永前等参考中厚板壳稳定性理论研究厚球壳屈曲问题，指出：由于厚度方向的剪切效应，厚球壳的实际临界屈曲载荷低于薄壳理论（Zolley 公式）的结果[3]。王自力、刘涛等认为，随着水深增加，耐压壳分析从薄壳问题转化为中厚壳问题，现有的潜水器规范不适用于深海耐压壳分析，而对于厚球壳可直接根据有限元计算确定其极限强度[4-5]。然而，在有限元建模过程中，模型简化、单元类型、网格密度、网格划分形式、边界条件、求解方法等对球形壳计算结果的影响很大，不同人员对同一问题的分析结果存在差异。一方面，缺少试验验证和厚壳理论支撑，数值解的可信度有待商榷。

为此，本文分别从理论和数值计算这两方面研究球形耐压壳的强度、稳定性、储备浮力等性能。在 $1 \sim 6$ km 水深条件下，分别按薄壳模型和厚壳模型，分析和对比壳体的强度、稳定性特性，并分析经验法和解析法求解浮力系数时存在的差异。建立球形耐压壳的壳单元数值模型，研究划分形式、单元类型、网格密度对壳体强度、稳定性的影响；最后，建立同比条件下体单元数值模型，研究单元类型、网格密度对耐压壳强度、稳定的影响规律，并与壳单元数值模型、理论模型结果作对比分析。研究成果可为深海球形耐压壳设计提供参数。

1 球形耐压壳理论研究

1.1 薄壳力学模型

根据薄壳强度理论，球形耐压壳中面应力 σ_m 按式（1）计算。该公式是船级社球形耐压壳强度校核的理论基础。

$$\sigma_m = \frac{P_S R}{2t} \qquad (1)$$

式中，P_S 为计算载荷，R 为球壳的半径，t 为球壳厚度。

假设 $\sigma_m = [\sigma]$，那么极限强度载荷 $P_{\sigma 1}$ 与 t/R（厚度半径比）的关系：

$$P_{\sigma 1} = 2[\sigma] \frac{t}{R} \qquad (2)$$

根据薄壳屈曲理论，球形耐压壳屈曲临界载荷 P_{cr1} 可用 Zolley 公式[6]表述，它也是为船级社球形耐压壳稳定性设计规范的理论基础，即：

$$P_{cr1} = \frac{2Et^2}{R^2} \sqrt{\frac{1}{3(1-\mu^2)}} \qquad (3)$$

1.2 厚壳力学模型

在设计时，耐压壳厚度随着工作水深的增加而增大，其强度和稳定性计算从薄壳变为厚壳计算，采用薄壳理论研究厚壳问题偏于危险。对于承受静水压力的厚球壳结构，内表面应力 σ_i 最大，外表面应力 σ_o 最小，分别如式(4)、(5) 所示，中面应力根据式(1) 确定。

$$\sigma_i = \frac{3P_s \left(2 + \frac{t}{R}\right)^3}{2\left[\left(2 + \frac{t}{R}\right)^3 - \left(2 - \frac{t}{R}\right)^3\right]} \qquad (4)$$

$$\sigma_o = \frac{3P_s \left(2 - \frac{t}{R}\right)^3}{2\left[\left(2 + \frac{t}{R}\right)^3 - \left(2 - \frac{t}{R}\right)^3\right]} \qquad (5)$$

根据用薄壳强度理论评价厚壳应力存在的偏差 Δ_σ，可由式（1）和式（4）求得：

$$\Delta_\sigma = \frac{|\sigma_i - \sigma_m|}{\sigma_i} \times 100\% = \left\{1 - \left[1 - \left(\frac{2 - \frac{t}{R}}{2 + \frac{t}{R}}\right)^3\right] \times \frac{3}{\frac{t}{R}}\right\} \times 100\% \qquad (6)$$

令 $\sigma_i = [\sigma]$，由式（4）可得到极限强度载荷 $P_{\sigma 2}$ 与 t/R 的关系：

$$P_{\sigma 2} = \frac{2[\sigma]\left[\left(2 + \frac{t}{R}\right)^3 - \left(2 - \frac{t}{R}\right)^3\right]}{3\left(2 + \frac{t}{R}\right)^3} \qquad (7)$$

深水球形耐压壳屈曲临界载荷采用式 8 表述[7]，该公式采用勒让德函数求解球形壳屈曲控制方程[8]，推导出厚球壳稳定性问题的解析解 P_{cr2}：

$$P_{cr2} = \frac{2Et}{R(1-\mu^2)}\left(\sqrt{\frac{(1-\mu^2)}{3}}\frac{t}{R} - \frac{\mu t^2}{2R^2}\right) \qquad (8)$$

将式(3)代入式(8)可得：

$$P_{cr2} = \left(1 - \frac{\sqrt{3}}{2}\frac{\mu}{\sqrt{1-\mu^2}}\frac{t}{R}\right)P_{cr1} \qquad (9)$$

则：

$$P_{cr2} = \left(1 - f\left(\frac{t}{R}\right)\right)P_{cr1} \quad 其中, \quad f\left(\frac{t}{R}\right) = \frac{\sqrt{3}}{2}\frac{\mu}{\sqrt{1-\mu^2}}\frac{t}{R} \qquad (10)$$

根据式 3、式 10，可得出经典 Zolley 公式在计算厚壳屈曲临界载荷的误差 Δ_c 为：

$$\Delta_c = \frac{|P_{cr1} - P_{cr2}|}{P_{cr2}} \times 100\% = \frac{f\left(\frac{t}{R}\right)}{1 - f\left(\frac{t}{R}\right)} \times 100\% \qquad (11)$$

1.3 球形耐压壳浮力系数

耐压壳浮力系数定义为耐压壳体重量与其排水量比值 δ：

$$\delta = \frac{\rho_{ph}V_{ph}}{\rho_w V_w} \qquad (12)$$

式中 V_{ph} 为耐压壳材料体积，V_w 为排水量体积。

在现有设计中，耐压壳材料体积可采用其中面面积与厚度乘积确定，耐压壳的排水体积可近似为中面围成区域的体积，因此，可得出球形耐压壳经验法浮力系数 δ_2：

$$\delta_1 = \frac{3\rho_{ph}}{\rho_w}\frac{t}{R} \qquad (13)$$

实际上，球形耐压壳材料体积应为外表面所谓围成区域的体积减去内表面所围成区域的体积，耐压壳的排水体积则为外表面所谓围成区域的体积，即解析法浮力系数 δ_2：

$$\delta_2 = \frac{\rho_{ph}\left[\left(2+\frac{t}{R}\right)^3 - \left(2-\frac{t}{R}\right)^3\right]}{\rho_w\left(2+\frac{t}{R}\right)^3} \tag{14}$$

根据式3、式14，可得出经验法计算球形耐压壳浮力系数的误差，即：

$$\Delta_\delta = \frac{|\delta_1 - \delta_2|}{\delta_2} = \left(\frac{3\frac{t}{R}}{1-\left(\frac{2-\frac{t}{R}}{2+\frac{t}{R}}\right)^3} - 1\right) \times 100\% \tag{15}$$

1.4 球形耐压壳力学特性分析

以直径为2m 球形耐压壳为对象，研究其强度和稳定性规律，计算载荷根据式（16）确定。假设球形耐压壳的材料为 Ti-6Al-4V（TC4），其基本力学参数：屈服强度为 $\sigma_b = 830MPa$，密度 $\rho_{ph} = 4.5g/cm^3$，弹性模量 $G = 110GPa$，泊松比 $\mu = 0.3$。由于本文目的在于探讨厚球壳的设计方法，故忽略其他因素（如材料物理非线性修正系数、制造效应系数等）的影响，假设许用应力 $[\sigma]$ 等于材料的屈服强度，得到计算载荷 P_S。

$$P_S = K\rho_w gh/0.9 \tag{16}$$

其中，K 为安全系数取1.5，ρ_w 为海水密度取 $1g/cm^3$，g 为重力加速度取 $9.8m/s^2$，h 为水深取 $0 \sim 6km$。

根据式2、式3、式7、式8，绘制出薄壳力学模型和厚壳力学模型在不同 t/R 下的极限强度载荷和屈曲临界载荷的分布曲线，如图（1）所示。可见，当 t/R 小于0.013时，屈曲临界载荷小于极限强度载荷，稳定性为耐压壳安全评估的主要影响因素；当 t/R 大于0.013时，屈曲临界载荷大于极限强度载荷，强度为耐压壳安全评估的主要影响因素，且随着水深的增加，强度因素的影响越来越大，而屈曲因素的影响越来越小。

由图（1）可知，经典 Zolley 公式所得出屈曲临界载荷偏于保守，其误差曲线如图（2）所示，随着厚度半径比的逐渐增加，Zolley 公式误差不断增大，与 t/R 成线性关系，当 t/R 为0.075时，误差最大，约为2.1%；由此可以认为，Zolley 公式在计算厚壳的临界屈曲载荷时，误差较小，可用于厚球壳的稳定性初步评估。马永前也研究厚球壳稳定性问题，基于板壳理论建立了厚球壳屈曲临界载荷的修正公式，指出 Zolley 公式所得出屈曲临界载荷偏于保守，但该方法依赖拟合有限元分析结果得到相关修正系数，不具备通用性，且不是厚球壳屈曲临界载荷解析解。

由图（1）还可以发现，随着厚度半径比的增加，球形耐压壳中面应力与内表面应力差值随着 t/R 增加逐渐增大，差值曲线如图（3）所示，当 t/R 增加到0.075时，中面应力与内表面应力差值达到最大的10.4%，即使 t/R 为1/20（厚壳、薄壳分界线）时，两种差值也达到了7.1%，此时薄壳强度理论（式2）进行球形耐压壳强度校核时，结果比较危险；当 t/R 小于0.015时，误差在2%以内，在这种情况下，薄壳强度理论可适用于球形耐压壳强度的初步评估。

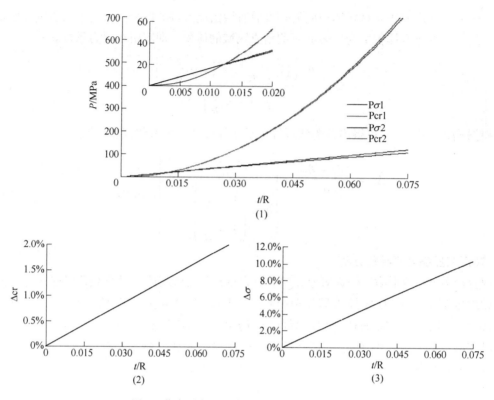

图1 薄壳厚壳理论模型公式及相对误差曲线
(1) 薄壳、厚壳力学模型计算结果 (2) 屈曲误差 (3) 应力偏差

1.5 球形耐压壳浮力系数分析

两种方法所得的浮力系数曲线如图2(1)所示。可见，两种计算方法得到的浮力系数均与 t/R 成近似的线性递增关系，但是经验法得到的浮力系数要比解析法高。且随着 t/R 的逐渐增大，经验法所得的浮力系数误差越来越大，如图2(2)所示；当 t/R 达到 0.075 时，误差值达到的 10.1%，即使 t/R 为 1/20（厚壳、薄壳分界线）时，两种差值也达到了 6.8%，故在进行中厚球壳浮力系数评估时，经验法不在适用；当 t/R 小于 0.015 时，经验法误差在 2% 以内，在这种情况下，经验法可适用于球形耐压壳浮力系数的初步评估。刘涛[9]关于球形耐压壳的浮力系数的研究也有相近的结论，说明采用经验法在进行深海耐压壳设计时偏于保守。

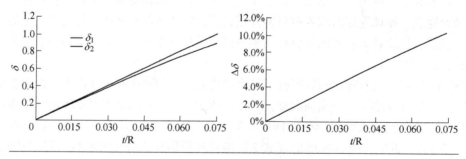

图2 浮力系数求解结果
(1) 两种方法所得浮力系数曲线 (2) 经验法浮力系数误差

2 球形耐压壳数值研究

以6km水深球形耐压壳为对象，研究其强度、稳定性数值分析方法，设计厚度为75mm。目前对球形耐压壳数值计算研究并未系统性考虑网格划分形式、单元类型和单元密度等因素对球形耐压壳数值分析的影响，本文为了系统研究这几种影响因素的影响规律，分别建立了多种数值方案来进行探讨这几种影响因素对球形耐压壳的数值计算分析的影响规律。

2.1 壳单元方案

采用pro/e软件，进行三维CAD建模，并抽取中面，采用ANSA前处理软件，进行网格划分；计算载荷以均布压力形式施加在耐压壳表面；理论上耐压壳是不受任何约束，为了消除方案的刚性位移，选择三个点限制其六个方向位移。所求得各约束反力接近0，说明所施加的约束为虚约束，仅限制了方案的刚体位移。定义2种工况进行分析：1）线性准静态分析；2）线性屈曲分析。采用ABAQUS/Standard对该方案进行求解计算，最后，运用ABAQUS/Viewer进行后处理。采用单因素控制变量法分别建立不同网格划分形式、单元类型、单元密度下的数值方案，进行分析计算。

采用随机划分、钱币划分、网球划分三者的划分形式，分别对应于方案1、方案2、方案3，如图3所示，单元类型为4节点完全积分线性壳单元（S4），网格单元数量约为6500。对于单元类型，采用4节点完全积分线性壳单元（S4）、4节点减缩积分壳单元(S4R)、每个节点5个自由度的4节点减缩积分壳单元（S4R5）、8节点双曲厚壳单元（S8R）、每节点5个自由度的8节点双曲厚壳单元（S8R5），分别对应于方案3、方案4、方案5、方案6、方案7，这些方案均采用网球划分的形式，单元数、节点数与方案3一致。对于数值方案，需要进行网格的收敛性检查来验证方案结果的正确性。故分别采用平均尺寸为200mm、120mm、100mm、70mm、60mm、45mm、35mm、20mm的网格进行分析，分别对应于方案8、方案9、方案10、方案11、方案3、方案12、方案13、方案14，单元类型均为S4，均采用网球划分，具体信息如表1所示。

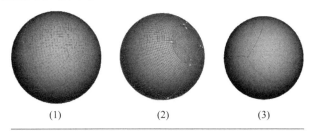

图3 球形耐压壳网格方案
(1) 随机划分 (2) 钱币划分 (3) 网球划分

表1 壳单元数值模型信息表

方案	划分形式	节点数	单元数	单元类型
方案1	随机	6514	6512	S4
方案2	钱币	6596	6594	S4
方案3	网球	6536	6534	S4
方案4	网球	6536	6534	S4R

(续)

方案	划分形式	节点数	单元数	单元类型
方案5	网球	6536	6534	S4R5
方案6	网球	6536	6534	S8R
方案7	网球	6536	6534	S8R5
方案8	网球	488	216	S4
方案9	网球	488	486	S4
方案10	网球	728	726	S4
方案11	网球	4058	4056	S4
方案12	网球	14408	14406	S4
方案13	网球	22328	22326	S4
方案14	网球	39368	39366	S4

2.2 体单元方案

体单元网格方案可以通过壳单元网格沿厚度方向偏移4层单元得到,其中载荷、边界、工况与壳单元一致。首先,根据方案3的网格,建立体单元方案,单元类型设定为三维8节点体单元(C3D8)、三维8节点减缩积分体单元(C3D8R)、三维8节点非协调模式体单元(C3D8I)、三维20节点体单元(C3D20)、三维20节点减缩积分体单元(C3D20R),分别对应于方案15、方案16、方案17、方案18、方案19。此外,分别采用周向平均尺寸为200mm、120mm、100mm、70mm、60mm、45mm、35mm、20mm的网格进行分析,分别对应于方案20、方案21、方案22、方案23、方案24、方案25、方案26、方案27,这些方案的网格分别由方案8、方案9、方案10、方案11、方案3、方案12、方案13、方案14的网格沿厚度方向偏移所得,单元类型均为C3D20R,具体信息如表2所示。

表2 不同单元类型体单元数值模型信息表

模型代号	划分形式	单元数	单元类型	单元平均尺寸/mm
方案15	网球	16224	C3D8	70
方案16	网球	16224	C3D8R	70
方案17	网球	16224	C3D8I	70
方案18	网球	16224	C3D20	70
方案19	网球	16224	C3D20R	70
方案20	网球	864	C3D20R	200
方案21	网球	1944	C3D20R	120
方案22	网球	2904	C3D20R	100
方案23	网球	16224	C3D20R	70
方案24	网球	57624	C3D20R	45
方案25	网球	89304	C3D20R	35
方案26	网球	157464	C3D20R	20

2.3 数值结果分析
2.3.1 壳单元数值结果

根据式1、式8求出6km球形耐压壳的中面应力和临界屈曲载荷分别为653.33Mpa、733.67Mpa。第3节所建立的14种壳单元数值方案的计算结果及误差如表4所示。由方案1、方案2、方案3的结果可知,在强度方面,随机形式的平均应力结果与理论值最为接近,钱币划分和网球划分形式的平均应力与理论值相差也较小,不足0.1%;但随机划分的最大最小应力相差太大,出现明显应力集中,网球划分和钱币划分的最大最小应力相差很小,较为吻合球形耐压壳的等强度特性。在稳定性方面,网球划分的临界屈曲载荷与理论值相差最小,为0.049%,而随机划分和钱币划分的临界屈曲载荷与理论值相差较大,分别为1.782%、0.167%。因此,从强度和稳定性两方面考虑,采用网球划分为球形耐压壳建模的最佳选择。

由方案3、方案4、方案5、方案6、方案7结果可知,在强度方面,无论是否采用减缩积分单元,得到的平均应力结果与理论值相差都非常小,几乎可以忽略不计;而从最大最小应力差值考虑,减缩积分单元S4R和S4R5较为理想,陆蓓、潘彬彬等在进行球形耐压壳数值分析时,也采用了S4R和S4R5单元。在稳定性方面,S4计算精度最高。因此,从强度和稳定性两方面考虑,4节点完全积分线性壳单元(S4)为球形耐压壳建模的最佳选择。

表3 壳单元数值方案结果

方案	σ_{max}	σ_{min}	$\sigma_{max}-\sigma_{min}$	$\sigma_{平均}$	P_{cr}	$\dfrac{\sigma-\sigma_t}{\sigma_t}\times 100\%$	$\dfrac{P_{cr}-P_{cr_t}}{P_{cr_t}}\times 100\%$
方案1	664.511	634.967	29.544	653.332	746.7404	0.00%	1.782%
方案2	655.075	651.919	3.156	652.871	734.8922	0.07%	0.167%
方案3	653.825	648.554	5.271	652.885	734.0298	0.07%	0.049%
方案4	653.942	651.251	2.691	652.889	732.4422	0.07%	0.167%
方案5	653.946	651.253	2.693	652.889	692.4974	0.07%	5.612%
方案6	654.926	648.65	6.276	652.803	690.4688	0.08%	5.888%
方案7	654.768	648.686	6.082	652.805	691.978	0.08%	5.683%
方案8	665.638	580.459	85.179	640.219	831.0596	2.01%	13.274%
方案9	659.112	613.638	45.474	647.367	772.0832	0.91%	5.236%
方案10	657.445	624.145	33.3	649.313	756.315	0.62%	3.087%
方案11	654.145	646.268	7.877	652.612	735.6762	0.11%	0.273%
方案12	653.559	650.934	2.625	653.13	733.0596	0.03%	0.083%
方案13	653.478	651.703	1.775	653.202	732.3442	0.02%	0.181%
方案14	653.417	652.348	1.069	653.259	731.7366	0.01%	0.264%

网格疏密对数值模拟的准确度影响很大,因此先进行网格无关性检验,只有当网格数的增加对计算结果影响不大时,这时的仿真结果才具有意义。单元密度的选取要综合考虑计算时间和结果精度[10]。由表1中的方案8、方案9、方案10、方案11、方案3、方案12、方案13、方案14结果,绘制应力误差曲线、屈曲临界载荷误差曲线,分别如图4(1)、(2)所示。图4(1)为球形耐压壳中面上最大应力,最小应力和平均应力与理论强度应力σ_{mid}的比值曲线,可见,单元平均尺寸与球形耐压壳半径比为0.07时,数值方案得到的结果就开始收敛,且网格尺寸越小,数值方案的平均应力越趋近于理论值,而最大最小值的差值也越

来越小，趋于解析解。

一般认为，网格尺寸的选取应该使屈曲临界载荷的相对浮动量小于等于1%，结果趋于收敛[12]。由图4（2）可知，当单元平均尺寸与球形耐压壳半径比达到0.07时，屈曲临界载荷的相对浮动量小于等于1%，数值方案得到的屈曲结果就开始收敛逼近于1，网格尺寸继续减小时得到的屈曲应力全部逼近于1。因此，从强度和稳定性两方面考虑，单元尺寸和半径比为0.07为球形耐压壳建模的最佳选择。

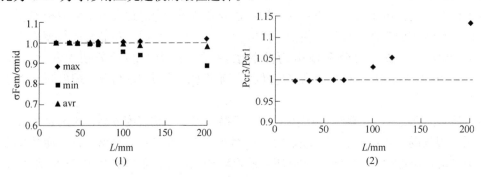

图4　壳单元数值方案网格收敛性曲线
（1）壳单元数值方案强度应力收敛曲线　（2）壳单元数值方案屈曲应力收敛曲线

图5为方案3计算所得的中面应力云图、内外表面应力云图、1阶屈曲振形图，显然，采用壳单元进行数值模拟时，中面和内外层面的应力相差仅仅不到1%，这与理论结果相差甚远，说明采用壳单元进行厚球壳强度分析是不合理的。

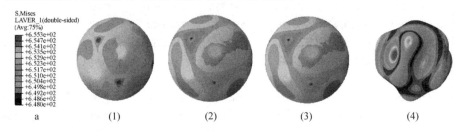

图5　S4壳单元方案应力与屈曲云图
（1）内层面　（2）中层面　（3）外层面　（4）1阶屈曲云图

2.3.2　体单元数值方案分析

根据式3、式4、式5、式8求出球形耐压壳的中面应力、内表面应力、外表面应力和临界屈曲载荷分别为653.33MPa、729.28MPa、582.28MPa、733.67MPa。第3节所建立的5种体单元数值方案的计算结果、及数值解误差如表4所示。由方案15、方案16、方案17、方案18、方案19的结果可知，在强度方面，采用减缩积分单元C3D20R，内中外三个面得到的平均应力结果与理论值最为接近，采用C3D8I单元和C3D20单元得到的三个表面应力与理论值相差相差都较小；而采用C3D8单元和C3D8R单元，三个面应力的最大最小值或者平均值都与理论值相差太大。在稳定性方面，采用C3D8I单元的临界屈曲载荷与理论值相差最小，为0.59%，而采用C3D20单元和C3D20R单元的临界屈曲载荷计算误差也较小，分别为0.89%、0.88%。因此，从强度和稳定性两方面考虑，采用C3D20R体单元为球形耐压壳建模最佳选择。

表4 不同单元类型体单元数值方案结果

Type		方案15	方案16	方案17	方案18	方案19
Inner Stress /Mpa	max	717.218	710.689	725.026	732.098	732.857
	min	714.201	707.792	720.358	726.644	727.796
	max−min	3.017	2.897	4.668	5.454	5.061
	average	715.124	708.128	720.811	728.604	729.603
	theory	729.282	729.282	729.282	729.282	729.282
	error	1.94%	2.90%	1.16%	0.09%	0.04%
Middle Stress /Mpa	max	650.569	650.612	650.151	649.874	651.006
	min	649.183	649.359	648.706	648.992	649.546
	max−min	1.386	1.253	1.445	0.882	1.46
	average	650.181	650.313	649.865	649.419	650.334
	theory	653.333	653.333	653.333	653.333	653.333
	error	0.48%	0.46%	0.53%	0.60%	0.46%
Outer Stress /Mpa	max	593.558	598.606	588.551	583.102	583.875
	min	589.119	593.97	582.256	578.027	578.584
	max−min	4.439	4.636	6.295	5.075	5.291
	average	592.594	598.007	587.841	581.395	582.127
	theory	582.282	582.282	582.282	582.282	582.282
	error	1.77%	2.70%	0.95%	0.15%	0.03%
Buckling Load /Mpa	PCr	760.8916	721.476	737.9694	740.194	740.1646
	theory	733.69	733.69	733.69	733.69	733.69
	error	3.71%	1.66%	0.58%	0.89%	0.88%

由方案20、方案21、方案22、方案23、方案24、方案25、方案26 结果，绘制应力误差曲线、屈曲临界载荷误差曲线，分别如图6（1）、（2）、（3）、（4）所示。图6（1）、（2）、（3）分别为球形耐压壳内表面、中面、外表面上最大应力，最小应力和平均应力与理论强度应力 σmid 的比值曲线，可见，体单元的单元平均尺寸与球形耐压壳半径比也为0.07时，

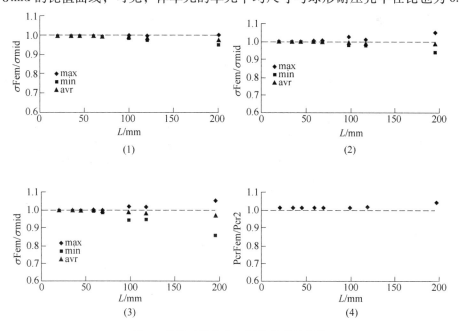

图6 体单元数值方案网格收敛性曲线
（1）内面应力 （2）中面应力 （3）外面应力 （4）临界屈曲载荷

数值方案得到的结果同样开始收敛，且网格尺寸越小，数值方案的平均应力越趋近于理论值，而最大最小值的差值越小，趋于解析解。由图6（4）可知，当单元平均尺寸与球形耐压壳半径比达到0.07时，屈曲临界载荷的相对浮动量小于等于1%，数值方案得到的屈曲结果就开始收敛逼近于1，网格尺寸继续减小时得到的屈曲应力全部逼近于1。因此，从强度和稳定性两方面考虑，体单元的单元尺寸和半径比为0.07为球形耐压壳建模的最佳选择。

图7为方案24计算所得的中面应力云图、内外表面应力云图、1阶屈曲振形图，可见，采用体单元进行数值模拟时，内表面和外表面的应力相差与与理论结果较为吻合，说明采用体单元进行厚球壳强度分析是合理的；而图5（4）所示的壳单元数值方案的1阶屈曲振形与图7所示体单元的1阶屈曲振形基本一致，结果相互佐证。

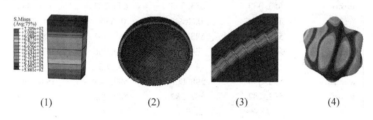

图7　C3D20体单元方案应力与屈曲云图
(1) 厚度方向　(2) 剖面方向　(3) 局部方向　(4) 1阶屈曲云图

3　结论

（1）强度是厚球壳设计主要影响因素，中面应力与内表面应力差值随着t/R增加而逐渐增大，当t/R增加到0.075时，两者差值达到最大为10.4%，即使t/R为1/20时，两者差值也达到了7.1%，建议以内表面应力为基准设计和评估深海球形耐压壳。Zolley公式误差随着t/R增加而逐渐增大，当t/R为0.075时，两者差值达到最大为2.1%，薄壳理论可用于厚球壳稳定性初步评估。经验法求解球形耐压壳浮力系数偏于保守，其误差随着t/R增加而逐渐增大，当σ_t达到0.075时，误差达到10.1%，即使P_{ct}为1/20时，误差也高达6.8%，建议采用解析法评估深海球形耐压壳的浮力系数。

（2）综合考虑计算精度和效率，建议采用网球划分、4节点完全积分线性壳单元、单元平均尺寸0.07R，建立球形耐压壳的壳单元数值方案；建议采用网球划分、三维20节点减缩积分体单元、周向单元平均尺寸0.07R、厚度方向4层单元，建立球形耐压壳的体单元数值方案。壳单元数值方案、薄壳理论方案可用于浅海耐压壳设计与评估，体单元数值方案、厚球壳理论方案可用于深海耐压壳设计与评估，建议船级社在进行深海耐压壳设计规范修订时，采用内表面应力、厚壳临界屈曲载荷作为评价指标。

参考文献

[1] Zhang J, Zuo X L, Wang W B, Tang W X. Overviews of Investigation on Submersible Pressure Hulls[J]. Advances in Natural Science, 2014, 7(4): 54-61.

[2] Pan B B, Cui W C. A Comparison of Different Rules for the Spherical Pressure Hull of Deep Manned Submersibles[J]. Journal of Ship Mechanics, 2011, 15(3): 276-285.

[3] Ma Y Q, Wang C M, Ang K K. Buckling of super ellipsoidal shells under uniform pressure[J]. Thin-Walled Structures, 2008, 46(6): 584-591.

[4] 王自力，王仁华，俞铭华，李良碧. 初始缺陷对不同深度载人潜水器耐压球壳极限承载力的影响［J］. 中国造船，2007, 02：45-50.

[5] 陆蓓,刘涛,崔维成. 深海载人潜水器耐压球壳极限强度研究 [J]. 船舶力学, 2004, 01: 51-58.
[6] Pan B B, Cui W C. An overview of buckling and ultimate strength of spherical pressure hull under external pressure[J]. Marine Structures, 2010, 23(3): 227-240.
[7] Wang C M, Wang C Y, Reddy J N. Exact Solutions for Buckling of Structural Members[M]. CRC Press, 2004.
[8] Timoshenko S P, Gere J M. Theory of Elastic Stability[M]. Dover Publications, 1961.
[9] 刘涛. 大深度潜水器结构分析与设计研究 [D]. 中国船舶科学研究中心. 2001, 3.
[10] Tomas A, Tovar J P. The influence of initial geometric imperfections on the buckling load of single and double curvature concrete shells[J]. Computers & Structures. 2012, 96(97): 34-45.

Investigation on Mechanical Properties of Deep Sea Spherical Pressure Hull

ZHANG Jian[1,2], GAO Jie[1], WANG Weibo[2], TANG Wenxian[1], ZHOU Tong[1]

(1. Jiangsu University of Science and Technology, Jiangsu Zhenjiang 212003, China
2. Chinese Ship Scientific Research Center, Jiangsu Wuxi 214082, China;)

Abstract

Calculating method for deep sea spherical pressure hull was systematically investigated. Mechanical models based on thin shell and thick shell, buoyancy factor equations for the hull were presented, respectively. Numerical models based on shell elements and solid elements for the hull with the water depth of 6 km were proposed as well. Strength, stability and buoyancy reserve capacity of the spherical hull with the water depth of 1~6 km were analyzed. Furthermore, effects of meshing, element type and density on the numerical results were studied. The results showed that, it is suitable to design and assess the deep sea spherical pressure hull using theory of thick shell and numerical models based on solid elements. Strength is the main influence factor during the thick spherical shell design process. Therefore, it is suggested to determine the thickness of the pressure hull based on the inner stress equation firstly. Then, the stability of the hull could be verified using buckling theory of thick shell and numerical analysis method.

Key words: spherical pressure hull; strength; stability; theory of thick shell

作者简介:

张 建 男, 1984 年生, 博士, 讲师。研究方向: 深海耐压装备现代设计理论与方法。
高 杰 男, 1992 年生, 硕士研究生。研究方向: 深海耐压壳 CAE 技术研究。
王纬波 男, 1969 年生, 博士, 研究院。研究方向: 舰船复合材料结构设计。
唐文献 男, 1963 年生, 博士, 教授。研究方向: 海洋工程结构设计与研究。
周 通 男, 1991 年生, 硕士研究生。研究方向: 深海耐压壳 CAE 技术研究。

9.1.4 二通意见答复与修改稿

(1) 编辑与专家意见

1) 专家邮件意见

张建:您好!
　　论文写作比较粗糙,需要继续改进。编辑部已对公式和符号作初步修改(体现在电子文档中),使其规范和格式化。请您在这个电子文档上继续进行修改。曲线图的质量须重点关注。

张编辑

2）专家纸质意见

深海球形耐压壳力学特性研究

张建[1,2]，高杰[1]，王纬波[2]，唐文献[1]，周通[1]

(1. 江苏科技大学，江苏 镇江 212003; 2. 中国船舶科学研究中心，江苏 无锡 214082)

摘　要

本文系统研究了深海球形耐压壳计算方法。分别建立了球形耐压壳薄壳和厚壳的力学模型、浮力系数求解公式以及6km水深球形耐压壳的壳单元、体单元数值模型，对比分析1~6km球形耐压壳强度、稳定性、储备浮力特性，并研究网格划分形式、单元类型、密度对数值结果的影响规律。结果表明，采用厚壳理论、体单元数值分析进行深海球形耐压壳设计与评估更为合理。强度是厚壳设计的主要影响因素，建议先根据内表面应力公式确定耐压壳厚度，再运用厚壳屈曲理论或数值分析校核其稳定性。

关键词： 球形耐压壳；强度；稳定性；厚壳理论

中图分类号： U661.4, TE58　**文献标识码：** A

0 引言

根据《中国制造2025》文件，国家将大力推动海洋工程装备突破发展。深海潜水器是大洋勘查与深海科学研究的重要海洋工程装备。作为潜水器的重要组成部分，在下潜过程中，耐压壳起着保障内部设备正常工作和人员健康安全的作用，其重量占潜水器总重的1/4~1/2[1]。

现有的球形耐压壳的设计与分析基于薄壳理论，也被各国船级社规范认同。潘彬彬等对比分析了现有深水球形耐压壳的设计规范，表明薄壳理论是这些规范的共性理论基础，但现有规范计算存在缺陷，需要修正[2]。然后通过原型试验和非线性有限元分析，建立了预测深海钛合金球形壳极限强度的经验公式。马永前等参考中厚板壳稳定性理论研究厚球壳屈曲问题，指出：由于厚度方向的剪切效应，厚球壳的实际临界屈曲载荷低于薄壳理论（Zolley公式）的结果[3]。王自力、刘涛等认为，随着水深增加，耐压壳分析从薄壳问题转化为中厚壳问题，现有的潜水器规范不适用于深海耐压壳分析，对于厚球壳可直接根据有限元计算确定其极限强度[4-5]。然而，在有限元建模过程中，模型简化、单元类型、网格密度、网格划分形式、边界条件、求解方法等对球形壳计算结果的影响很大，不同人员对同一问题的分析结果存在差异。一方面，缺少试验验证和厚壳理论支撑，数值解的可信度有待商榷。

为此，本文分别从理论和数值计算这两方面研究球形耐压壳的强度、稳定性、储备浮力等性能。在1~6km水深条件下，分别按薄壳模型和厚壳模型，分析和对比壳体的强度、稳定性特性，并分析经验法和解析法求解浮力系数间存在的差异。建立球形耐压壳的壳单元数值模型，研究划分形式、单元类型、网格密度对壳体强度、稳定性的影响。最后，建立同类体单元数值模型，研究单元类型、网格密度对耐压壳强度、稳定的影响规律，并与壳单元数值模型、理论模型结果作对比分析。研究成果可为深海球形耐压壳设计提供参考。

1 球形耐压壳理论研究

1.1 薄壳力学模型

根据薄壳强度理论，球形耐压壳中面应力σ_m按式（1）计算。该公式是船级社球形耐压壳强度校核的理论基础。

$$\sigma_m = \frac{P_s R}{2t} \tag{1}$$

收稿日期：2015-06-01　修改稿收稿日期：
基金项目：国家自然科学基金项目（51205173）

式中，P_s 为计算载荷，R 为球壳的半径，t 为球壳厚度。

假设 $\sigma_m = [\sigma]$，那么极限强度载荷 $P_{\sigma 1}$ 与 t/R（厚度半径比）的关系

$$P_{\sigma 1} = 2[\sigma]\frac{t}{R} \tag{2}$$

根据薄壳屈曲理论，球形耐压壳屈曲临界载荷 P_{c1} 可用 Zolley 公式[6]表述，它也是为船级社球形耐压壳稳定性设计规范的理论基础，即：

$$P_{c1} = \frac{2Et^2}{R^2}\sqrt{\frac{1}{3(1-\mu^2)}} \tag{3}$$

1.2 厚壳力学模型

在设计时，耐压壳厚度随着工作水深的增加而增大，其强度和稳定性计算从薄壳变为厚壳计算，采用薄壳理论研究厚壳问题偏于危险。对于承受静水压力的厚壳壳结构，内表面应力 σ_i 最大，外表面应力 σ_o 最小，分别如式（4）、（5）所示，中面应力根据式（1）确定。

$$\sigma_i = \frac{3P_s(2+\frac{t}{R})^3}{2\left[(2+\frac{t}{R})^3 - (2-\frac{t}{R})^3\right]} \tag{4}$$

$$\sigma_o = \frac{3P_s(2-\frac{t}{R})^3}{2\left[(2+\frac{t}{R})^3 - (2-\frac{t}{R})^3\right]} \tag{5}$$

根据用薄壳强度理论评价厚壳应力存在的偏差 Δ_σ，可由式（1）和式（4）求得：

$$\Delta_\sigma = \frac{|\sigma_o - \sigma_m|}{\sigma_o}\times 100\% = \left\{1 - \left[1 - \left(\frac{2-\frac{t}{R}}{2+\frac{t}{R}}\right)^3\right]\times \frac{3}{\frac{t}{R}}\right\}\times 100\% \tag{6}$$

令 $\sigma_i = [\sigma]$，由式（4）可得到极限强度载荷 $P_{\sigma 2}$ 与 t/R 的关系：

$$P_{\sigma 2} = \frac{2[\sigma]\left[(2+\frac{t}{R})^3 - (2-\frac{t}{R})^3\right]}{3(2+\frac{t}{R})^3} \tag{7}$$

深水球形耐压壳屈曲临界载荷采用式 8 表述[7]，该公式采用勒让德函数求解球形壳屈曲控制方程[8]，推导出厚球壳稳定性问题的解析解：

$$P_{c2} = \frac{2Et}{R(1-\mu^2)}\left(\sqrt{\frac{(1-\mu^2)}{3}}\frac{t}{R} - \frac{\mu t^2}{2R^2}\right) \tag{8}$$

将式（3）代入式（8）可得：

$$P_{c2} = (1 - \frac{\sqrt{3}}{2}\frac{\mu}{\sqrt{1-\mu^2}}\frac{t}{R}) P_{c1} \qquad (9)$$

则：

$$P_{c2} = (1 - f(\frac{t}{R})) P_{c1} \qquad (10)$$

其中 $f(\frac{t}{R}) = \frac{\sqrt{3}}{2}\frac{\mu}{\sqrt{1-\mu^2}}\frac{t}{R}$。

根据式(3)、式(10)，可得出经典 Zolley 公式在计算厚壳屈曲临界载荷的误差 Δ_c 为：

$$\Delta_c = \frac{|P_{c1} - P_{c2}|}{P_{c2}} \times 100\% = \frac{f(\frac{t}{R})}{1 - f(\frac{t}{R})} \times 100\% \qquad (11)$$

1.3 球形耐压壳浮力系数

耐压壳浮力系数定义为耐压壳体重量与其排水量比值 δ：

$$\delta = \frac{\rho_p V_p}{\rho_w V_w} \qquad (12)$$

式中 V_p 为耐压壳材料体积，V_w 为排水量体积。

在现有设计中，耐压壳材料体积可采用其中面面积与厚度乘积确定，耐压壳的排水体积可近似为中面围成区域的体积，因此，可得出球形耐压壳经验法浮力系数 δ_1：

$$\delta_1 = \frac{3\rho_p}{\rho_w}\frac{t}{R} \qquad (13)$$

实际上，球形耐压壳材料体积应为外表面所谓围成区域的体积减去内表面所围成区域的体积，耐压壳的排水体积则为外表面所谓围成区域的体积，即解析法浮力系数 δ_2：

$$\delta_2 = \frac{\rho_p\left[\left(2+\frac{t}{R}\right)^3 - \left(2-\frac{t}{R}\right)^3\right]}{\rho_w\left(2+\frac{t}{R}\right)^3} \qquad (14)$$

根据式(13)、式(14)，可得出经验法计算球形耐压壳浮力系数的误差，即：

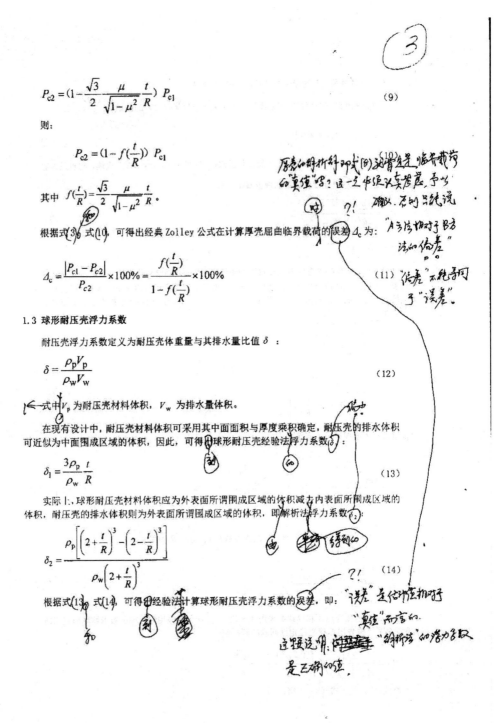

$$\Delta_\delta = \frac{|\delta_1 - \delta_2|}{\delta_2} = \left(\frac{3\frac{t}{R}}{1-\left(\frac{2-\frac{t}{R}}{2+\frac{t}{R}}\right)^3} - 1 \right) \times 100\% \qquad (15)$$

1.4 球形耐压壳力学特性分析

以直径为 2m 球形耐压壳为对象，研究其强度和稳定性规律，计算载荷根据式（16）确定。假设球形耐压壳的材料为 Ti-6Al-4V(TC4)，其基本力学参数：屈服强度 σ_b=830MPa，密度 ρ_p=4.5g/cm³，弹性模量 G=110GPa，泊松比 μ=0.3。由于本文目的在于探讨厚球壳的设计方法，故忽略其它因素（如材料物理非线性修正系数、制造效应系数等）的影响，假设许用应力$[\sigma]$等于材料的屈服强度，得到计算载荷 P_s

$$P_s = K\rho_w gh/0.9 \qquad (16)$$

式中，K 为安全系数取 1.5，ρ_w 为海水密度 1g/cm³，g 为重力加速度取 9.8m/s²，h 为水深取 0~6km。

根据式(2)、式(3)、式(7)、式(8)，绘制出薄壳力学模型和厚壳力学模型在不同 t/R 的极限强度载荷和屈曲临界载荷的分布曲线，如图 1(a)所示。当 t/R 小于 0.013 时，屈曲临界载荷小于极限强度载荷，稳定性为耐压壳安全评估的主要影响因素；当 t/R 大于 0.013 时，屈曲临界载荷大于极限强度载荷，强度为耐压壳安全评估的主要影响因素，且随着水深的增加，强度因素的影响越来越大，而屈曲因素的影响越来越小。

由图 1(a)可知，经典 Zolley 公式所得的屈曲临界载荷偏于保守，其误差曲线如图 1(b)所示，随着厚度半径比的逐渐增加，Zolley 公式误差不断增大，与 t/R 成线性关系，当 t/R 为 0.075 时，误差最大，约为 2.1%；由此可以认为，Zolley 公式在计算厚壳的临界屈曲载荷时，误差较小，可用于厚球壳的稳定性初步评估。马永前也研究厚球壳稳定性问题，基于板壳理论建立了厚球壳屈曲临界载荷的修正公式，指出 Zolley 公式所得的屈曲临界载荷偏于保守，但该方法依赖拟合有限元分析结果得到相关修正系数，不具备通用性，且不是厚球壳屈曲临界载荷解析解。

由图 1(f)还可以发现，随着厚度半径比的增加，球形耐压壳中面应力与内表面应力差值随着 t/R 增加逐渐增大，差值曲线如图 1(c)所示，当 t/R 增加到 0.075 时，中面应力与内表面应力差值达到最大的 10.4%，即使 t/R 为 1/20（厚壳、薄壳分界线）时，两种差值也达到了 7.1%，此时薄壳强度理论（式(2)）进行球形耐压壳强度校核时，结果比较危险，当 t/R 小于 0.015 时，误差在 2%以内，在这种情况下，薄壳强度理论可适用于球形耐压壳强度的初步评估。

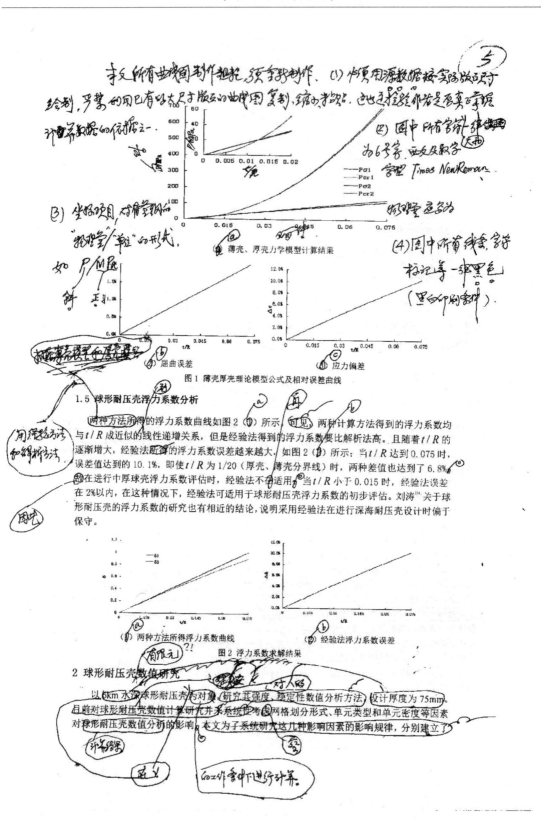

图 1 薄壳厚壳理论模型公式及相对误差曲线

1.5 球形耐压壳浮力系数分析

两种方法所得的浮力系数曲线如图 2 所示。两种计算方法得到的浮力系数均与 t/R 成近似的线性递增关系,但是经验法得到的浮力系数要比解析法高。且随着 t/R 的逐渐增大,经验法所得的浮力系数误差越来越大,如图 2 所示:当 t/R 达到 0.075 时,误差值达到 10.1%,即使 t/R 为 1/20(厚壳、薄壳分界线)时,两种差值也达到了 6.8%。在进行中厚球壳浮力系数评估时,经验法不再适用;当 t/R 小于 0.015 时,经验法误差在 2%以内,在这种情况下,经验法可适用于球形耐压壳浮力系数的初步评估。刘涛[14] 关于球形耐压壳的浮力系数的研究也有相近的结论,说明采用经验法在进行深海耐压壳设计时偏于保守。

图 2 浮力系数求解结果

2 球形耐压壳数值研究

以 6km 水深球形耐压壳为对象,研究其强度、稳定性数值分析方法,设计厚度为 75mm。目前对球形耐压壳数值计算研究并未系统地考虑网格划分形式、单元类型和单元密度等因素对球形耐压壳数值分析的影响,本文为了系统研究这几种影响因素的影响规律,分别建立了多种数值方案来进行探讨这几种影响因素对球形耐压壳的数值计算分析的影响规律。

2.1 壳单元方案

采用 pro/e 软件，进行三维 CAD 建模，并抽取中面，采用 ANSA 前处理软件，进行网格划分，计算载荷以均布压力形式施加在耐压壳表面。理论上耐压壳是不受任何约束，为了消除方案的刚性位移，选择三个点限制其六个方向位移。要求得约束反力接近 0，说明所施加的约束为虚约束，仅限制了方案的刚体位移。定义 2 种工况进行分析：(1) 线性准静态分析；(2) 线性屈曲分析。采用 ABAQUS/Standard 对该方案进行求解计算，最后运用 ABAQUS/Viewer 进行后处理。采用单因素控制变量法分别建立不同网格划分形式，单元类型、单元密度下的数值方案，进行分析计算。

采用随机划分、钱币划分、网球划分三种划分形式，分别对应方案 1、方案 2、方案 3，如图 3 所示。单元类型为 4 节点完全积分线性壳单元（S4），网格单元数量约为 6500。对于单元类型，采用 4 节点完全积分线性壳单元（S4）、4 节点减缩积分壳单元（S4R）、每个节点 5 个自由度的 4 节点减缩积分壳单元（S4R5）、8 节点双曲厚壳单元（S8R）、每节点 5 个自由度的 8 节点双曲厚壳单元（S8R5），分别对应方案 3、方案 4、方案 5、方案 6、方案 7。这些方案均采用网球划分的形式，单元数、节点数与方案 3 一致。对于数值方案，需要进行网格的收敛性检查来验证方案结果的正确性。分别采用平均尺寸为 200mm、120mm、100mm、70mm、60mm、45mm、35mm、20mm 的网格进行求解，分别对应方案 8、方案 9、方案 10、方案 11、方案 3、方案 12、方案 13、方案 14，单元类型均为 S4，均采用网球划分，具体信息如表 1 所示。

（1）随机划分　　（2）钱币划分　　（3）网球划分

图 3 球形耐压壳网格方案

表 1 壳单元数值模型信息表

方案	划分形式	节点数	单元数	单元类型
方案 1	随机	6514	6512	S4
方案 2	钱币	6596	6594	S4
方案 3	网球	6536	6534	S4
方案 4	网球	6536	6534	S4R
方案 5	网球	6536	6534	S4R5
方案 6	网球	6536	6534	S8R
方案 7	网球	6536	6534	S8R5
方案 8	网球	488	216	S4
方案 9	网球	488	486	S4
方案 10	网球	728	726	S4
方案 11	网球	4058	4056	S4
方案 12	网球	14408	14406	S4
方案 13	网球	22328	22326	S4

方案 14	网球	39368	39366	S4

2.2 体单元方案

体单元网格方案可以通过壳单元网格沿厚度方向偏移 4 层单元得到,其中载荷、边界、工况与壳单元一致。首先,根据方案 3 的网格,建立体单元方案,单元类型设定为三维 8 节点体单元(C3D8)、三维 8 节点减缩积分体单元(C3D8R)、三维 8 节点非协调模式体单元(C3D8I)、三维 20 节点体单元(C3D20)、三维 20 节点减缩积分体单元(C3D20R),分别对应于方案 15、方案 16、方案 17、方案 18、方案 19。此外,分别采用周向平均尺寸为 200mm、120mm、100mm、70mm、60mm、45mm、35mm、20mm 的网格进行分析,分别对应于方案 20、方案 21、方案 22、方案 23、方案 24、方案 25、方案 26、方案 27,这些方案的网格分别由方案 8、方案 9、方案 10、方案 11、方案 3、方案 12、方案 13、方案 14 的网格沿厚度方向偏移所得,单元类型均为 C3D20R,具体信息如表 2 所示。

表 2 不同单元类型体单元数值模型信息表

模型代号	划分形式	单元数	单元类型	单元平均尺寸/mm
方案 15	网球	16224	C3D8	70
方案 16	网球	16224	C3D8R	70
方案 17	网球	16224	C3D8I	70
方案 18	网球	16224	C3D20	70
方案 19	网球	16224	C3D20R	70
方案 20	网球	864	C3D20R	200
方案 21	网球	1944	C3D20R	120
方案 22	网球	2904	C3D20R	100
方案 23	网球	16224	C3D20R	70
方案 24	网球	57624	C3D20R	45
方案 25	网球	89304	C3D20R	35
方案 26	网球	157464	C3D20R	20

2.3 数值结果分析

2.3.1 壳单元数值结果

根据式(1)与式(8)求出 6km 球形耐压壳的中面应力和临界屈曲载荷分别为 653.33Mpa 和 733.67Mpa。第 3 节所建立的 14 种壳单元数值方案的计算结果及误差如表 4 所示。由方案 1、方案 2、方案 3 的结果可知,在强度方面,随机形式的平均应力结果与理论值最为接近,钱币划分和网球划分形式的平均应力与理论值相差也较小,不足 0.1%;但随机划分的最大最小应力相差太大,出现明显应力集中,网球划分和钱币划分的最大最小应力相差很小,较为物合球形耐压壳的等强度特性。在稳定性方面,网球划分的临界屈曲载荷与理论值相差最小,为 0.049%,而随机划分和钱币划分的临界屈曲载荷与理论值相差较大,分别为 1.782%、0.167%。因此,从强度和稳定性两方面考虑,采用网球划分为球形耐压壳建模的最佳选择。

由方案 3、方案 4、方案 5、方案 6、方案 7 结果可知,在强度方面,无论是否采用减缩积分单元,得到的平均应力结果与理论值相差都非常小,几乎可以忽略不计;而从最大最小应力差值考虑,减缩积分单元 S4R 和 S4R5 较为理想,陆蓓、潘彬彬等在进行球形耐压壳数值分析时,也采用了 S4R 和 S4R5 单元。在稳定性方面,S4 计算精度最高。因此,从强度和稳定性两方面考虑,4 节点完全积分线性壳单元(S4)为球形耐压壳建模的最佳选择。

表 3 壳单元数值方案结果

方案	σ_{max}	σ_{min}	$\sigma_{max}-\sigma_{min}$	$\sigma_{平均}$	P_c	$\dfrac{\sigma-\sigma_t}{\sigma_t}\times100\%$	$\dfrac{P_c-P_{c_t}}{P_{c_t}}\times100\%$
方案 1	664.511	634.967	29.544	653.332	746.7404	0.00%	1.782%
方案 2	655.075	651.919	3.156	652.871	734.8922	0.07%	0.167%
方案 3	653.825	648.554	5.271	652.885	734.0298	0.07%	0.049%
方案 4	653.942	651.251	2.691	652.889	732.4422	0.07%	0.167%
方案 5	653.946	651.253	2.693	652.889	692.4974	0.07%	5.612%
方案 6	654.926	648.65	6.276	652.803	690.4688	0.08%	5.888%
方案 7	654.768	648.686	6.082	652.805	691.978	0.08%	5.683%
方案 8	665.638	580.459	85.179	640.219	831.0596	2.01%	13.274%
方案 9	659.112	613.638	45.474	647.367	772.0832	0.91%	5.236%
方案 10	657.445	624.145	33.3	649.313	756.315	0.62%	3.087%
方案 11	654.145	646.268	7.877	652.612	735.6762	0.11%	0.273%
方案 12	653.559	650.934	2.625	653.13	733.0596	0.03%	0.083%
方案 13	653.478	651.703	1.775	653.202	732.3442	0.02%	0.181%
方案 14	653.417	652.348	1.069	653.059	731.7366	0.01%	0.264%

网格疏密对数值模拟的准确度影响很大,因此先进行网格无关性检验,只有当网格数的增加对计算结果影响不大时,这时的仿真结果才具有意义。单元密度的选取要综合考虑计算时间和结果精度[10]。表 1 中的方案 8、方案 9、方案 10、方案 11、方案 3、方案 12、方案 13、方案 14 结果,绘制应力误差曲线、屈曲临界载荷误差曲线,分别如图 4(a)、(b)所示。图 4(a)为球形耐压壳中面上最大应力,最小应力和平均应力与理论强度应力的比值曲线,可见,单元平均尺寸与球形耐压壳半径比为 0.07 时,数值方案得到的结果就开始收敛,且网格尺寸越小,数值方案的平均应力越接近于理论值,而最大最小值的差值也越来越小,趋于解析解。

一般认为,网格尺寸的选取应该使屈曲临界载荷的相对浮动量小于等于 1%,结果趋于收敛[12]。由图 4(b)可知,当单元平均尺寸与球形耐压壳半径比达到 0.07 时,屈曲临界载荷的相对浮动量小于等于 1%,数值方案得到的屈曲结果就开始收敛逼近于 1,网格尺寸继续减小时得到的屈曲应力全部逼近于 1。因此,从强度和稳定性两方面考虑,单元尺寸和半径比为 0.07 为球形耐压壳建模的最佳选择。

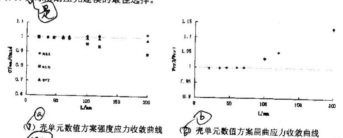

(a) 壳单元数值方案强度应力收敛曲线　　(b) 壳单元数值方案屈曲应力收敛曲线

图 4 壳单元数值方案网格收敛性曲线

图 5 为方案 3 计算所得的中面应力云图、内外表面应力云图、1 阶屈曲振形图。显然,采用壳单元进行数值模拟时,中面和内外层面的应力相差仅仅不到 1%,这与理论结果相差

甚远,说明采用壳单元进行厚球壳强度分析是不合理的。

(a) 内层面　　(b) 中层面　　(c) 外层面　　(d) 1阶屈曲云图

图5 S4壳单元方案应力与屈曲云图

2.3.2 体单元数值方案分析

根据式(1)、式(4)、式(5)、式(8)求出球形耐压壳的中面应力、内表面应力、外表面应力和临界屈曲载荷分别为653.33Mpa、729.28Mpa、582.28Mpa、733.67Mpa。第3节所建立的5种体单元数值方案的计算结果、及数值解误差如表4所示。由方案15、方案16、方案17、方案18、方案19的结果可知,在强度方面,采用减缩积分单元C3D20R,内中外三个面得到的平均应力结果与理论值最为接近,采用C3D8I单元和C3D20单元得到的三个表面应力与理论值相差相差都较小;而采用C3D8单元和C3D8R单元,三个面应力的最大最小值或者平均值都与理论值相差太大。在稳定性方面,采用C3D8I单元的临界屈曲载荷与理论值相差最小,为0.59%,而采用C3D20单元和C3D20R单元的临界屈曲载荷计算误差也较小,分别为0.89%、0.88%。因此,从强度和稳定性两方面考虑,采用C3D20R体单元为球形耐压壳建模最佳选择。

表4 不同单元类型体单元数值方案结果

Type		方案15	方案16	方案17	方案18	方案19
Inner Stress /Mpa	max	717.218	710.689	725.026	732.098	732.857
	min	714.201	707.792	720.358	726.644	727.796
	max-min	3.017	2.897	4.668	5.454	5.061
	average	715.124	708.128	720.811	728.604	729.603
	theory	729.282	729.282	729.282	729.282	729.282
	error	1.94%	2.90%	1.16%	0.09%	0.04%
Middle Stress /Mpa	max	650.569	650.612	650.151	649.874	651.006
	min	649.183	649.359	648.706	648.992	649.546
	max-min	1.386	1.253	1.445	0.882	1.46
	average	650.181	650.313	649.865	649.419	650.334
	theory	653.333	653.333	653.333	653.333	653.333
	error	0.48%	0.46%	0.53%	0.60%	0.46%
Outer Stress /Mpa	max	593.558	598.606	588.551	583.102	583.875
	min	589.119	593.97	582.256	578.027	578.584
	max-min	4.439	4.636	6.295	5.075	5.291
	average	592.594	598.007	587.841	581.395	582.127
	theory	582.282	582.282	582.282	582.282	582.282
	error	1.77%	2.70%	0.95%	0.15%	0.03%
Buckling Load	PCr	760.8916	721.476	737.9694	740.194	740.1646
	theory	733.69	733.69	733.69	733.69	733.69

| Mpa | error | 3.71% | 1.66% | 0.58% | 0.89% | 0.88% |

由方案 20、方案 21、方案 22、方案 23、方案 24、方案 25、方案 26 结果，绘制应力差曲线、屈曲临界载荷误差曲线，分别如图 6 (1)、(2)、(3)、(4) 所示。图 6 (1)、(2)、(3) 分别为球形耐压壳内表面、中面、外表面上最大应力、最小应力和平均应力与理论强度应力 σ_{mid} 的比值曲线，可见，体单元的单元平均尺寸与球形耐压壳半径比也为 0.07 时，数值方案得到的结果同样开始收敛，且网格尺寸越小，数值方案的平均应力越趋近于理论值，而最大最小值的差值越小，趋于解析解。由图 6 (4) 可知，当单元平均尺寸与球形耐压壳半径比达到 0.07 时，屈曲临界载荷的相对浮动量小于等于 1%，数值方案得到的屈曲结果开始收敛，逼近于 1。网格尺寸继续减小时得到的屈曲应力全部逼近于 1，因此，从强度和稳定性两方面考虑，体单元的单元尺寸和半径比为 0.07 为球形耐压壳建模的最佳选择。

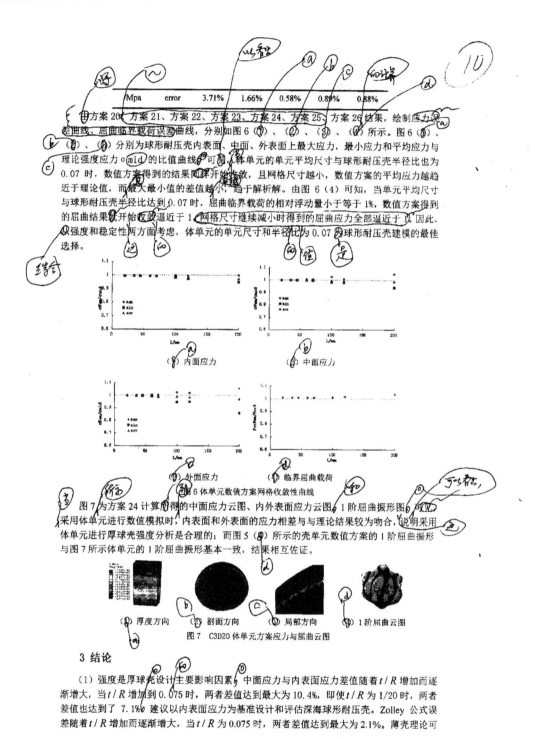

(a) 内面应力　　　(b) 中面应力

(c) 外面应力　　　(d) 临界屈曲载荷

图 6 体单元数值方案网格收敛性曲线

图 7 为方案 24 计算所得的中面应力云图、内外表面应力云图 1 阶屈曲振形图。采用体单元进行数值模拟时，内表面和外表面的应力相差与理论结果较为吻合，说明采用体单元进行厚球壳强度分析是合理的；而图 5 (d) 所示的壳单元数值方案的 1 阶屈曲振形与图 7 所示体单元的 1 阶屈曲振形基本一致，结果相互佐证。

(a) 厚度方向　(b) 剖面方向　(c) 局部方向　(d) 1 阶屈曲云图

图 7 C3D20 体单元方案应力与屈曲云图

3 结论

(1) 强度是厚球壳设计主要影响因素，中面应力与内表面应力差值随着 t/R 增加而逐渐增大，当 t/R 增加到 0.075 时，两者差值达到最大为 10.4%，即使 t/R 为 1/20 时，两者差值也达到了 7.1%，建议以内表面应力为基准设计和评估深海球形耐压壳。Zolley 公式误差随着 t/R 增加而逐渐增大，当 t/R 为 0.075 时，两者差值达到最大为 2.1%，薄壳理论可用于厚球壳稳定性初步评估。经验法求解球形耐压壳浮力系数偏于保守，其误差随着t/R增加而逐渐增大，当t/R达到0.075时，误差达到10.1%，即使t/R为1/20时，误差也高达6.8%。建议采用解析法评估深海球形耐压壳的浮力系数。

（2）综合考虑计算精度和效率，建议采用网球划分、4节点完全积分线性壳单元、单元平均尺寸0.07R，建立球形耐压壳的壳单元数值方案；建议采用网球划分、三维20节点减缩积分体单元、周向单元平均尺寸0.07R，厚度方向4层单元，建立球形耐压壳的体单元数值方案。壳单元数值方案、薄壳理论方案可用于浅海耐压壳设计与评估，体单元数值方案、厚球壳理论方案可用于深海耐压壳设计与评估。建议船级社在进行深海耐压壳设计规范修订时，采用内表面应力、厚壳临界屈曲载荷作为评价指标。

参考文献

[1] Zhang J, Zuo X L, Wang W B, Tang W X. Overviews of Investigation on Submersible Pressure Hulls[J]. Advances in Natural Science, 2014, 7(4): 54-61.
[2] Pan B B, Cui W C. A Comparison of Different Rules for the Spherical Pressure Hull of Deep Manned Submersibles[J]. Journal of Ship Mechanics, 2011, 15(3): 276-285.
[3] Ma Y Q, Wang C M, Ang K K. Buckling of super ellipsoidal shells under uniform pressure[J]. Thin-Walled Structures, 2008, 46(6): 584-591.
[4] 王自力,王仁华,俞铭华,李良碧. 初始缺陷对不同深度载人潜水器耐压球壳极限承载力的影响[J] 中国造船, 2007, 02:45-50.
[5] 陆蓓,刘涛,崔维成. 深海载人潜水器耐压球壳极限强度研究[J]. 船舶力学, 2004, 01: 51-58.
[6] Pan B B, Cui W C. An overview of buckling and ultimate strength of spherical pressure hull under external pressure[J]. Marine Structures, 2010,23(3):227-240.
[7] Wang C M, Wang C Y, Reddy J N. Exact Solutions for Buckling of Structural Members[M]. CRC Press. 2004.
[8] Timoshenko S P, Gere J M. Theory of Elastic Stability[M]. Dover Publications, 1961.
[9] 刘涛. 大深度潜水器结构分析与设计研究[D].中国船舶科学研究中心.2001,3.
[10] Tomas A, Tovar J P. The influence of initial geometric imperfections on the buckling load of single and double curvature concrete shells[J]. Computers & Structures. 2012, 96(97):34–45.

Investigation on Mechanical Properties of Deep Sea Spherical Pressure Hull

ZHANG Jian[1,2], GAO Jie[1], WANG Weibo[2], TANG Wenxian[1], ZHOU Tong[1]

(1. Jiangsu University of Science and Technology, Jiangsu Zhenjiang 212003, China
2. Chinese Ship Scientific Research Center, Jiangsu Wuxi 214082, China;)

Abstract

Calculating method for deep sea spherical pressure hull was systematically investigated. Mechanical models based on thin shell and thick shell, buoyancy factor equations for the hull were presented, respectively. Numerical models based on shell elements and solid elements for the hull with the water depth of 6 km were proposed as well. Strength, stability and buoyancy reserve capacity of the spherical hull with the water depth of 1~6 km were analyzed. Furthermore, effects of meshing, element type and density on the numerical results were studied. The results showed that, it is suitable to design and assess the deep sea spherical pressure hull using theory of thick shell and numerical models based on solid elements. Strength is the main influence factor during the thick spherical shell design process. Therefore, it is suggested to determine the thickness of the pressure hull based on the inner stress equation firstly. Then, the stability of the hull could be

(2) 专家意见答复及修改说明

专家意见邮件答复：

尊敬的张编辑，您好！

　　再次感谢您和专家为本论文付出了大量劳动。针对专家意见，作者对论文作了全面详细修改，请见附件"15086 修改稿"。此外，作者对专家的主要意见作了逐一答复，并附上相应的修改说明，具体请见附件"专家意见及修改说明"。请您及专家对本论文作进一步考察。

祝：工作顺利，万事如意！

张建

2015.12.15

联系人：张建

手机：15896387748

邮箱：zhjian127@163.com

专家意见答复及修改说明

　　意见之一：厚壳的解析式（8）就肯定是临界载荷的真值吗？这一点必须认真考虑，予以确认，否则只能说 A 方法相对于 B 方法的偏差。偏差不能等同于误差。

　　答：解析式（8）是王昌逸教授在 Zolley 公式的基础上考虑了高阶无穷小后推导的结果，但推导过程并非绝对的真值，在修改稿中已将误差改为偏差。

　　意见之二：误差是估计值相对于真值而言的，这里要说明解析法的浮力系数是正确的值。

　　答：在修改稿中第 1.3 节第四段开头增加了说明"由解析法得到的浮力系数为正确的值"。

　　意见之三：计算载荷和这里说的假设有因果关系吗？

　　答：公式 16 中计算载荷和第 1.4 节的假设没有因果关系，在修改稿中已将该假设予以删除。

　　意见之四：本文所有曲线图制作粗糙，须重新制作。（1）必须用源数据按实际版的尺寸绘制，严禁利用已有的大尺寸的曲线图复制、缩小、粘贴，这也是检验作者是否真正掌握计算数据的依据之一（2）图中所有字符一律为 6 号字，西文及数字字形 Times New Roman（3）坐标项目，对有量纲的物理量应写为"物理量/单位"的形式如 P（斜体）/MPa（正体）（4）图中所有线条字符标记等一律黑色（黑白印刷条件）。

　　答：本文所有的图形已在制图软件 AI 下重新按 1∶1 比例采用黑白线条重新进行了制作，修改了物理量单位的表示方法，并将图中所有字符一律改为 6 号字，西文及数字字形选为 Times New Roman。

　　意见之五：空间方向只有三个是相互独立的，方向改为自由度。

　　答：在修改稿中已将 2.1 节的限制其六个方向的位移改为了限制其六个自由度的位移。

意见之六：像这样的图能让人们看到什么？能说明什么问题？不能对论述有帮助的图应予以删除。

答：图 3 的表达没有说明什么实际意义的问题，已在修改稿中第二节将图 3 全部予以删除，并重新调整了图符的顺序编码。

意见之七：作者对表 3 中的第 7 列和第 8 列表示什么予以说明，如果读者连表格的内容都不清楚还谈什么分析？至于"误差"到底是什么含义？

答：在修改稿中第 2.3 节第一段增加了对表 3 中第 7 列和第 8 列公式符号的解释"对表 1 中列出的 14 个壳单元数值方案的计算结果及与理论中面应力 σ_t 和理论临界屈曲载荷 P_{ct} 偏差列于表 3。"原始稿中的"误差"为有限元计算结果和理论计算结果的偏差，已在修改稿中进行修改。

意见之八：符号不规范，不要使用中文字作为下标，应使用统计数学中习惯的符号如 $\bar{\sigma}$。

答：已将表 3 中的中文字下标符号予以删除，并在修改稿中将平均应力的符合改为专家建议的统计数学中习惯的符号 $\bar{\sigma}$

意见之九：σ_{mid} 下表不规范，宜用单字母。

答：在修改稿中已将中面应力的表述 σ_{mid} 全部予以删除，并改为单字母下标 σ_m。

意见之十：表 4 中项目类别不该用英文改用中文。

答：在修改稿中将表 4 中的英文表述的项目类别全部予以删除，并全部采用中文表述，具体修改见修改稿。

其他——专家纸面意见修改

根据专家在论文的详细修改意见，如语句表述、部分词汇、标点符号、图符字型和字体类型等，均在修改稿中按专家意见作了仔细、严格修改。具体内容见修改稿。

(3) 附件"15086 修改稿"

深海球形耐压壳力学特性研究

张建[1,2]，高杰[1]，王纬波[2]，唐文献[1]，周通[1]

（1. 江苏科技大学，江苏 镇江 212003；2. 中国船舶科学研究中心，江苏 无锡 214082）

摘 要

研究了深海球形耐压壳计算方法。分别建立了球形耐压壳薄壳和厚壳的力学模型、浮力系数求解公式以及壳单元、体单元数值模型。分析 1～6km 球形耐压壳强度、稳定性、储备浮力特性，并研究网格划分形式、单元类型、密度对数值计算结果的影响。研究结果表明，采用厚壳理论、体单元数值分析进行深海球形耐压壳设计与评估更为合理。在设计时，建议

收稿日期：2015-06-01　修改稿收稿日期：

基金项目：国家自然科学基金项目（51205173）；江苏省自然科学基金（BK20150469）

先根据内表面应力公式确定耐压壳厚度,再运用厚壳屈曲理论或数值分析校核其稳定性。

关键词:球形耐压壳;强度;稳定性;厚壳理论

中图分类号:U661.4,TE58 **文献标识码**:A

0 引言

根据《中国制造2025》文件,国家将大力推动海洋工程装备突破发展。深海潜水器是大洋勘查与深海科学研究的重要海洋工程装备。在下潜过程中,潜水器的耐压壳起着保障内部设备正常工作和人员健康安全的作用,其重量占潜水器总重的1/4~1/2[1]。

现有的球形耐压壳的设计与分析基于薄壳理论,且已被各国船级社规范认同。潘彬彬等对现有深水球形耐压壳的设计规范进行了对比和分析,指出规范计算中存在的缺陷[2]。然后通过原型试验和非线性有限元分析,建立了预测深海钛合金球形壳极限强度的经验公式。马永前等参考中厚板壳稳定性理论,研究厚球壳的屈曲问题,指出:由于厚度方向的剪切效应,厚球壳的实际临界屈曲载荷低于薄壳理论(Zolley公式)的结果[3]。王自力、刘涛等的研究表明,随着水深增加,对于耐压壳的分析将从薄壳问题转化为中厚壳问题,然而现有的潜水器规范不适用于深海耐压壳分析,应直接根据有限元计算确定其极限强度[4-5]。在有限元建模过程中,模型简化、单元类型、网格密度、网格划分形式、边界条件、求解方法等对球形壳计算结果的影响很大,不同人员对同一问题的计算结果存在差异,数值解的可信度有待商榷。

本文从理论分析和数值计算这两方面研究球形耐压壳的强度、稳定性、储备浮力等性能。在1~6km水深条件下,分别按薄壳模型和厚壳模型,分析和对比壳体的强度和稳定性。建立球形耐压壳的壳单元和体单元数值模型,研究单元类型、网格密度对耐压壳强度和稳定性的影响。

1 球形耐压壳理论研究

1.1 薄壳力学模型

根据薄壳强度理论,球形耐压壳中面应力σ_m按式(1)计算。该公式是船级社球形耐压壳强度校核的理论基础。

$$\sigma_m = \frac{P_s R}{2t} \tag{1}$$

式中,P_s为计算载荷,R为球壳的半径,t为球壳厚度。

假设$\sigma_m = [\sigma]$,那么极限强度载荷$P_{\sigma1}$与t/R(厚度半径比)的关系为

$$P_{\sigma1} = 2[\sigma]\frac{t}{R} \tag{2}$$

根据薄壳屈曲理论,球形耐压壳屈曲临界载荷P_{c1}可用Zolley公式[6]表述,它也是船级社球形耐压壳稳定性设计规范的理论基础,即:

$$P_{c1} = \frac{2Et^2}{R^2}\sqrt{\frac{1}{3(1-\mu^2)}} \tag{3}$$

1.2 厚壳力学模型

在设计时,耐压壳厚度随着工作水深的增加而增大,其强度和稳定性计算从薄壳变为厚壳计算,采用薄壳理论研究厚壳问题偏于危险。对于承受静水压力的厚球壳结构,内表面应力σ_i最大,外表面应力σ_o最小,分别如式(4)、(5)所示,中面应力根据式(1)确定。

$$\sigma_i = \frac{3P_S \left(2 + \frac{t}{R}\right)^3}{2\left[\left(2 + \frac{t}{R}\right)^3 - \left(2 - \frac{t}{R}\right)^3\right]} \qquad (4)$$

$$\sigma_o = \frac{3P_S \left(2 - \frac{t}{R}\right)^3}{2\left[\left(2 + \frac{t}{R}\right)^3 - \left(2 - \frac{t}{R}\right)^3\right]} \qquad (5)$$

根据用薄壳强度理论评价厚壳应力存在的偏差 Δ_σ，可由式（1）和式（4）求得：

$$\Delta_\sigma = \frac{|\sigma_i - \sigma_m|}{\sigma_i} \times 100\% = \left\{1 - \left[1 - \left(\frac{2 - \frac{t}{R}}{2 + \frac{t}{R}}\right)^3\right] \times \frac{3}{\frac{t}{R}}\right\} \times 100\% \qquad (6)$$

令 $\sigma_i = [\sigma]$，由式（4）可得到极限强度载荷 $P_{\sigma 2}$ 与 t/R 的关系：

$$P_{\sigma 2} = \frac{2[\sigma]\left[\left(2 + \frac{t}{R}\right)^3 - \left(2 - \frac{t}{R}\right)^3\right]}{3\left(2 + \frac{t}{R}\right)^3} \qquad (7)$$

深水球形耐压壳屈曲临界载荷采用式(8) 表述[7]，该公式采用勒让德函数求解球形壳屈曲控制方程[8]，推导出厚球壳稳定性问题的解析解 P_{c2}：

$$P_{c2} = \frac{2Et}{R(1-\mu^2)}\left(\sqrt{\frac{(1-\mu^2)}{3}}\frac{t}{R} - \frac{\mu t^2}{2R^2}\right) \qquad (8)$$

将式（3）代入式（8）可得：

$$P_{c2} = \left(1 - \frac{\sqrt{3}}{2}\frac{\mu}{\sqrt{1-\mu^2}}\frac{t}{R}\right)P_{c1} \qquad (9)$$

则：

$$P_{c2} = \left(1 - f\left(\frac{t}{R}\right)\right)P_{c1} \qquad (10)$$

其中 $f\left(\frac{t}{R}\right) = \frac{\sqrt{3}}{2}\frac{\mu}{\sqrt{1-\mu^2}}\frac{t}{R}$。

根据式(3) 和式（10），可得出经典 Zolley 公式在计算厚壳屈曲临界载荷时的偏差 Δ_c 为：

$$\Delta_c = \frac{|P_{c1} - P_{c2}|}{P_{c2}} \times 100\% = \frac{f\left(\frac{t}{R}\right)}{1 - f\left(\frac{t}{R}\right)} \times 100\% \qquad (11)$$

1.3 球形耐压壳浮力系数

耐压壳浮力系数定义为耐压壳体重量与其排水量比值 δ：

$$\delta = \frac{\rho_p V_p}{\rho_w V_w} \qquad (12)$$

式中，V_p 为耐压壳材料体积，V_w 为排水量体积。

在现有设计中，耐压壳材料体积可采用其中面面积与厚度乘积确定，耐压壳的排水体积可近似为中面围成区域的体积，因此，可得到球形耐压壳经验法的浮力系数 δ_1：

$$\delta_1 = \frac{3\rho_p}{\rho_w} \frac{t}{R} \tag{13}$$

实际上，球形耐压壳材料体积应为外表面所谓围成区域的体积减去内表面所围成区域的体积，耐压壳的排水体积则为外表面所谓围成区域的体积，即由解析法得到的浮力系数 δ_2：

$$\delta_2 = \frac{\rho_p \left[\left(2+\frac{t}{R}\right)^3 - \left(2-\frac{t}{R}\right)^3 \right]}{\rho_w \left(2+\frac{t}{R}\right)^3} \tag{14}$$

由解析法得到的浮力系数为正确的值，根据式（13）和式（14），可得到经验法计算球形耐压壳浮力系数的误差，即：

$$\Delta_\delta = \frac{|\delta_1 - \delta_2|}{\delta_2} = \left(\frac{3\frac{t}{R}}{1-\left(\frac{2-\frac{t}{R}}{2+\frac{t}{R}}\right)^3} - 1 \right) \times 100\% \tag{15}$$

1.4 球形耐压壳力学特性分析

考虑一个直径为 2m 的球形耐压壳，计算载荷由式（16）确定。假设球形耐压壳的材料为 Ti-6Al-4V(TC4)，其基本力学参数为：屈服强度 $\sigma_b = 830MPa$，密度 $\rho_p = 4.5 g/cm^2$，弹性模量 $G = 110GPa$，泊松比 $\mu = 0.3$。计算载荷取 P_S 为

$$P_S = K\rho_w gh/0.9 \tag{16}$$

式中，K 为安全系数，取 1.5，为海水密度，ρ_w 取 $1g/cm^3$；g 为重力加速度，取 $9.8m/s^2$；h 为水深，取 0~6km。

根据式（2）、式（3）、式（7）和式（8），绘制按薄壳模型和厚壳模型计算的极限强度载荷和屈曲临界载荷随 t/R 变化的曲线，如图 1（a）所示。当 t/R 小于 0.013 时，屈曲临界载荷小于极限强度载荷，稳定性为耐压壳安全评估的主要影响因素；当 t/R 大于 0.013 时，屈曲临界载荷大于极限强度载荷，强度为耐压壳安全评估的主要影响因素，且随着水深的增加，强度因素的影响越来越大，而屈曲因素的影响越来越小。

由图 1（a）可知，由经典 Zolley 公式得到的屈曲临界载荷偏于保守，偏差曲线如图 1（b）所示。随着厚度半径比的逐渐增加，Zolley 公式偏差不断增大，且与 t/R 成线性关系，当 t/R 为 0.075 时，误差最大，约为 2.1%；由此可以认为，Zolley 公式在计算厚壳的临界屈曲载荷时，误差较小，可用于厚球壳的稳定性初步评估。马永前也研究厚球壳稳定性问题，基于板壳理论建立了厚球壳屈曲临界载荷的修正公式，指出 Zolley 公式得到的屈曲临界载荷偏于保守。

随着厚度半径比的增加，球形耐压壳中面应力与内表面应力差值随着 t/R 增加逐渐增大，差值曲线如图 1（c）所示，当 t/R 增加到 0.075 时，中面应力与内表面应力差值达到最大的 10.4%，即使 t/R 为 1/20（厚壳、薄壳分界线）时，两种差值也达到了 7.1%，此时用薄壳强度理论（式（2））进行球形耐压壳强度校核得到的结果偏于危险。当 t/R 小于

0.015 时，误差在 2% 以内，在这种情况下，薄壳强度理论可适用于球形耐压壳强度的初步评估。

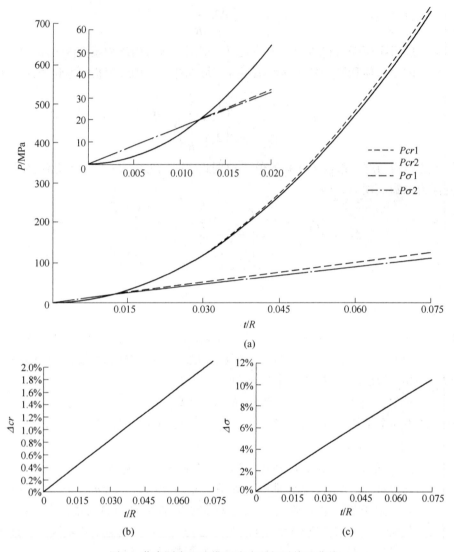

图 1　薄壳厚壳理论模型公式及相对偏差曲线
（a）薄壳、厚壳力学模型计算结果　（b）屈曲偏差　（c）应力偏差

1.5　球形耐压壳浮力系数分析

用经验方法和解析方法得到的浮力系数曲线如图 2（a）所示。两种计算方法得到的浮力系数均与 t/R 成近似的线性递增关系，但是经验法得到的浮力系数要比解析法高。且随着 t/R 的逐渐增大，经验法的浮力系数误差越来越大，如图 2（b）所示；当 t/R 达到 0.075 时，误差值达到的 10.1%，即使 t/R 为 1/20（厚壳、薄壳分界线）时，两种差值也达到了 6.8%。因此在进行中厚球壳浮力系数评估时，经验法不再适用。当 t/R 小于 0.015 时，经验法误差在 2% 以内，在这种情况下，经验法可适用于球形耐压壳浮力系数的初步评估。刘涛[9]关于球形耐压壳的浮力系数的研究也有相近的结论，说明采用经验法在进行深海耐压壳设计时偏于保守。

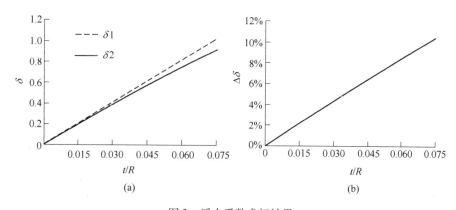

图 2 浮力系数求解结果
(a) 经验法和解析法得到的浮力系数曲线 (b) 经验法浮力系数误差

2 球形耐压壳有限元数值研究

以对人的球形耐压壳在6km水深的工作条件下进行计算,设计厚度为75mm。考察网格划分形式、单元类型和单元密度等因素对计算结果的影响。

2.1 壳单元方案

采用pro/e软件,进行三维CAD建模,并抽取中面,采用ANSA前处理软件,进行网格划分。计算载荷以均布压力形式施加在耐压壳表面。耐压壳理论上是不受任何约束的,为了消除模型的刚性位移,选择三个点,限制其六个自由度的位移。求得的各约束反力接近0,说明所施加的约束为虚约束,仅限制了方案的刚体位移。现对2种工况进行分析:(1) 线性准静态分析;(2) 线性屈曲分析。采用ABAQUS/Standard进行计算,并运用ABAQUS/Viewer进行后处理。采用单因素控制变量法建立不同网格划分形式、单元类型、单元密度下的数值方案,进行分析计算。

采用随机划分、钱币划分、网球划分三种划分形式,它们分别对应于方案1、方案2、方案3。单元类型为4节点完全积分线性壳单元(S4),网格单元数量约为6500。对于单元类型,采用4节点完全积分线性壳单元(S4)、4节点减缩积分壳单元(S4R)、每个节点5个自由度的4节点减缩积分壳单元(S4R5)、8节点双曲厚壳单元(S8R)、每节点5个自由度的8节点双曲厚壳单元(S8R5),它们分别对应于方案3、方案4、方案5、方案6、方案7。这些方案均采用网球划分的形式,单元数、节点数与方案3一致。对于数值方案,需要进行网格的收敛性检查来验证方案结果的正确性。分别采用平均尺寸为200mm、120mm、100mm、70mm、60mm、45mm、35mm、20mm的网格进行计算,分别对应于方案8、方案9、方案10、方案11、方案3、方案12、方案13、方案14,单元类型均为S4,均采用网球划分,具体信息如表1所示。

表1 壳单元数值模型信息表

方案	划分形式	节点数	单元数	单元类型
方案1	随机	6514	6512	S4
方案2	钱币	6596	6594	S4
方案3	网球	6536	6534	S4
方案4	网球	6536	6534	S4R

(续)

方案	划分形式	节点数	单元数	单元类型
方案5	网球	6536	6534	S4R5
方案6	网球	6536	6534	S8R
方案7	网球	6536	6534	S8R5
方案8	网球	488	216	S4
方案9	网球	488	486	S4
方案10	网球	728	726	S4
方案11	网球	4058	4056	S4
方案12	网球	14408	14406	S4
方案13	网球	22328	22326	S4
方案14	网球	39368	39366	S4

2.2 体单元方案

体单元网格方案可以通过壳单元网格沿厚度方向偏移4层单元得到，其中的载荷、边界、工况与壳单元一致。首先，根据方案3的网格，建立体单元方案，单元类型设定为三维8节点体单元（C3D8）、三维8节点减缩积分体单元（C3D8R）、三维8节点非协调模式体单元（C3D8I）、三维20节点体单元（C3D20）、三维20节点减缩积分体单元（C3D20R），它们分别对应于方案15、方案16、方案17、方案18、方案19。此外，分别采用周向平均尺寸为200mm、120mm、100mm、70mm、45mm、35mm、20mm的网格进行计算，分别对应于方案20、方案21、方案22、方案23、方案24、方案25、方案26，这些方案的网格分别由方案8、方案9、方案10、方案11、方案12、方案13、方案14的网格沿厚度方向偏移所得，单元类型均为C3D20R，具体信息如表2所示。

表2 不同单元类型体单元数值模型信息表

模型代号	划分形式	单元数	单元类型	单元平均尺寸/mm
方案15	网球	16224	C3D8	70
方案16	网球	16224	C3D8R	70
方案17	网球	16224	C3D8I	70
方案18	网球	16224	C3D20	70
方案19	网球	16224	C3D20R	70
方案20	网球	864	C3D20R	200
方案21	网球	1944	C3D20R	120
方案22	网球	2904	C3D20R	100
方案23	网球	16224	C3D20R	70
方案24	网球	57624	C3D20R	45
方案25	网球	89304	C3D20R	35
方案26	网球	157464	C3D20R	20

2.3 数值结果分析

2.3.1 壳单元数值结果

根据式（1）和式（8），6km水深下球形耐压壳的理论中面应力 σ_t 和理论临界屈曲载荷

P_{ct} 分别为 653.33 MPa 和 733.67 MPa。对表 1 中列出的 14 个壳单元数值方案的计算结果及与理论中面应力 σ_t 和理论临界屈曲载荷 P_{ct} 偏差列于表 3。由方案 1、方案 2、方案 3 的结果可知，在强度方面，随机形式的平均应力结果与理论值最为接近，钱币划分和网球划分形式的平均应力与理论值相差也较小，不足 0.1%；但随机划分的最大最小应力相差太大，出现明显的应力集中，网球划分和钱币划分的最大最小应力相差很小，较为符合球形耐压壳的等强度特性。在稳定性方面，网球划分的临界屈曲载荷与理论值相差最小，为 0.049%，而随机划分和钱币划分的临界屈曲载荷与理论值相差较大，分别为 1.782%、0.167%。因此，从强度和稳定性两方面考虑，采用网球划分为球形耐压壳建模的最佳选择。

由方案 3、方案 4、方案 5、方案 6、方案 7 结果可知，在强度方面，无论是否采用减缩积分单元，得到的平均应力结果与理论值相差都非常小，几乎可以忽略不计；而从最大最小应力差值考虑，减缩积分单元 S4R 和 S4R5 较为理想。陆蓓、潘彬彬等在进行球形耐压壳数值分析时，也采用了 S4R 和 S4R5 单元。在稳定性方面，S4 计算精度最高。因此，从强度和稳定性两方面考虑，4 节点完全积分线性壳单元（S4）为球形耐压壳建模的最佳选择。

表 3 壳单元数值方案结果

方案	σ_{max}	σ_{min}	$\sigma_{max}-\sigma_{min}$	$\overline{\sigma}$	P_c	$\dfrac{\overline{\sigma}-\sigma_t}{\sigma_t}\times 100\%$	$\dfrac{P_c-P_{ct}}{P_{ct}}\times 100\%$
方案 1	664.511	634.967	29.544	653.332	746.7404	0.00%	1.782%
方案 2	655.075	651.919	3.156	652.871	734.8922	0.07%	0.167%
方案 3	653.825	648.554	5.271	652.885	734.0298	0.07%	0.049%
方案 4	653.942	651.251	2.691	652.889	732.4422	0.07%	0.167%
方案 5	653.946	651.253	2.693	652.889	692.4974	0.07%	5.612%
方案 6	654.926	648.65	6.276	652.803	690.4688	0.08%	5.888%
方案 7	654.768	648.686	6.082	652.805	691.978	0.08%	5.683%
方案 8	665.638	580.459	85.179	640.219	831.0596	2.01%	13.274%
方案 9	659.112	613.638	45.474	647.367	772.0832	0.91%	5.236%
方案 10	657.445	624.145	33.3	649.313	756.315	0.62%	3.087%
方案 11	654.145	646.268	7.877	652.612	735.6762	0.11%	0.273%
方案 12	653.559	650.934	2.625	653.13	733.0596	0.03%	0.083%
方案 13	653.478	651.703	1.775	653.202	732.3442	0.02%	0.181%
方案 14	653.417	652.348	1.069	653.259	731.7366	0.01%	0.264%

网格疏密对数值模拟的准确度影响很大。先进行网格无关性检验。只有当网格数的增加对计算结果影响不大时，这时的仿真结果才具有意义。单元密度的选取要综合考虑计算时间和精度[10]。对表 1 中的方案 8、方案 9、方案 10、方案 11、方案 3、方案 12、方案 13、方案 14 的计算结果，绘制应力误差曲线、屈曲临界载荷误差曲线，分别如图 3（a）、（b）所示。图 3（a）所示为球形耐压壳中面上最大应力，最小应力和平均应力与理论强度应力 σ_m 的比值曲线，当单元平均尺寸与球形耐压壳半径比为 0.07 时，数值方案得到的结果就开始收敛，且网格尺寸越小，数值方案的平均应力越趋近于理论值，而最大最小值的差值也越来越小，趋于解析解。

一般认为，网格尺寸的选取应该使屈曲临界载荷的相对浮动量小于等于 1%，那么结果趋于收敛。由图 3（b）可知，当单元平均尺寸与球形耐压壳半径比达到 0.07 时，屈曲临界载荷的相对浮动量小于等于1%，数值方案得到的屈曲结果就开始收敛逼近于1，网格尺寸继续减小时得到的屈曲应力全部逼近于1。因此，从强度和稳定性两方面考虑，单元尺寸和半径的比值为0.07是球形耐压壳建模的最佳选择。

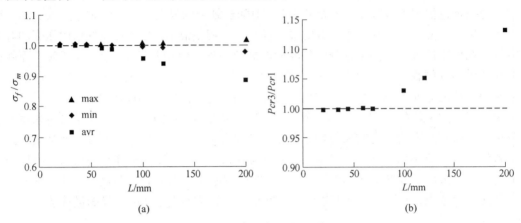

图3　壳单元数值方案网格收敛性曲线
(a) 壳单元数值方案强度应力收敛曲线　(b) 壳单元数值方案屈曲应力收敛曲线

图4所示为方案3计算所得的中面应力云图、内外表面应力云图、1阶屈曲振形图。显然，采用壳单元进行数值模拟时，中面和内外层面的应力相差仅仅不到1%，这与理论结果相差甚远，表明采用壳单元进行厚球壳强度分析是不合理的。

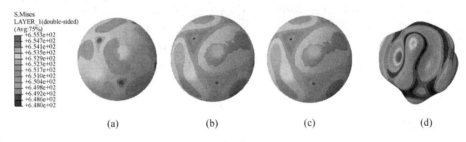

图4　S4壳单元方案应力与屈曲云图
(a) 内层面　(b) 中层面　(c) 外层面　(d) 1阶屈曲云图

2.3.2　体单元数值方案分析

根据式(1)、式(4)、式(5)和式(8)求得球形耐压壳的中面应力、内表面应力、外表面应力和临界屈曲载荷分别为653.33MPa、729.28MPa、582.28MPa、733.67MPa。由表2中方案15~方案19这5种体单元数值方案的计算结果、及数值误差如表4所示。在强度方面，采用减缩积分单元C3D20R，内中外三个面得到的平均应力结果与理论值最为接近，采用C3D8I单元和C3D20单元得到的三个表面应力与理论值相差相差都较小；而采用C3D8单元和C3D8R单元，三个面应力的最大最小值或者平均值都与理论值相差太大。在稳定性方面，采用C3D8I单元的临界屈曲载荷与理论值相差最小，为0.59%，而采用C3D20单元和C3D20R单元的临界屈曲载荷计算误差也较小，分别为0.89%、0.88%。综合强度和稳定性这两方面考虑，采用C3D20R体单元为球形耐压壳建模最佳选择。

表4　不同单元类型体单元数值方案结果

Type		方案15	方案16	方案17	方案18	方案19
内表面应力/MPa	max	717.218	710.689	725.026	732.098	732.857
	min	714.201	707.792	720.358	726.644	727.796
	max−min	3.017	2.897	4.668	5.454	5.061
	avcrage	715.124	708.128	720.811	728.604	729.603
	theory	729.282	729.282	729.282	729.282	729.282
	error	1.94%	2.90%	1.16%	0.09%	0.04%
中面应力/MPa	max	650.569	650.612	650.151	649.874	651.006
	min	649.183	649.359	648.706	648.992	649.546
	max−min	1.386	1.253	1.445	0.882	1.46
	average	650.181	650.313	649.865	649.419	650.334
	theory	653.333	653.333	653.333	653.333	653.333
	error	0.48%	0.46%	0.53%	0.60%	0.46%
外表面应力/MPa	max	593.558	598.606	588.551	583.102	583.875
	min	589.119	593.97	582.256	578.027	578.584
	max−min	4.439	4.636	6.295	5.075	5.291
	average	592.594	598.007	587.841	581.395	582.127
	theory	582.282	582.282	582.282	582.282	582.282
	error	1.77%	2.70%	0.95%	0.15%	0.03%
屈曲载荷/MPa	Pcr	760.8916	721.476	737.9694	740.194	740.1646
	theory	733.69	733.69	733.69	733.69	733.69
	error	3.71%	1.66%	0.58%	0.89%	0.88%

将方案20~方案26的计算结果，绘制曲线，分别如图5（a）、（b）、（c）、（d）所示。图5（a）、（b）、（c）分别为球形耐压壳内表面、中面、外表面上最大应力，最小应力和平

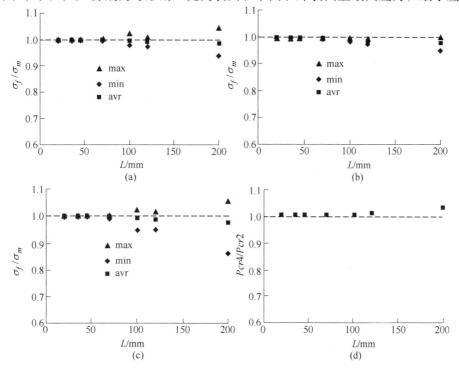

图5　体单元数值方案网格收敛性曲线
（a）内面应力　（b）中面应力　（c）外面应力　（d）临界屈曲载荷

均应力与理论强度应力 σ_m 的比值曲线。可以看出，当体单元的单元平均尺寸与球形耐压壳半径比也为 0.07 时，数值方案得到的结果开始收敛，且网格尺寸越小，数值方案的平均应力越趋近于理论值，而且最大最小值的差值越来越小，趋于解析解。由图5（4）可知，当单元平均尺寸与球形耐压壳半径比达到 0.07 时，屈曲临界载荷的相对浮动量小于等于 1%，数值方案得到的屈曲结果开始逼近于 1。因此，综合强度和稳定性这两方面的考虑，体单元的单元尺寸和半径的比值为 0.07 是球形耐压壳建模的最佳选择。

图6 所示为方案23 计算得到的中面应力云图、内外表面应力云图和 1 阶屈曲振形图。可以看出，当采用体单元进行数值模拟时，内表面和外表面的应力相差与理论结果较为吻合，这说明采用体单元进行厚球壳强度分析是合理的；而图4（d）所示的壳单元数值方案的 1 阶屈曲振形与图6 所示体单元的 1 阶屈曲振形基本一致，结果相互佐证。

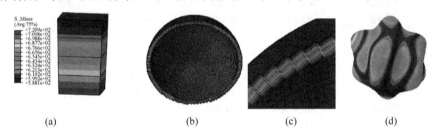

图6 C3D20R 体单元方案应力与屈曲云图
（a）厚度方向 （b）剖面方向 （c）局部方向 （d）1 阶屈曲云图

3 结论

（1）强度是厚球壳设计的主要影响因素。中面应力与内表面应力差值随着 t/R 增加而逐渐增大，当 t/R 增加到 0.075 时，两者差值达到最大为 10.4%，即使 t/R 为 1/20 时，两者差值也达到了 7.1%。建议以内表面应力为基准设计和评估深海球形耐压壳。Zolley 公式误差随着 t/R 增加而逐渐增大，当 t/R 为 0.075 时，两者差值达到最大为 2.1%，薄壳理论可用于厚球壳稳定性初步评估。经验法求解球形耐压壳浮力系数偏于保守，其误差随着 t/R 增加而逐渐增大，当 t/R 达到 0.075 时，误差达到 10.1%，即使 t/R 为 1/20 时，误差也高达 6.8%。建议采用解析法评估深海球形耐压壳的浮力系数。

（2）综合考虑计算精度和效率，建议采用网球划分、4 节点完全积分线性壳单元、单元平均尺寸 $0.07R$，建立球形耐压壳的壳单元数值方案。建议采用网球划分、三维 20 节点减缩积分体单元、周向单元平均尺寸 $0.07R$、厚度方向 4 层单元，建立球形耐压壳的体单元数值方案。壳单元数值方案、薄壳理论方案可用于浅海耐压壳设计与评估，体单元数值方案、厚球壳理论方案可用于深海耐压壳设计与评估。建议船级社在进行深海耐压壳设计规范修订时，采用内表面应力、厚壳临界屈曲载荷作为评价指标。

参考文献

［1］ ZHANG J, ZUO X L, WANG W B, TANG W X. Overviews of investigation on submersible pressure Hulls[J]. Advances in Natural Science, 2014, 7(4): 54-61.

［2］ PAN B B, CUI W C. A comparison of different rules for the spherical pressure hull of deep manned submersibles [J]. Journal of Ship Mechanics, 2011, 15(3): 276-285.

［3］ MA Y Q, WANG C M, ANG K K. Buckling of super ellipsoidal shells under uniform pressure[J]. Thin-Walled Structures, 2008, 46(6): 584-591.

[4] 王自力,王仁华,俞铭华,李良碧. 初始缺陷对不同深度载人潜水器耐压球壳极限承载力的影响[J]. 中国造船, 2007, 02: 45-50.
[5] 陆蓓,刘涛,崔维成. 深海载人潜水器耐压球壳极限强度研究[J]. 船舶力学, 2004, 01: 51-58.
[6] PANB B, CUI W C. An overview of buckling and ultimate strength of spherical pressure hull under external pressure[J]. Marine Structures, 2010, 23(3): 227-240.
[7] WANG C M, WANG C Y, REDDY J N. Exact solutions for buckling of structural members[M]. CRC Press, 2004.
[8] TIMOSHENKOS P, GERE J M. Theory of elastic stability[M]. Dover Publications, 1961.
[9] 刘涛. 大深度潜水器结构分析与设计研究[D]. 中国船舶科学研究中心. 2001, 3.
[10] TOMASA, TOVAR J P. The influence of initial geometric imperfections on the buckling load of single and double curvature concrete shells[J]. Computers & Structures. 2012, 96(97): 34-45.

Investigation on Mechanical Properties of Deep Sea Spherical Pressure Hull

ZHANG Jian[1,2], GAO Jie[1], WANG Weibo[2], TANG Wenxian[1], ZHOU Tong[1]

(1. Jiangsu University of Science and Technology, Zhenjiang 212003, China;
2. Chinese Ship Scientific Research Center, Jiangsu Wuxi 214082, China)

Abstract

Calculation method for deep sea spherical pressure hull was systematically investigated. Mechanical models for thin shell and thick shell were presented respectively. Effects of meshing, element types and density on numerical results were studied. The results show that, it is suitable to design and assess deep sea spherical pressure hull s using theory of thick shell and numerical models with solid elements. Strength is the primary influence factor in the design. It is suggested that the thickness of the pressure hull should be determined based on the inner stress equation, and then the stability of the hull could be verified by using buckling theory of thick shell and numerical method.

Key words: spherical pressure hull; strength; stability; theory of thick shell

作者简介:
张　建　男,1984年生,博士,讲师。研究方向:深海耐压装备现代设计理论与方法。
高　杰　男,1992年生,硕士研究生。研究方向:深海耐压壳CAE技术研究。
王纬波　男,1969年生,博士,研究院。研究方向:舰船复合材料结构设计。
唐文献　男,1963年生,博士,教授。研究方向:海洋工程结构设计与研究。
周　通　男,1991年生,硕士研究生。研究方向:深海耐压壳CAE技术研究。

9.1.5 稿件录用及后续

(1) 录用邮件

张建:您好!

　　您的论文经审稿后同意在《中国造船》上发表,编辑部就稿件修改还可能和您进一步联系。现将录用通知扫描件发送给您(费用中已包含审稿费和发表后的期刊邮寄(快递)费),请尽快办理汇款等相关事项。并请在回信中给出版面费发票的抬头(单位名)及发票收件人的姓名、联系电话和详细地址。若需要录用通知的原件,我们在收到您的汇款后会将录用通知原件和版面费发票一起寄给您。

收到后请回复。

《中国造船》编辑部　张编辑

注：关于经费，发票等事项，若有问题，请和郑编辑具体联系。

郑编辑的电话：021-63152172-3171；13020187882

邮箱：zhongguozaochuan@aliyun.com（主题栏写郑编辑收）

(2) 录用通知书

稿件录用及收取版面费的通知

张建 同志：

您的论文"深海球形耐压壳力学特性研究"

（作者：张建，高杰，王纬波，唐文献，周通　稿件编号：15086）

通过专家审稿，决定录用，并将在完成全文修改、编辑和定稿后由本刊安排刊登。

本刊根据上级有关指示，收取论文发表版面费，版面费可由作者所在单位支付（可以从课题费中支付）。为此，请您落实将本篇论文的版面费人民币 3900 元，在 30 天内由银行汇寄：

开户：上海中船编印社

账号：1001219709003800450

银行：102290021971-工行中华路支行

或由邮局汇寄：

上海市高雄路 185 号中国造船编辑部（邮政编码:200011）

编辑部收款后将用挂号寄给您电子打印发票。

请您必须把正确的通讯地址、电话号码（最好有手机号码）及时通知编辑部，以便需用。同时，遵照公开出版物保密管理规定，作者需向编辑部提交单位出具的该论文可公开发表的无涉密证明。此外，请您同意论文书面出版后一次性发放稿费（已包括网站、电子出版物出版等全部稿费）的办法，并附上第一作者的身份证复印件，供发放稿费使用；如有不同意见请告之，本刊将另作处理。十分感谢您的支持和合作。

《中国造船》编辑部

2015 年 12 月 23 日

9.2 英文论文实例

9.2.1 《thin-walled structures》投稿指南

DESCRIPTION

Thin-walled structures comprises an important and growing proportion of **engineering construction** with areas of application becoming increasingly diverse, ranging from **aircraft**, **bridges**, **ships** and **oil rigs** to **storage vessels**, **industrial buildings** and **warehouses**.

Many factors, including cost and weight economy, new materials and processes and the growth of powerful methods of analysis have contributed to this growth, and led to the need for a journal which concentrates specifically on structures in which problems arise due to the thinness of the walls. This field includes cold-formed sections, plate and shell structures, reinforced plastics structures and aluminium structures, and is of importance in many branches of engineering.

The primary criterion for consideration of papers in *Thin-Walled Structures* is that they must be concerned with thin-walled structures or the basic problems inherent in thin-walled structures. Provided this criterion is satisfied no restriction is placed on the type of construction, material or field of application. Papers on theory, experiment, design, etc., are published and it is expected that many papers will contain aspects of all three.

Submission

Our online submission system guides you stepwise through the process of entering your article details and uploading your files. The system converts your article files to a single PDF file used in the peer-review process. Editable files (e.g., Word, LaTeX) are required to typeset your article for final publication. All correspondence, including notification of the Editor's decision and requests for revision, is sent by e-mail.

Referees

Please submit the names and institutional e-mail addresses of several potential referees. For more details, visit ourSupport site. Note that the editor retains the sole right to decide whether or not the suggested reviewers are used.

Additional information

Double spacing and a font size of 10 or 12 should be used.

All contributions are read by two or more referees to ensure both accuracy and relevance, and revisions to the script may thus be required. On acceptance, contributions may be subject to editorial amendment to suit house style if necessary. When a manuscript is returned for revision prior to final acceptance, the revised version must be submitted as soon as possible after the author's receipt of the referees' reports. Revised manuscripts returned after two months will be considered as new submissions subject to full rereview.

PREPARATION

Use of word processing software

It is important that the file be saved in the native format of the word processor used. The text should be in single-column format. Keep the layout of the text as simple as possible. Most formatting codes will be removed and replaced on processing the article. In particular, do not use the word processor's options to justify text or to hyphenate words. However, do use bold face, italics, subscripts, superscripts etc. When preparing tables, if you are using a table grid, use only one grid for each individual table and not a grid for each row. If no grid is used, use tabs, not spaces, to align columns. The electronic text should be prepared in a way very similar to that of conventional manuscripts (see also theGuide to Publishing with Elsevier). Note that source files of figures, tables and text graphics will be required whether or not you embed your figures in the text. See also the section on Electronic artwork.

To avoid unnecessary errors you are strongly advised to use the 'spell-check' and 'grammar-check' functions of your word processor.

LaTeX

You are recommended to use the Elsevier article classelsarticle.cls to prepare your manuscript and BibTeX to generate your bibliography.

Our LaTeX site has detailed submission instructions, templates and other information.

Article structure

Subdivision-numbered sections

Divide your article into clearly defined and numbered sections. Subsections should be numbered 1.1 (then 1.1.1, 1.1.2, ⋯), 1.2, etc. (the abstract is not included in section numbering). Use this numbering also for internal cross-referencing: do not just refer to 'the text'. Any subsection may be given a brief heading. Each heading should appear on its own separate line.

Introduction

State the objectives of the work and provide an adequate background, avoiding a detailed literature survey or a summary of the results.

Theory/calculation

A Theory section should extend, not repeat, the background to the article already dealt with in the Introduction and lay the foundation for further work. In contrast, a Calculation section represents a practical development from a theoretical basis.

Results

Results should be clear and concise.

Discussion

This should explore the significance of the results of the work, not repeat them. A combined Results and Discussion section is often appropriate. Avoid extensive citations and discussion of published literature.

Conclusions

The main conclusions of the study may be presented in a short Conclusions section, which may stand alone or form a subsection of a Discussion or Results and Discussion section.

Appendices

If there is more than one appendix, they should be identified as A, B, etc. Formulae and equations in appendices should be given separate numbering: Eq. (A.1), Eq. (A.2), etc.; in a subsequent appendix, Eq. (B.1) and so on. Similarly for tables and figures: Table A.1; Fig. A.1, etc.

Essential title page information
- ***Title.*** Concise and informative. Titles are often used in information-retrieval systems. Avoid abbreviations and formulae where possible.
- ***Author names and affiliations.*** Please clearly indicate the given name(s) and family name(s) of each author and check that all names are accurately spelled. Present the authors' affiliation addresses (where the actual work was done) below the names. Indicate all affiliations with a lowercase superscript letter immediately after the author's name and in front of the appropriate address.

Provide the full postal address of each affiliation, including the country name and, if available, the email address of each author.

- ***Corresponding author.*** Clearly indicate who will handle correspondence at all stages of refereeing and publication, also post-publication. **Ensure that the e-mail address is given and that contact details are kept up to date by the corresponding author.**
- ***Present/permanent address.*** If an author has moved since the work described in the article was done, or was visiting at the time, a 'Present address' (or 'Permanent address') may be indicated as a footnote to that author's name. The address at which the author actually did the work must be retained as the main, affiliation address. Superscript Arabic numerals are used for such footnotes.

Abstract

A concise and factual abstract not exceeding 100 words is required. The abstract should state briefly the purpose of the research, the principal results and major conclusions. An abstract is often presented separately from the article, so it must be able to stand alone. For this reason, References should be avoided, but if essential, then cite the author(s) and year(s). Also, non-standard or uncommon abbreviations should be avoided, but if essential they must be defined at their first mention in the abstract itself.

Graphical abstract

Although a graphical abstract is optional, its use is encouraged as it draws more attention to the online article. The graphical abstract should summarize the contents of the article in a concise, pictorial form designed to capture the attention of a wide readership. Graphical abstracts should be submitted as a separate file in the online submission system. Image size: Please provide an image with a minimum of 531×1328 pixels (h × w) or proportionally more. The image should be readable at a size of 5×13 cm using a regular screen resolution of 96 dpi. Preferred file types: TIFF, EPS, PDF or MS Office files. You can viewExample Graphical Abstracts on our information site. Authors can make use of Elsevier's Illustration and Enhancement service to ensure the best

presentation of their images and in accordance with all technical requirements: Illustration Service.

Highlights

Highlights are mandatory for this journal. They consist of a short collection of bullet points that convey the core findings of the article and should be submitted in a separate editable file in the online submission system. Please use 'Highlights' in the file name and include 3 to 5 bullet points (maximum 85 characters, including spaces, per bullet point). You can viewexample Highlights on our information site.

Keywords

Immediately after the abstract, provide a maximum of 6 keywords, and avoiding general and plural terms and multiple concepts (avoid, for example, " and ", " of"). Be sparing with abbreviations: only abbreviations firmly established in the field may be eligible. These keywords will be used for indexing purposes.

Immediately following the abstract provide a maximum of six keywords which reflect the entries the authors would like to see in an index.

Abbreviations

Define abbreviations that are not standard in this field in a footnote to be placed on the first page of the article. Such abbreviations that are unavoidable in the abstract must be defined at their first mention there, as well as in the footnote. Ensure consistency of abbreviations throughout the article.

Acknowledgements

Collate acknowledgements in a separate section at the end of the article before the references and do not, therefore, include them on the title page, as a footnote to the title or otherwise. List here those individuals who provided help during the research (e.g., providing language help, writing assistance or proof reading the article, etc.).

Formatting of funding sources

List funding sources in this standard way to facilitate compliance to funder's requirements:

Funding: This work was supported by the National Institutes of Health [grant numbers xxxx, yyyy]; the Bill & Melinda Gates Foundation, Seattle, WA [grant number zzzz]; and the United States Institutes of Peace [grant number aaaa].

It is not necessary to include detailed descriptions on the program or type of grants and awards. When funding is from a block grant or other resources available to a university, college, or other research institution, submit the name of the institute or organization that provided the funding.

If no funding has been provided for the research, please include the following sentence:

This research did not receive any specific grant from funding agencies in the public, commercial, or not-for-profit sectors.

Nomenclature and units

Follow internationally accepted rules and conventions: use the international system of units (SI). If other quantities are mentioned, give their equivalent in SI. You are urged to consultIUPAC: Nomenclature of Organic Chemistry for further information.

Math formulae

Please submit math equations as editable text and not as images. Present simple formulae in line with normal text where possible and use the solidus (/) instead of a horizontal line for small fractional terms, e. g., X/Y. In principle, variables are to be presented in italics. Powers of e are often more conveniently denoted by exp. Numberconsecutively any equations that have to be displayed separately from the text (if referred to explicitly in the text).

Footnotes

Footnotes should be used sparingly. Number them consecutively throughout the article. Many word processors can build footnotes into the text, and this feature may be used. Otherwise, please indicate the position of footnotes in the text and list the footnotes themselves separately at the end of the article. Do not include footnotes in the Reference list.

Artwork

Electronic artwork

General points

- Make sure you use uniform lettering and sizing of your original artwork.
- Embed the used fonts if the application provides that option.
- Aim to use the following fonts in your illustrations: Arial, Courier, Times New Roman, Symbol, or use fonts that look similar.
- Number the illustrations according to their sequence in the text.
- Use a logical naming convention for your artwork files.
- Provide captions to illustrations separately.
- Size the illustrations close to the desired dimensions of the published version.
- Submit each illustration as a separate file.

A detailedguide on electronic artwork is available.

You are urged to visit this site; some excerpts from the detailed information are given here.

Formats

If your electronic artwork is created in a Microsoft Office application (Word, PowerPoint, Excel) then please supply 'as is' in the native document format.

Regardless of the application used other than Microsoft Office, when your electronic artwork is finalized, please 'Save as' or convert the images to one of the following formats (note the resolution requirements for line drawings, halftones, and line/halftone combinations given below):

EPS (or PDF): Vector drawings, embed all used fonts.

TIFF (or JPEG): Color or grayscale photographs (halftones), keep to a minimum of 300 dpi.

TIFF (or JPEG): Bitmapped (pure black & white pixels) line drawings, keep to aminimum of 1000 dpi.

TIFF (or JPEG): Combinations bitmapped line/half-tone (color or grayscale), keep to a minimum of 500 dpi.

Please do not:

- Supply files that are optimized for screen use (e. g., GIF, BMP, PICT, WPG); these typically have a low number of pixels and limited set of colors;

- Supply files that are too low in resolution;
- Submit graphics that are disproportionately large for the content.

Color artwork

Please make sure that artwork files are in an acceptable format (TIFF (or JPEG), EPS (or PDF), or MS Office files) and with the correct resolution. If, together with your accepted article, you submit usable color figures then Elsevier will ensure, at no additional charge, that these figures will appear in color online (e. g., ScienceDirect and other sites) regardless of whether or not these illustrations are reproduced in color in the printed version. **For color reproduction in print, you will receive information regarding the costs from Elsevier after receipt of your accepted article.** Please indicate your preference for color: in print or online only. Further information on the preparation of electronic artwork.

Figure captions

Ensure that each illustration has a caption. Supply captions separately, not attached to the figure. A caption should comprise a brief title (**not** on the figure itself) and a description of the illustration. Keep text in the illustrations themselves to a minimum but explain all symbols and abbreviations used.

Tables

Please submit tables as editable text and not as images. Tables can be placed either next to the relevant text in the article, or on separate page(s) at the end. Number tables consecutively in accordance with their appearance in the text and place any table notes below the table body. Be sparing in the use of tables and ensure that the data presented in them do not duplicate results described elsewhere in the article. Please avoid using vertical rules and shading in table cells.

References

Citation in text

Please ensure that every reference cited in the text is also present in the reference list (and vice versa). Any references cited in the abstract must be given in full. Unpublishedresults and personal communications are not recommended in the reference list, but may be mentioned in the text. If these references are included in the reference list they should follow the standard reference style of the journal and should include a substitution of the publication date with either 'Unpublished results' or 'Personal communication'. Citation of a reference as 'in press' implies that the item has been accepted for publication.

Reference links

Increased discoverability of research and high quality peer review are ensured by online links to the sources cited. In order to allow us to create links to abstracting and indexing services, such as Scopus, CrossRef and PubMed, please ensure that data provided in the references are correct. Please note that incorrect surnames, journal/book titles, publication year and pagination may prevent link creation. When copying references, please be careful as they may already contain errors. Use of the DOI is encouraged.

A DOI can be used to cite and link to electronic articles where an article is in-press and full citation details are not yet known, but the article is available online. A DOI is guaranteed never to change, so you can use it as a permanent link to any electronic article. An example of a citation using DOI for an article not yet in an issue is: VanDecar J. C., Russo R. M., James D. E., Ambeh W. B., Franke M. (2003). Aseismic continuation of the Lesser Antilles slab beneath northeastern Venezuela. Journal of Geophysical Research, https://doi.org/10.1029/2001JB000884. Please note the format of such citations should be in the same style as all other references in the paper.

Web references

As a minimum, the full URL should be given and the date when the reference was last accessed. Any further information, if known (DOI, author names, dates, reference to a source publication, etc.), should also be given. Web references can be listed separately (e. g., after the reference list) under a different heading if desired, or can be included in the reference list.

Data references

This journal encourages you to cite underlying or relevant datasets in your manuscript by citing them in your text and including a data reference in your Reference List. Data references should include the following elements: author name(s), dataset title, data repository, version (where available), year, and global persistent identifier. Add [dataset] immediately before the reference so we can properly identify it as a data reference. The [dataset] identifier will not appear in your published article.

References in a special issue

Please ensure that the words 'this issue' are added to any references in the list (and any citations in the text) to other articles in the same Special Issue.

Reference management software

Most Elsevier journals have their reference template available in many of the most popular reference management software products. These include all products that supportCitation Style Language styles, such as Mendeley and Zotero, as well as EndNote. Using the word processor plug-ins from these products, authors only need to select the appropriate journal template when preparing their article, after which citations and bibliographies will be automatically formatted in the journal's style.

If no template is yet available for this journal, please follow the format of the sample references and citations as shown in this Guide.

Users of Mendeley Desktop can easily install the reference style for this journal by clicking the following link:

http://open.mendeley.com/use-citation-style/thin-walled-structures

When preparing your manuscript, you will then be able to select this style using the Mendeley plugins for Microsoft Word or LibreOffice.

Reference formatting

There are no strict requirements on reference formatting at submission. References can be in any style or format as long as the style is consistent. Where applicable, author(s) name(s), journal title/book title, chapter title/article title, year of publication, volume number/book chapter and the pagination must be present. Use of DOI is highly encouraged. The reference style used by the journal will be applied to the accepted article by Elsevier at the proof stage. Note that missing data will be highlighted at proof stage for the author to correct. If you do wish to format the references yourself they should be arranged according to the following examples:

Reference style

   Text: Indicate references by number(s) in square brackets in line with the text. The actual authors can be referred to, but the reference number(s) must always be given.

   Example: '.....as demonstrated [3,6]. Barnaby and Jones [8] obtained a different result ....'

   List: Number the references (numbers in square brackets) in the list in the order in which they appear in the text.

Examples:

Reference to a journal publication:

[1] J. van der Geer, J. A. J. Hanraads, R. A. Lupton, The art of writing a scientific article, J. Sci. Commun. 163 (2010) 51-59.

Reference to a book:

[2] W. Strunk Jr., E. B. White, The Elements of Style, fourth ed., Longman, New York, 2000.

Reference to a chapter in an edited book:

[3] G. R. Mettam, L. B. Adams, How to prepare an electronic version of your article, in: B. S. Jones, R. Z. Smith (Eds.), Introduction to the Electronic Age, E-Publishing Inc., New York, 2009, pp. 281-304.

Reference to a website:

[4] Cancer Research UK, Cancer statistics reports for the UK. http://www.cancerresearchuk.org/aboutcancer/statistics/cancerstatsreport/, 2003 (accessed 13.03.03).

Reference to a dataset:

[dataset] [5] M. Oguro, S. Imahiro, S. Saito, T. Nakashizuka, Mortality data for Japanese oak wilt disease and surrounding forest compositions, Mendeley Data, v1, 2015. https://doi.org/10.17632/xwj98nb39r.1.

Journal abbreviations source

   Journal names should be abbreviated according to theList of Title Word Abbreviations.

9.2.2 投稿信与原始稿

(1) 投稿信

Dear Editor,

   We would like to submit our manuscript entitled "Buckling of spherical shells subjected to external pressure: A comparison of experimental and theoretical data" to "Thin-walled Structures" for publication. No conflict of interest exits in the submission of this manuscript, and manuscript is approved by all authors for publication. The work described was original research that has not been published previously, and not under consideration for publication elsewhere, in whole or in part.

In this work, we tested the geometric and buckling properties of ten laboratory scale spherical shells. The buckling behaviors of these shells were demonstrated analytically and numerically according to experimental data. Moreover, the effects of pure elastic and elastic-perfectly plastic models on the buckling loads of spherical shells were examined numerically. We found that the real load-carrying capacity of a spherical shell can be obtained numerically from measured geometric shape and average wall thickness, as well as from the assumption of elastic-perfectly plastic material properties. The current approach appears to be effective for other shells of revolution with typical or nontypical meridional profiles. We hope this paper is suitable for "Thin-walled Structures".

The following is a list of possible reviewers for your consideration:

1) J. Blachut E-mail: em20@ liverpool. ac. uk

2) P. Jasion E-mail: pawel. jasion@ put. poznan. pl

We deeply appreciate your consideration of our manuscript, and we look forward to receiving comments from the reviewers.

Thank you very much four your time and consideration.

Yours Sincerely,

Jian Zhang, Meng zhang, Wenxian Tang, Weibo Wang, Minglu Wang

Corresponding author:

Name: Meng Zhang

E-mail: zmeng1227@163. com

(2) 原始稿

Buckling of spherical shells subjected to external pressure: A comparison of experimental and theoretical data

Jian Zhang[a, b], Meng Zhang[a*], Wenxian Tang[a], Weibo Wang[b], Minglu Wang[a]

[a]Jiangsu University of Science and Technology, Zhenjiang, Jiangsu, 212003, China

[b]Chinese Ship Scientific Research Center, Wuxi, Jiangsu, 214082, China

* Corresponding author:

Meng Zhang

E-mail: zmeng1227 @ 163. com

Tel & Fax: +86-51184401142

Abstract: This paper focuses on spherical shells under uniform external pressure. Ten laboratory scale models, each with a nominal diameter of 150 mm, were tested. Half of them were manufactured from a 0.4-mm stainless steel sheet, whereas the remaining five shells were manufactured from a 0.7-mm sheet. The geometry, wall thickness, buckling load, and final collapsed mode of each spherical shell were measured, as well as the material properties of the corresponding sheet. The buckling behaviors of these shells were demonstrated analytically and numerically according to experimental data. Analyses involved considering the average geometry, average wall thicknesses, and average elastic material properties. Numerical calculations entailed considering the true geometry, average wall thicknesses, and elastic-plastic modeling of true stress-strain curves. Moreover, the effects of purely elastic and elastic-perfectly plastic models on the buckling loads of spherical shells were examined numerically. The results of the experimental, analytical, and numerical investigations were compared in tables and figures.

Keywords: spherical shell, buckling, external pressure, numerical solution

1. Introduction

For more than 100 years, research has been published on spherical shells subjected to uniform external pressure. Knowledge about this type of loading has been widely applied in various engineering fields such as those involving underwater pressure hulls, underground pressure vessels, and underpressure tanks[1]. In particular, the spherical configuration is broadly considered an ideal structure for the pressure hulls of deep submersibles. This is due to the extremely efficient stress and strain distributions in the material [2, 3]. Although the theoretical buckling loads are high, spherical shells have been found to be highly sensitive to imperfections, and the experimental buckling loads are even lower than theoretical ones.

The difference between theory and experiment has prompted numerous studies regarding the buckling of spherical shells loaded by external pressure. For example, Pan et al. performed a set of experimental and numerical studies on the ultimate strength levels of spherical pressure hulls[4, 5]. Their numerical models were elaborated on the basis of initial equivalent geometric imperfections in the shape of the first eigenmode and a local dimple. Their numerical predictions were verified by pressurizing four laboratory scale spherical hulls to collapse. More recently, Quilliet carried out elasticity theory calculations to predict the collapsed mode of a spherical shell [6]. Quillet's prediction resembled previously published experimental results. However, little attention has been paid to true geometry, including deterministic imperfections and the effects of constitutive models on the buckling of spherical shells. Further study is still necessary in this branch of mechanics.

For investigating the buckling of spherical shells loaded with external pressure, spherical shells were manufactured from 304 stainless steel sheets through stamping and butt-welding processes. The geometric and buckling properties of these spherical shells were demonstrated by aseries of tests. The buckling and postbuckling behaviors were determined numerically and verified experimentally. The numerical analysis was based on deterministic imperfections obtained from measured geometric shapes and elastic-plastic modeling of true stress-strain curves. Furthermore, the effects of constitutive models, such as purely elastic and elastic-perfectly plastic modeling of material, on the buckling loads were studied numerically. This paper aims to provide a rational approach to predicting the real load-carrying capacities of spherical shells.

2. Materials and methods

This study involved sampling and analyzing 10 spherical shells to determine their buckling behaviors. A series of tests were performed to obtain the geometric and buckling properties of these shells in addition to their material properties.

2.1. Shell manufacturing and testing

Each spherical shell was manufactured using the tungsten inert gas butt welding of two coupled hemispherical shells. Each hemispherical shell was cut and stamped from 304 thin stainless steel sheets with a nominal thickness of either 0.4 mm or 0.7 mm. Ten spherical shells with a nominal diameter of 150 mm were manufactured for the tests. Five of them were fabricated from a 0.4-mm-thick sheet and were denoted as t0.4-1, t0.4-2, t0.4-3, t0.4-4, and t0.4-5. Five other shells were fabricated from a 0.7-mm-thick sheet and were denoted as t0.7-1, t0.7-2, t0.7-3, t0.7-4, and t0.7-5. In addition, all the shells were not stress relieved during the manufacturing process because the ratios of the wall thickness to the nominal diameter were very low. Before the spherical shells were tested, the wall thickness and geometric shape were measured for all the shells.

First, the thickness of each wall was measured using an ultrasonic probe at 13 equidistant points along a meridian for eight equally spaced meridians, as detailed in Fig. 1. Each shell was measured at $8 \times 11 + 2 = 90$ points. The values of the minimum (t_{min}), maximum (t_{max}), and average wall thicknesses (t_{ave}), as well as the corresponding standard deviations (t_{std}), are listed in Table 1. The average variation between the maximal and minimal wall thicknesses was approximately 17%, which may be attributed to the stamping process. Second, the geometries of all the spherical shells were obtained using a three-dimensional optical scanner, developed by Open Technologies Corporation. Each shell surface was scanned in the form of a point cloud and automatically transformed into a CAD model. Each model demonstrated the real geometric shape of the corresponding shell, which contained deterministic geometric imperfections caused by manufacturing processes. Furthermore, the minimum (r_{min}), maximum (r_{max}), and average radii (r_{ave}) of each shell were also obtained from the CAD model in addition to the corresponding standard deviations (r_{std}); these values are listed in the final four columns of Table 1.

Thereserve buoyancy values of the spherical shells were considerably high because their buoyant loads were higher than their dead-weight values. For example, the difference between a buoyant load and a dead weight of a $t = 0.4$-mm spherical shell can be as much as 15.12 N, whereas the difference can be approximately 13.50 N for a $t = 0.7$-mm spherical shell. In the experiments, each spherical shell was subjected to a concentrated load inside a pressure chamber. The load was expected to exert a strong influence on the buckling behavior of its spherical shell. To minimize this effect, each spherical shell was encased in a string bag connected to a ballast pig. The weight of the pig was slightly higher than the buoyant load of the spherical shell. The shell, bag, and pig were then immersed together in a cylindrical pressure chamber with a 200-mm inner diameter, 400-mm total length, and 20-MPa maximum pressure. The chamber (located at Jiangsu University of Science and Technology) entailed using water as a pressurizing medium. The pressure inside the chamber was controlled automatically by a programmable logic controller and measured using a pressure transducer. All the spherical shells failed suddenly with substantial decreases in pressure. Thus, determining the buckling load was very simple.

2.2. Material properties

In cases of uniform external pressure, the buckling behaviors of spherical shells are determined according to the compression stress-strain behavior of the relevant material. However, experiments to demonstrate such behaviors with thin-walled structures are extremely difficult to conduct. Therefore, the compression behavior of steel is assumed to be the same as its tension behavior. This hypothesis has been frequently used in the buckling prediction of various shells of revolution loaded by external pressure [7-9]. Thus, the material properties of steel sheets can be established by testing a series of flat tension coupons.

The coupons for this work were designed and tested according to Chinese Standard (GB/T 228.1-2010) [10], which is in line with ISO 6892-1: 2009 [11]. They were cut from the same sheets that were used to manufacture spherical shells for ensuring accurate material data. Five coupons were selected for each thickness and subjected to uniaxial tension. Two of them were strain-gauged in the transverse and longitudinal directions to obtain Poisson's ratio (ν) for the material and to verify the extensometer readings. The average values were 0.277 for the 0.4-mm-thick sheet and 0.291 for the 0.7-mm-thick sheet. Other coupons were tested to obtain accurate stress-strain curves, which can be demonstrated in the following form:

$$\sigma = E\varepsilon, \quad for \sigma < \sigma_y \tag{1a}$$

and

$$\sigma = \sigma_y \sqrt[k]{\left(\frac{E\varepsilon}{\sigma_y} - 1\right)n}, \tag{1b}$$

where E is Young's modulus, σ_{yp} is the yield strength based on 0.2% proof stress, and n and k are the strain hardening parameters. The values of these coefficients, as well as the average values, are listed in Table 2. The testing coupons were numbered and named according to the thickness and coupon number; one name, for example, was t0.4-c1, where t0.4 indicates that the thickness of the sheet was 0.4 mm, and c1 indicates that the coupon number was one. The variance of coefficients for each thickness was very small.

3. Results and discussion

Previous studies have indicated that the experimental buckling loads of spherical shells are lower than theoretical predictions [3, 12]. This phenomenon may result from inevitable geometric imperfections and from nonlinear material properties. This problem of classical mechanics is far from being solved; the buckling analysis of spherical shells remains to be vivid and is still challenging.

This section reports how the buckling loads and final collapsed modes of a family of spherical shells were determined from hydrostatic tests. The results of analytical and numerical investigations into these shells are presented and compared with the experimental findings. The effects of constitutive models on the buckling load are discussed.

3.1. Experimental and analytical results analysis

The experimental buckling loads are listed in column 2 of Table 3, and graphed in Fig. 2. Photographs of the final collapsed modes for 10 spherical shells are presented in Fig. 3. Notably, the buckling load of the t0.7-2 spherical shell was not recorded because of an incorrect operation during the testing process. However, the final collapsed mode of this shell was still obtained. The buckling loads of the 0.4-mm-thick spherical shells ranged between 1.330 and

1.956 MPa, whereas the 0.7-mm-thick shell buckling loads ranged between 3.178 and 4.692 MPa. The buckling loads of the 0.7-mm-thick shell loads were more than twice those of the 0.4-mm-thick shell loads. This variance mainly affected by the ratio of the average wall thickness (t_{ave}) to the average radius (r_{ave}), as illustrated in Fig. 2. The experimental buckling load increased monotonically with an increase in t_{ave}/r_{ave}. As shown in Fig. 3, the final collapsed modes of all shells are identical, and all of them have the form of a local dent because of the high ductility of stainless steel and the initial geometric imperfections of the shells. This failure mode is consistent with previous experimental results regarding shells of revolution with a positive Gaussian curvature, such as those for spherical shells reported by Quilliet [6], for ellipsoidal shells reported by Healey [13], and for barreled shells reported by Blachut [8, 14].

Atheory derived by Zoelly [15] predicts the elastic buckling load (p_{cr}) of spherical shells, which is obtained using

$$P_{cr} = \frac{2E}{\sqrt{3(1-\nu^2)}}\left(\frac{t}{R}\right)^2, \tag{2}$$

where the wall thickness t, radius r, Young's modulus E, and Poisson's ratio ν are assumed to be average values of the experimental results (Tables 1 and 2). This analytical formula is widely accepted in ocean and aerospace engineering as a rule for designing spherical shells [3, 16, 17]. The results of Eq. (2) are listed in column 3 of Table 3, followed by the ratio of the experimental load p_{test} to the elastic buckling load p_{zoelly} in parentheses. As shown in the table, the experimental load of a spherical shell was as little as 15.07%-24.55% of that shell's elastic buckling load, confirming that the spherical shell is a highly imperfection-sensitive structure. A small imperfection may lead to a substantial decrease in the magnitude of the buckling load. Furthermore, the average ratio of the experimental load p_{test} to the elastic buckling load p_{zoelly} for 0.4-mm-thick spherical shells was approximately 3% lower than the ratio for 0.7-mm-thick shells. It appears that the nonlinear properties of spherical shells' materials may play a major role in the buckling behaviors of shells with various wall thicknesses.

3.2. Comparison of experimental and numerical results

Prior work has demonstrated the effectiveness of the finite element method in predicting the buckling behaviors of thin-walled structures. Schmidt, for example, suggested that the real buckling load of a shell can be determined using geometrically and materially nonlinear analyses of shells that include imperfections [18, 19]. However, most studies have focused on equivalent geometric imperfections, such as eigenmode imperfections, in numerically analyzing the buckling of spherical shells.

In thisstudy, we carried out nonlinear buckling analysis for the same types of spherical shells as would be tested for deterministic imperfections. The analysis was performed using the modified Riks method in ABAQUS software [20]. The finite element model of each spherical shell was established according to the real geometric shape obtained from the experimental data. The shapes and sizes of the initial geometric imperfections were automatically included in the models. A fully integrated S4 shell was selected to avoid hourglassing. The number of elements was determined using mesh density convergence analysis in line with [21]. In all the analyses, a $p_0 = 1$ MPa external pressure was applied on the whole area of each shell. To avoid rigid body motion, three random spatial points were respectively constrained in the three orthogonal directions. These constraints did not lead to overconstrained models because the pressure was equally applied. The steel was assumed to be elastic-plastic as described in Eq. (1). In addition, the average wall thickness (column 4 of Table 1) and material properties (Table 2) were defined in the analyses. Fig. 4 and the final column of Table 3 show the results obtained using numerical analysis.

Becausethe equilibrium paths, critical buckling, and postbuckling modes of all the analyzed shells were similar, detailed results are provided only for the case of t0.4-1. Fig. 4 shows the equilibrium path of a shell; the vertical axis shows the applied load normalized by the initial applied load $p_0 = 1$ MPa, and the horizontal axis shows the maximum deflection (Δ) normalized by the wall thickness (t). The path has an unstable characteristic that is typical of shell structures: At first, the load increases nearly linearly with an increase in the deflection up to a peak corresponding to the critical buckling load, beyond which the load decreases sharply. The same figure shows that the buckling and postbuckling modes are similar and assume the form of a local dent. This may have been caused by the initial deterministic imperfections of the shell. Comparing Figs. 3 and 4 show that the predicted final failure mode is highly consistent with the experimental one. In addition, as indicated in the final column of Table 3, excellent correlation between the numerical buckling loads and the experimental ones was obtained ($\pm 7\%$). This slight difference may be attributed to small variations of the material properties for the steel sheets, in addition to the assumption of the average wall thickness used to perform numerical calculation. These findings indicate that the real buckling resistance of a spherical shell can be determined numerically on the basis of its true geometry as well as its average wall thickness and material properties.

In the same figure, the first yield load of t0.4-1 is plotted at the value of 1.466 MPa, which was obtained using the postprocessing procedure as in Ref. [22]. The first yield load was approximately 84% of the critical buckling load. At the first stage of testing up to this value, the spherical shell had an elastic characteristic. At the second stage of testing higher than this value, the spherical shell appeared to be elastic-plastic. This phenomenon was observed for all the cases shown in Table 4. For spherical shells, the ratio of the first yield to the critical buckling load, $p_{ABAQUS}^{fyd}/p_{ABAQUS}^{elastic-plastic}$, varied between 0.681 and 0.895. It is suggested that all the spherical shells could lose stability within the elastic-plastic regime. This finding is similar to those regarding medium-thick conical shells subjected to external pressure [9].

3.3. Effect ofconstitutive models

It iswell known that the modeling of materials strongly influences the accuracy of numerical results. Most recent numerical investigations on the buckling of shell structures have assumed the material properties to be either purely elastic [23] or elastic-perfectly plastic [8, 14]. To examine this assumption, the effect of constitutive models on the buckling of spherical shells was investigated in the present study. The same numerical models as those mentioned in Section 3.2 were employed, except that the steel was assumed to be elastic and elastic-perfectly plastic. The material parameters were determined on the basis of the average values listed in Table 2; 20 models were accounted for. Because the equilibrium paths, critical buckling modes, and postbuckling modes of these cases were almost identical with the elastic-plastic results for t0.4-1 shown in Fig. 4, the effects of constitutive models were examined according to the critical buckling load only. Table 5 shows the buckling loads $p_{ABAQUS}^{elastic}$ and $p_{ABAQUS}^{elastic\text{-}perfectly\ plastic}$ obtained from elastic and elastic-perfectly plastic assumptions, respectively, and the values normalized by elastic-plastic $p_{ABAQUS}^{elastic\text{-}plastic}$ and experimental p_{test} buckling loads are in parentheses.

As shown in Table 5, the elastic assumption yielded an increase of 53.98%-135.55% in the magnitude of the buckling load over that of the elastic-plastic assumption. A fairly large difference existed between the results obtained according to the purely elastic assumption and those of the experiments. This finding indicates that numerical predictions based on the purely elastic assumption are extremely nonconservative and are not suitable for engineering applications. However, the differences between the elastic and elastic-plastic results for 0.4-mm-thick spherical shells are always higher than those for 0.7-mm-thick shells. This implies that the failures of spherical shells vary gradually from elastic buckling to elastic-plastic buckling as the wall thicknesses increase. It is more reasonable to include plastic material properties when performing buckling analysis on a medium-thick shell structure.

As shown in Table 5, the elastic-perfectly plastic predictions deviated from the elastic-plastic predictions by as little as 6%. Excellent agreement was obtained between the elastic-plastic and elastic-perfectly plastic results. The maximum difference between a prediction from the elastic-perfectly plastic assumption and that from the experiment was only 8%. This confirms that the buckling of a shell is greatly determined according to its stress behavior, particularly its yield [24]. It could be inferred that aside from the elastic material properties, the buckling load of a shell strongly depends on the yield strength of the material. This finding extends those of Bluchat [8, 14], confirming that the elastic-perfectly plastic assumption can be made in the buckling analysis of shells, and tends to result in extremely accurate predictions.

4. Conclusions

In the present work, the results of experimental, analytical, and numerical study into the buckling behaviors of spherical shells are presented, as well as the effects of constitutive modes on the buckling loads of these shells. The experimental buckling load increased monotonically with an increase in t_{ave}/r_{ave}, which was as little as 15.07%-24.55% of the elastic buckling load determined using Zoelly's equation. The experimental collapsed modes of all the shells were identical; all of them assumed the form of a local dent, which is typical of shells of revolution with a positive Gaussian curvature.

Geometrically and materially nonlinear buckling analyses were performed on the spherical shells for deterministic imperfections. Excellent correlation was obtained between the numerical buckling loads and the experimental ones. The path of each spherical shell had an unstable characteristic typical of shell structures. All the shells buckled within an elastic-plastic range. The buckling and postbuckling modes of all the analyzed shells were similar and assumed the form of a local dent, which was in excellent agreement with the experimental results.

Theeffects of constitutive models on the buckling of spherical shells were demonstrated numerically according to the buckling load. The failures of spherical shells varied gradually from elastic buckling to elastic-plastic buckling as the wall thicknesses increased. Excellent agreement was obtained among the elastic-plastic, elastic-perfectly plastic, and experimental results. The elastic-perfectly plastic assumption resulted in a highly accurate prediction. The elastic assumption yielded a fairly large increase in the magnitude of the buckling load above the elastic-plastic assumption and experiment.

Thiswork therefore indicates that the real load-carrying capacity of a spherical shell can be obtained numerically from measured geometric shape and average wall thickness, as well as from the assumption of elastic-perfectly plastic material properties. The current approach appears to be effective for other shells of revolution with typical meridional profiles, such as cylindrical and conical shells, as well as for shells of revolution with nontypical meridional profiles, such as barreled and egg-shaped shells. However, some limitations merit attention. Although the predicted buckling loads and final failure modes were verified experimentally, the critical buckling modes were not examined through testing. Moreover, the manufacturing process caused some variance in the wall thicknesses, and that variance exerted an effect on the buckling of spherical shells; however, this effect was not studied. These limitations require further investigation in the near future.

Acknowledgments

This work was supported by two grants from the Natural Science Foundation of Jiangsu Province, China (BK20140512, BK20150469).

References

[1] J. Blachut, Experimental perspective on the buckling of pressure vessel components, Appl. Mech. Rev. 66 (2013) 010803-1-010803-24.

[2] B. B. Pan, W. C. Cui, An overview of buckling and ultimate strength of spherical pressure hull under external pressure, Mar. Struct. 23 (2010) 227-240.

[3] B. B. Pan, W. C. Cui, A comparison of different rules for the spherical pressure hull of deep manned submersibles, J. Ship Mech. 15 (2011) 276-285.

[4] B. B. Pan, W. C. Cui, Y. S. Shen, T. Liu, Further study on the ultimate strength analysis of spherical pressure hulls, Mar. Struct. 23 (2010) 444-461.

[5] B. B. Pan, W. C. Cui, Y. S. Shen, Experimental verification of the new ultimate strength equation of spherical pressure hulls, Mar. Struct. 29 (2012) 169-176.

[6] C. Quilliet, Depressions at the surface of an elastic spherical shell submitted to external pressure, Phys. Rev. E. 74 (2006) 046608-1-046608-6.

[7] H. Schmidt, P. Swadlo, Part C-Shells of revolution with Arbitrary meridional shapes-Buckling design by use of computer analysis, ECSC contract No. 7210-SA/208: Enhancement of ECCS design recommendations and development of Eurocode 3 parts related to shell buckling, Final Report, Universität GH Essen, FB Bauwesen· Stahlbau, 1996.

[8] J. Błachut, Optimal barreling of steel shells via simulated annealing algorithm, Comput. Struct. 81 (2003) 1941-1956.

[9] J. Błachut, A. Muc, J. Ryś, Plastic buckling of cones subjected to axial compression and external pressure,

J. Press. Vessel. Technol. 135 (2013) 011205-1-011205-9.

[10] GB/T 228.1: Metallic materials-Tensile testing-Part 1: Method of test at room temperature, Chinese Standard Institute, china, 2010.

[11] ISO 6892-1: Metallic materials-Tensile testing-Part 1: Method of test at room temperature, International Organization for Standardization, 2009.

[12] T. Von Kármán, H. S. Tsien, The buckling of Spherical Shells by External Pressure, J. Aeronaut. Sci. 7 (1939) 43-50 (doi: 10.2514/8.1019).

[13] J. J. Healey, Hydrostatic tests of two prolate spheroidal shells, J. Ship Res. 9 (1965) 77-78.

[14] J. Błachut, Buckling of externally pressurised barrelled shells: a comparison of experiment and theory, Int. J. Press. Vessel. Pip. 79 (2002) 507-517.

[15] R. Zoelly, Über ein Knickungs problem an der Kugelschale, Zürich, 1915.

[16] CCS. Rules for the classification and construction of diving systems and submersibles, China Classification Society, china, 1996.

[17] NASA SP-8032. Buckling of thin-walled doubly curved shells, National Aeronautics and Space Administration, Washington, 1969.

[18] H. Schmidt, Stability of steel shell structures: General Report, J. Constr. Steel Res. 55 (2000) 159-181.

[19] EN 1993-1-6: Eurocode 3-Design of steel structures-Part 1.6: Strength and Stability of shell structures, CEN, Brussels, 2007.

[20] K. Hibbitt, S. Inc, ABAQUS-Theory and Standard User's Manual Version 6.3, USA, 2006.

[21] P. Jasion, K. Magnucki, Elastic buckling of clothoidal-spherical shells under external pressure-theoretical study, Thin-Walled Struct. 86 (2015) 18-23.

[22] J. Błachut, O. Ifayefunmi, Buckling of unstiffened steel cones subjected to axial compression and external pressure, J. Offshore Mech. Arct. Eng. 134 (2012) 031603-1-031603-9.

[23] P. Jasion, K. Magnucki, Elastic buckling of classini ovaloidal shells under external pressure-theoretical study, Arch. Mech. 67 (2015) 179-192.

[24] M. Barski, J. Krużelecki, Optimal design of shells against buckling under overall bending and external pressure, Thin-Walled Struct. 43 (2005) 1677-1698.

Table 1

Testing values of the wall thickness and radius for spherical shells (minimum, maximum, average, and standard deviation)

	t_{min} (mm)	t_{max} (mm)	t_{ave} (mm)	t_{std} (mm)	r_{min} (mm)	r_{max} (mm)	r_{ave} (mm)	r_{std} (mm)
t0.4-1	0.382	0.476	0.422	0.022	73.903	74.485	74.248	0.174
t0.4-2	0.396	0.496	0.432	0.024	73.843	74.517	74.163	0.170
t0.4-3	0.378	0.488	0.426	0.024	74.067	74.285	74.157	0.046
t0.4-4	0.382	0.436	0.401	0.010	74.304	74.754	74.548	0.133
t0.4-5	0.382	0.476	0.414	0.016	73.817	74.501	74.185	0.158
t0.7-1	0.650	0.754	0.708	0.024	74.231	75.005	74.710	0.249
t0.7-2	0.614	0.766	0.715	0.024	74.391	75.291	74.926	0.242
t0.7-3	0.644	0.746	0.723	0.02	74.282	75.102	75.023	0.142
t0.7-4	0.652	0.756	0.724	0.019	74.300	75.062	74.840	0.184
t0.7-5	0.648	0.762	0.716	0.021	74.317	75.001	74.983	0.252

Table 2

Material properties of 304 stainless steel obtained from uniaxial tension tests (E-Young's modulus; σ_{yp}-yield strength; n and k-strain hardening parameter)

	E(GPa)	σ_{yp}(MPa)	n	k
t0.4-c1	193.1	250.9	0.108	4.154
t0.4-c2	188.4	241.4	0.101	3.896
t0.4-c3	190.5	246.2	0.091	4.319
t0.4-average	190.7	246.1	0.100	4.123
t0.7-c1	187.2	288.5	0.081	4.291
t0.7-c2	180.3	292.0	0.088	4.733
t0.7-c3	197.1	294.2	0.118	4.972
t0.7-average	188.2	291.6	0.096	4.665

Table 3

Experimental (p_{test}), analytical (p_{zoelly}), and numerical ($p_{ABAQUS}^{elastic-plastic}$) buckling loads of spherical shells. The analytical and numerical values were normalized by the experimental values and are in parentheses

	p_{test}(MPa)	p_{zoelly}(MPa)	($p_{ABAQUS}^{elastic-plastic}$(MPa)
t0.4-1	1.708	7.586(4.44)	1.745(1.02)
t0.4-2	1.956	7.968(4.07)	1.946(0.99)
t0.4-3	1.773	7.749(4.37)	1.708(0.96)
t0.4-4	1.330	6.795(5.11)	1.332(1.00)
t0.4-5	1.594	7.313(4.59)	1.708(1.07)
t0.7-1	3.178	21.089(6.64)	3.155(0.99)
t0.7-2	NA	21.384(NA)	4.317(NA)
t0.7-3	4.496	21.809(4.85)	4.716(1.05)
t0.7-4	4.692	21.976(4.68)	4.397(0.94)
t0.7-5	3.974	21.412(5.39)	4.006(1.01)

Table 4

First yield load p_{ABAQUS}^{fyd} values of spherical shells and the ratio of the first yield and critical buckling load $p_{ABAQUS}^{fyd}/p_{ABAQUS}^{elastic-plastic}$

	p_{ABAQUS}^{fyd}(MPa)	$p_{ABAQUS}^{fyd}/p_{ABAQUS}^{elastic-plastic}$
t0.4-1	1.466	0.840
t0.4-2	1.407	0.723
t0.4-3	1.531	0.896
t0.4-4	0.907	0.681
t0.4-5	1.528	0.895
t0.7-1	2.392	0.758
t0.7-2	3.401	0.788
t0.7-3	3.904	0.828
t0.7-4	3.905	0.888
t0.7-5	3.402	0.849

Table 5
Buckling loads of spherical shells obtained from elastic and elastic-perfectly plastic models. Values in parentheses were normalized by the elastic-plastic and experimental buckling loads, respectively

	$p_{ABAQUS}^{elastic}$ (MPa)	$p_{ABAQUS}^{elastic-perfectly\ plastic}$ (MPa)
t0.4-1	3.146(1.80, 1.84)	1.722(0.99, 1.01)
t0.4-2	3.389(1.74, 1.73)	1.823(0.94, 0.93)
t0.4-3	2.941(1.72, 1.65)	1.630(0.95, 0.92)
t0.4-4	2.051(1.54, 1.54)	1.332(1.00, 1.00)
t0.4-5	3.174(1.86, 1.99)	1.712(1.00, 1.07)
t0.7-1	5.930(1.88, 1.87)	2.953(0.94, 0.92)
t0.7-2	9.549(2.21, NA)	4.206(0.97, NA)
t0.7-3	10.174(2.16, 2.31)	4.483(0.95, 1.02)
t0.7-4	10.357(2.36, 2.21)	4.383(1.00, 0.93)
t0.7-5	9.035(2.26, 2.27)	3.953(0.99, 0.99)

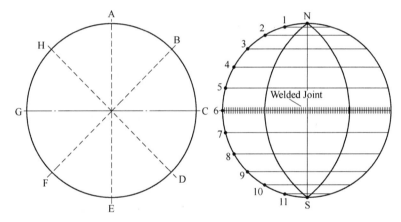

Fig. 1. Typical distribution of testing points for wall thickness.

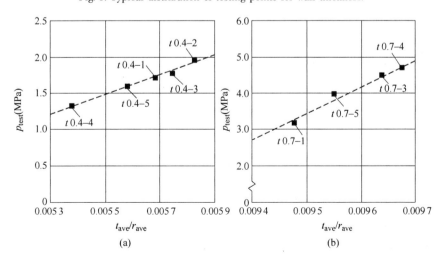

Fig. 2. Plots of experimental buckling load versus ratio of average wall thickness (t_{ave}) to average radius (r_{ave}) of spherical shells; a = 0.4-mm spherical shells, b = 0.7-mm spherical shells.

Fig. 3. Views of spherical shells after collapse caused by external hydrostatic pressure; all final failure modes assumed the form of a local dimple.

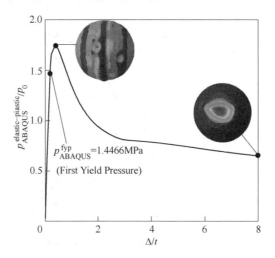

Fig. 4. Equilibrium path, critical buckling mode, and postbuckling mode of a t0.4-1 spherical shell.

9.2.3　一通意见答复与修改稿

（1）编辑与专家意见

Comments from the editors and reviewers:

TWS_ 2016_ 349

Buckling of spherical shells subjected to external pressure: a comparison of experimental and theoretical data

The manuscript reports experimental data on collapse of ten stainless steel full spheres (D/t = 375 & 214). Some FE results are also provided. Spheres were made by back-to-back welding of two stamped hemispheres.

The manuscript is chaotically arranged and it should not be considered for publication in its present form but it merits publication once the following concerns are fully addressed:

1. Most of the references provided are not cited in the manuscript. Those which are-are not uniquely identified. The list appears to be adequate.

2. Introduction has to be re-written in order to give the state-of-the-art of the field, and reason why this research has been undertaken.

3. In keywords please include '304 steel'

4. Thin steel sheets usually show anisotropy caused by manufacturing process. Elaborate how the test specimens were cut with respect to rolling directions?

5. On page 4 provide details of calculations showing how the net buoyancy of 15.1N was derived. It might be worth expanding the text here saying that the spheres were empty and they were floating in the test vessel. A sketch here would be helpful. The expression "... a concentrated load inside..." is unclear-please remove.

6. Describe the weld-prep. Was the excess of the weld removed by grinding or left? Another sketch (or close) photograph of the equatorial weld would be helpful.

7. The wall thickness of stamped hemispheres varies along the meridian. Two actions are requested here: (i) provide overall average wall thickness profile from the North-Pole to the South Pole for a single sphere (by summing all readings at the same lattitude and then dividing by number of measuring points), and (ii) provide contours of wall thickness on a plane.

8. Elaborate on the spring-back after stamping (has there been any, if not how big this was, ec.).

9. Provide contours of local radii of curvature for a typical hemisphere.

10. Provide the number of the FE elements used in the models, and elaborate whether the mesh was uniform and how you have handled the apex area. Adding a mesh, as a figure, would be advisable.

11. In conlusions substitute 'excellent' by 'very good'.

12. Fig. 3 indicates that (probably) only in two cases the buckles were close to the weld line. In all other cases spheres failed in either North or South hemispheres. It would be beneficial to add another set of photograps showing the weld line.

13. It is suggested that that the following paper is added to references: J. Blachut, G. D. Galletly, D. N. Moreton, "Buckling of near-perfect steel torispherical and hemispherical shells subjected to external pressure", AIAA J., vol. 28, 1990, 1971-1975. It is directly relevant to the substance of this manuscript.

(2) 专家意见答复及修改说明
1) 专家意见回复信

Ref: TWST_ 2016_ 349
Dear Editor,

Thank you very much for your email with reviewers' comments to our paper "Buckling of spherical shells subjected to external pressure: A comparison of experimental and theoretical data".

We have made some revisions to our paper according to the reviewers' suggestions. And also we have formed the explanations to questions which reviewers were concerned in their comments.

Please find attached word documents of the revised version of our paper together with responses to the comments of reviewers respectively. If there is anything else, please just let me know.

Many thanks for your attention and looking forward to your response.

Faithfully Yours

Mr. Zhang

Research Assistant of Mechanical Engineering

Jiangsu University of Science and Technology

2) 专家意见答复及修改说明

Responses to the reviewers' comments

1. **Reviewer's comments**: Most of the references provided are not cited in the manuscript. Those which are-are not uniquely identified. The list appears to be adequate.

1. Accepted. Every reference provided in the reference list has been cited in the revised manuscript. This has been done according to "GUIDE FOR AUTHORS" of "THIN-WALLED STRUCTURES".

2. **Reviewer's comments**: Introduction has to be re-written in order to give the state-of-the-art of the field, and reason why this research has been undertaken.

2. Accepted. We have rewritten the Introduction section in order to present the state-of-the-art of the field, and the reason why this research has been undertaken:

3. **Reviewer's comments**: In keywords please include '304 steel'.

3. Accepted. The correction has been made in the revised version.

4. **Reviewer's comments**: Thin steel sheets usually show anisotropy caused by manufacturing process. Elaborate how the test specimens were cut with respect to rolling directions?

4. Accepted. The correction has been made in the revised version. "They were cut from the same sheets that were used to manufacture spherical shells for ensuring accurate material data." has been replaced by "They were cut along the rolling directions of the same sheets that were used to manufacture spherical shells for ensuring accurate material data.".

5. **Reviewer's comments**: On page 4 provide details of calculations showing how the net buoyancy of 15.1N was derived. It might be worth expanding the text here saying that the spheres were empty and they were floating in the test vessel. A sketch here would be helpful. The expression "... a concentrated load inside..." is unclear-please remove.

5. Accepted. We have provided details of calculations showing how the net buoyancy of 15.1N was derived, in the revised version.

6. **Reviewer's comments**: Describe the weld-prep. Was the excess of the weld removed by grinding or left? Another sketch (or close) photograph of the equatorial weld would be helpful.

6. Accepted. The excess of the weld for each spherical shell has been removed by grinding and then been polished. We have added this description in the the revised version. However, another sketch (or close) photograph of the equatorial weld was not readily available, because it is difficult to identify the weld line on the polished spherical shells.

7. **Reviewer's comments**: The wall thickness of stamped hemispheres varies along the meridian. Two actions are requested here: (i) provide overall average wall thickness profile from the North-Pole to the South Pole for a single sphere (by summing all readings at the same lattitude and then dividing by number of measuring points), and (ii) provide contours of wall thickness on a plane.

7. **Accepted.** We have provided overall average wall thickness profile from the North-Pole to the South Pole for a t0.4-1 spherical shell in the revised version. However, giving the contours of wall thickness on a plane seems to be inappropriate because of a few measuring points. Therefore, we have provided thicknesses of all measure points for a t0.4-1 spherical shell in the revised version. The added graph and table are as follows:

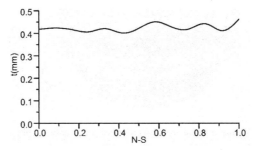

Fig. 2. Overall average wall thickness profile from the North-Pole to the South Pole for a t0.4-1 spherical shell.

Table 2   Thickness (in mm) at 13 equidistant points along 8 meridians for a t0.4-1 spherical shell

Longtitude no.	Lattitude no.							
	A	B	C	D	E	F	G	H
1	0.416	0.422	0.420	0.41	0.426	0.458	0.426	0.412
2	0.436	0.410	0.408	0.404	0.436	0.416	0.410	0.408
3	0.426	0.426	0.398	0.382	0.422	0.408	0.394	0.396
4	0.428	0.432	0.412	0.464	0.410	0.422	0.398	0.4
5	0.402	0.396	0.418	0.388	0.402	0.398	0.408	0.398
6	0.425	0.415	0.418	0.42	0.419	0.416	0.432	0.431
7	0.406	0.466	0.408	0.408	0.392	0.396	0.396	0.418
8	0.414	0.434	0.432	0.432	0.456	0.47	0.476	0.424
9	0.398	0.438	0.418	0.406	0.416	0.416	0.446	0.414
10	0.428	0.446	0.406	0.414	0.424	0.42	0.458	0.414
11	0.456	0.446	0.436	0.45	0.446	0.45	0.472	0.454

The thicknesses atthe North-Pole and South-pole are 0.418 and 0.462 respectively.

8. **Reviewer's comments**: Elaborate on the spring-back after stamping (has there been any, if not how big this was, ec.).

8. It is really true, as the reviewer suggested, that the spring-back exists after stamping of each spherical shell. We did not consider this phenomenon because it seems to be beyond the scope of this study. Nevertheless, the geometric properties of manufactured spherical shells including spring-back were tested experimentally. Hence, we think it will not influence our research conclusion.

9. Reviewer's comments: Provide contours of local radii of curvature for a typical hemisphere.

9. Accepted. We have provided contours of local radii of curvature for a t0.4-1 spherical shell in the revised version, as follows:

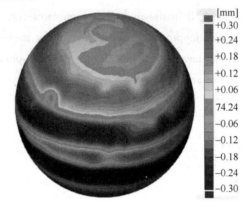

Fig. 3. Contours of local radii of curvature for a t0.4-1 spherical shell.

10. Reviewer's comments: Provide the number of the FE elements used in the models, and elaborate whether the mesh was uniform and how you have handled the apex area. Adding a mesh, as a figure, would be advisable.

10. Accepted. The correction has been made in the revised version, as follows:

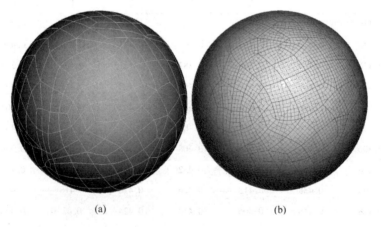

Fig. 6. Scanned CAD model (a) for a t0.4-1 spherical shell and its mesh (b).

Table 5 Number of the FE elements for each spherical shell.

	t0.4-1	t0.4-2	t0.4-3	t0.4-4	t0.4-5	t0.7-1	t0.7-2	t0.7-3	t0.7-4	t0.7-5
S4	6746	6643	6820	6298	6264	6430	6348	6287	6436	6447
S3	1064	448	1110	1134	1064	1118	1212	1180	1170	1216

11. **Reviewer's comments**: In conclusions substitute 'excellent' by 'very good'.

11. Accepted. The correction has been made in the revised version.

12. **Reviewer's comments**: Fig. 3 indicates that (probably) only in two cases the buckles were close to the weld line. In all other cases spheres failed in either North or South hemispheres. It would be beneficial to add another set of photographs showing the weld line.

12. Accepted. We have added a red line showing the weld line in Fig. 3, as follows:

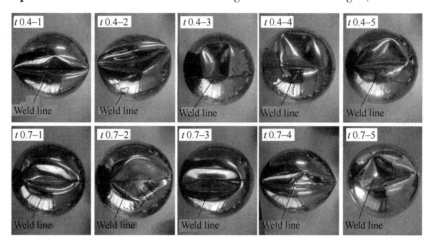

Fig. 3. Views of spherical shells after collapse caused by external hydrostatic pressure; All final failure modes assumed the form of a local dimple.

13. **Reviewer's comments**: It is suggested that the following paper be added to references: J. Blachut, G. D. Galletly, D. N. Moreton, "Buckling of near-perfect steel torispherical and hemispherical shells subjected to external pressure", AIAA J., vol. 28, 1990, 1971-1975. It is directly relevant to the substance of this manuscript.

13. Accepted. We have added this reference in Introduction section.

(3) 修改稿

Buckling of Spherical Shells Subjected to External Pressure: A Comparison of Experimental and Theoretical Data

Jian Zhang[a, b], Meng Zhang[a*], Wenxian Tang[a], Weibo Wang[b], Minglu Wang[a]

[a]Jiangsu University of Science and Technology, Zhenjiang, Jiangsu, 212003, China

[b]Chinese Ship Scientific Research Center, Wuxi, Jiangsu, 214082, China

* Corresponding author:

Meng Zhang

E-mail: zmeng1227@163.com

Tel & Fax: +86-51184401142

Abstract: This paper focuses on spherical shells under uniform external pressure. Ten laboratory scale models, each with a nominal diameter of 150 mm, were tested. Half of them were manufactured from a 0.4-mm stainless steel sheet, whereas the remaining five shells were manufactured from a 0.7-mm sheet. The geometry, wall thickness, buckling load, and final collapsed mode of each spherical shell were measured, as well as the material properties of the corresponding sheet. The buckling behaviors of these shells were demonstrated analytically and numerically according to experimental data. Analyses involved considering the average geometry, average wall thicknesses, and average elastic material properties. Numerical calculations entailed considering the true geometry, average wall thicknesses, and elastic-plastic modeling of true stress-strain curves. Moreover, the effects of purely elastic and elastic-perfectly plastic models on the buckling loads of spherical shells were examined numerically. The results of the experimental, analytical, and numerical investigations were compared in tables and figures.

Keywords: spherical shell, 304 steel, buckling, external pressure, numerical solution

1. Introduction

For more than 100 years, research has been published on spherical shells subjected to uniform external pressure. Knowledge about this type of loading has been widely applied in various engineering fields such as those involving underwater pressure hulls, underground pressure vessels, and underpressure tanks [1, 2]. In particular, the spherical configuration is broadly considered an ideal structure for the pressure hulls of deep submersibles. This is due to the extremely efficient stress and strain distributions in the material [3, 4]. Although the theoretical elastic buckling loads are high, the spherical shells have been found to be highly imperfection sensitive and be strongly affected by plastic material properties. The experimental buckling loads are even lower than the theoretical ones.

The difference between theory and experiment has prompted numerous studies regarding the buckling of spherical shells loaded by external pressure. For example, Blachut et al. presented a series of experimental and numerical studies concerning elastic-plastic buckling of spherical [5], torispherical [6], conical [7, 8] or barreled shells [9, 10] under external pressure. In most of their studies, the material was assumed to be elastic-perfectly plastic. The effects of initial geometric imperfections were also taken into account, which included eigenmode imperfections derived from linear elastic buckling analysis of the perfect geometries or deterministic ones derived from a limited number of measuring points. Moreover, Pan et al. performed a set of experimental and numerical studies on the ultimate strength levels of spherical pressure hulls used in deep submersibles [11, 12]. Their numerical models were elaborated on the basis of initial equivalent geometric imperfections in the shape of the first eigenmode and a local dimple. Their numerical predictions were verified by pressurizing four laboratory scale spherical hulls to collapse. More recently, Quilliet carried out elasticity theory calculations to predict the collapsed mode of a spherical shell [13]. Quillet's prediction resembled previously published experimental results. However, little attention has been paid to true geometry, including deterministic imperfections, derived from a more precise measurement. And the effects of plastic material properties including or excluding yield strengths and hardening parameters on the buckling of spherical shells were rarely investigated as well. Further study is still necessary in this branch of mechanics.

For investigating the buckling of spherical shells loaded with external pressure, spherical shells were manufactured from 304 stainless steel sheets through stamping and butt-welding processes. The geometric and buckling properties of these spherical shells were demonstrated by a series of tests. The buckling and postbuckling behaviors were determined numerically and verified experimentally. The numerical analysis was based on deterministic imperfections obtained from measured geometric shapes and elastic-plastic modeling of true stress-strain curves. Furthermore, the effects of constitutive models, such as purely elastic and elastic-perfectly plastic modeling of material, on the buckling loads were studied numerically. This paper aims to provide a rational approach to predicting the real load-carrying capacities of spherical shells.

2. Materials and methods

This study involved sampling and analyzing 10 spherical shells to determine their buckling behaviors. A series of tests were performed to obtain the geometric and buckling properties of these shells in addition to their material properties.

2.1. Shell manufacturing and testing

Each spherical shell was manufactured using the tungsten inert gas butt welding of two coupled hemispherical shells, <u>after which the excess of the weld has been removed by grinding and then been polished.</u> Each hemispherical shell was cut and stamped from 304 thin stainless steel sheets with a nominal thickness of either 0.4 mm or 0.7 mm. Ten spherical shells with a nominal diameter of 150 mm were manufactured for the tests. Five of them were fabricated from a 0.4-mm-thick sheet and were denoted as t0.4-1, t0.4-2, t0.4-3, t0.4-4, and t0.4-5. Five other shells were fabricated from a 0.7-mm-thick sheet and were denoted as t0.7-1, t0.7-2, t0.7-3, t0.7-4, and t0.7-5. In addition, all the shells were not stress relieved during the manufacturing process because the ratios of the wall thickness to the nominal diameter were very low. Before the spherical shells were tested, the wall thickness and geometric shape were measured for all the shells.

First, the thickness of each wall was measured using an ultrasonic probe at 13 equidistant points along a meridian for eight equally spaced meridians, as detailed in Fig. 1. Each shell was measured at $8 \times 11 + 2 = 90$ points. The values of the minimum (t_{min}), maximum (t_{max}), and average wall thicknesses (t_{ave}), as well as the corresponding standard deviations (t_{std}), are listed in Table 1. <u>Overall average wall thickness profile from the North-Pole to the South Pole for a t0.4-1 spherical shell and its thicknesses of all measure points are also showed in Fig. 2 and Table 2 respectively.</u> The average variation between the maximal and minimal wall thicknesses was approximately 17%, which may be attributed to the stamping process. Second, the geometries of all the spherical shells were obtained using a three-dimensional optical scanner, developed by Open Technologies Corporation. Each shell surface was scanned in the form of a point cloud and automatically transformed into a CAD model. Each model demonstrated the real geometric shape of the corresponding shell, which contained deterministic geometric imperfections caused by manufacturing processes. Furthermore, the minimum (r_{min}), maximum (r_{max}), and average radii (r_{ave}) of each shell were also obtained from the CAD model in addition to the corresponding standard deviations (r_{std}); these values are listed in the final four columns of Table1, while contours of local radii of curvature for a t0.4-1 spherical shell are presented in Fig. 3.

The spheres were empty and they were floating in the test vessel. This floating was expected to exert a strong influence on the buckling behavior of spherical shells. The net buoyancy values of the spherical shells were considerably high because their buoyant loads were higher than their dead-weight values. The net buoyancy was obtained by:

$$F_{net\ buoyant} = \frac{4}{3}\pi r^3 g\rho_{water} - \frac{4}{3}\pi(r^3 - (r-t)^3)g\rho_{steel}, \quad (1)$$

where, r, t are the nominal radius and nominal thickness of a spherical shell, ρ_{steel} is the density of strainless steel, ρ_{water} is the density of water inside the vessel, g is the gravitational acceleration. Assume that: $r = 75mm$, $t = 0.4mm$ for a t = 0.4-mm spherical shell, $t = 0.7mm$ for a t = 0.7-mm spherical shell, $\rho_{steel} = 7930\ kg/m^3$, $\rho_{water} = 1000\ kg/m^3$, $g = 9.8\ m/s^2$. Therefore, the net buoyancy of a $t = 0.4$-mm spherical shell is 15.12N, whereas the results of calculation can be approximately is 13.50N for a$t = 0.7$-mm spherical shell. To minimize this effect, each spherical shell was encased in a string bag connected to a ballast pig. The weight of the pig was slightly higher than the buoyant load of the spherical shell. The shell, bag, and pig were then immersed together in a cylindrical pressure chamber with a 200-mm inner diameter, 400-mm total length, and 20-MPa maximum pressure. The chamber (located at Jiangsu University of Science and Technology) entailed using water as a pressurizing medium. The pressure inside the chamber was controlled automatically by a programmable logic controller and measured using a pressure transducer. All the spherical shells failed suddenly with substantial decreases in pressure. Thus, determining the buckling load was very simple.

2.2. Material properties

In cases of uniform external pressure, the buckling behaviors of spherical shells are determined according to the compression stress-strain behavior of the relevant material. However, experiments to demonstrate such behaviors with thin-walled structures are extremely difficult to conduct. Therefore, the compression behavior of steel is assumed to be the same as its tension behavior. This hypothesis has been frequently used in the buckling prediction of various shells of revolution loaded by external pressure [7, 9, 14]. Thus, the material properties of steel sheets can be established by testing a series of flat tension coupons.

The coupons for this work were designed and tested according to Chinese Standard (GB/T 228.1-2010) [15], which is in line with ISO 6892-1: 2009 [16]. They were cut along the rolling directions of the same sheets that were used to manufacture spherical shells for ensuring accurate material data. Five coupons were selected for each thickness and subjected to uniaxial tension. Two of them were strain-gauged in the transverse and longitudinal directions to obtain Poisson's ratio (ν) for the material and to verify the extensometer readings. The average values were 0.277 for the 0.4-mm-thick sheet and 0.291 for the 0.7-mm-thick sheet. Other coupons were tested to obtain accurate stress-strain curves, which can be demonstrated in the following form:

$$\sigma = E\varepsilon, \quad for \sigma < \sigma_y \quad (2a)$$

and

$$\sigma = \sigma_y \sqrt[k]{\left(\frac{E\varepsilon}{\sigma_y} - 1\right)n}, \quad (2b)$$

where E is Young's modulus, σ_{yp} is the yield strength based on 0.2% proof stress, and n and k are the strain hardening parameters. The values of these coefficients, as well as the average values, are listed in Table 3. The testing coupons were numbered and named according to the thickness and coupon number; one name, for example, was t0.4-c1, where t0.4 indicates that the thickness of the sheet was 0.4 mm, and c1 indicates that the coupon number was one. The variance of coefficients for each thickness was very small.

3. Results and discussion

Previous studies have indicated that the experimental buckling loads of spherical shells are lower than theoretical predictions [4, 17]. This phenomenon may result from inevitable geometric imperfections and from nonlinear material properties. This problem of classical mechanics is far from being solved; the buckling analysis of spherical shells remains to be vivid and is still challenging.

This section reports how the buckling loads and final collapsed modes of a family of spherical shells were determined from hydrostatic tests. The results of analytical and numerical investigations into these shells are presented and compared with the experimental findings. The effects of constitutive models on the buckling load are discussed.

3.1. Experimental and analytical results analysis

The experimental buckling loads are listed in column 2 of Table 4, and graphed in Fig. 4. Photographs of the final collapsed modes for 10 spherical shells are presented in Fig. 5. Notably, the buckling load of the t0.7-2 spherical shell was not recorded because of an incorrect operation during the testing process. However, the final collapsed mode of this shell was still obtained. The buckling loads of the 0.4-mm-thick spherical shells ranged between 1.330 and 1.956 MPa, whereas the 0.7-mm-thick shell buckling loads ranged between 3.178 and 4.692 MPa. The buckling loads of the 0.7-mm-thick shell loads were more than twice those of the 0.4-mm-thick shell loads. This variance mainly affected by the ratio of the average wall thickness (t_{ave}) to the average radius (r_{ave}), as illustrated in Fig. 4. The experimental buckling load increased monotonically with an increase in t_{ave}/r_{ave}. As shown in Fig. 5, the final collapsed modes of all shells are identical, and all of them have the form of a local dent because of the high ductility of stainless steel and the initial geometric imperfections of the shells. This failure mode is consistent with previous experimental results regarding shells of revolution with a positive Gaussian curvature, such as those for spherical shells reported by Quilliet [13], for ellipsoidal shells reported by Healey [18], and for barreled shells reported by Blachut [9, 10].

A theory derived by Zoelly [19] predicts the elastic buckling load (p_{cr}) of spherical shells, which is obtained using

$$P_{cr} = \frac{2E}{\sqrt{3(1-\nu^2)}}\left(\frac{t}{R}\right)^2 \quad (3)$$

where the wall thickness t, radius r, Young's modulus E, and Poisson's ratio ν are assumed to be average values of the experimental results (Tables 1 and 3). This analytical formula is widely accepted in ocean and aerospace engineering as a rule for designing spherical shells [4, 20, 21]. The results of Eq. (3) are listed in column 3 of Table 4, followed by the ratio of the experimental load p_{test} to the elastic buckling load p_{zoelly} in parentheses. As shown in the table, the experimental load of a spherical shell was as little as 15.07%-24.55% of that shell's elastic buckling load, confirming that the spherical shell is a highly imperfection-sensitive structure. A small imperfection may lead to a substantial decrease in the magnitude of the buckling load. Furthermore, the average ratio of the experimental load p_{test} to the elastic buckling load p_{zoelly} for 0.4-mm-thick spherical shells was approximately 3% lower than the ratio for 0.7-mm-thick shells. It appears that the nonlinear properties of spherical shells' materials may play a major role in the buckling behaviors of shells with various wall thicknesses.

3.2. Comparison of experimental and numerical results

Prior work has demonstrated the effectiveness of the finite element method in predicting the buckling behaviors of thin-walled structures. Schmidt, for example, suggested that the real buckling load of a shell can be determined using geometrically and materially nonlinear analyses of shells that include imperfections [22, 23]. However, most studies have focused on equivalent geometric imperfections, such as eigenmode imperfections, in numerically analyzing the buckling of spherical shells.

In this study, we carried out nonlinear buckling analysis for the same types of spherical shells as would be tested for deterministic imperfections. The analysis was performed using the modified Riks method in ABAQUS software [24]. The finite element model of each spherical shell was established according to the real geometric shape obtained from the experimental data. The shapes and sizes of the initial geometric imperfections were automatically included in the models. A fully integrated S4 and S3 shell was selected to avoid hourglassing and the number of elements was determined using mesh density convergence analysis in line with [25], shown in Fig. 6 and Table 5. The mesh of each spherical shell was generated freely based on its real geometry in the form of numerous small surface pieces, where the local apex area was included. In all the analyses, a $p_0 = 1$ MPa external pressure was applied on the whole area of each shell. To avoid rigid body motion, three random spatial points were respectively constrained in the three orthogonal directions. These constraints did not lead to overconstrained models because the pressure was equally applied. The steel was assumed to be elastic-plastic as described in Eq. (2). In addition, the average wall thickness (column 4 of Table 1) and material properties (Table 3) were defined in the analyses. Fig. 7 and the final column of Table 4 show the results obtained using numerical analysis.

Because the equilibrium paths, critical buckling, and postbuckling modes of all the analyzed shells were similar, detailed results are provided only for the case of t0.4-1. Fig. 7 shows the equilibrium path of a shell; the vertical axis shows the applied load normalized by the initial applied load $p_0 = 1$ MPa, and the horizontal axis shows the maximum deflection (Δ) normalized by the wall thickness (t). The path has an unstable characteristic that is typical of shell structures: At first, the load increases nearly linearly with an increase in the deflection up to a peak corresponding to the critical buckling load, beyond which the load decreases sharply. The same figure shows that the buckling and postbuckling modes are similar and assume the form of a local dent. This may have been caused by the initial deterministic imperfections of the shell. Comparing Figs. 5 and 7 show that the predicted final failure mode is highly consistent with the experimental one. In addition, as indicated in the final column of Table 4, very good correlation between the numerical buckling loads and the experimental ones was obtained (±7%). This slight difference may be attributed to small variations of the material properties for the steel sheets, in addition to the assumption of the average wall thickness used to perform numerical calculation. These findings indicate that the real buckling resistance of a spherical shell can be determined numerically on the basis of its true geometry as well as its average wall thickness and material properties.

In the same figure, the first yield load of t0.4-1 is plotted at the value of 1.466 MPa, which was obtained using the postprocessing procedure as in Ref. [8]. The first yield load was approximately 84% of the critical buckling load. At the first stage of testing up to this value, the spherical shell had an elastic characteristic. At the second stage of testing higher than this value, the spherical shell appeared to be elastic-plastic. This phenomenon was observed for all the cases shown in Table 6. For spherical shells, the ratio of the first yield to the critical buckling load, $p_{ABAQUS}^{fyd}/p_{ABAQUS}^{elastic-plastic}$, varied between 0.681 and 0.895. It is suggested that all the spherical shells could lose stability within the elastic-plastic regime. This finding is similar to those regarding medium-thick conical shells subjected to external pressure [7].

3.3. Effect of constitutive models

It is well known that the modeling of materials strongly influences the accuracy of numerical results. Most recent numerical investigations on the buckling of shell structures have assumed the material properties to be either purely elastic [26] or elastic-perfectly plastic [9, 10]. To examine this assumption, the effect of constitutive models on the buckling of spherical shells was investigated in the present study. The same numerical models as those mentioned in Section 3.2 were employed, except that the steel was assumed to be elastic and elastic-perfectly plastic. The material parameters were determined on the basis of the average values listed in Table 3; 20 models were accounted for. Because the equilibrium paths, critical buckling modes, and postbuckling modes of these cases were almost identical with the elastic-plastic results for t0.4-1 shown in Fig. 7, the effects of constitutive models were examined according to the critical buckling load only. Table 7 shows the buckling loads $p_{ABAQUS}^{elastic}$ and $p_{ABAQUS}^{elastic-perfectly\ plastic}$ obtained from elastic and elastic-perfectly plastic assumptions, respectively, and the values normalized by elastic-plastic $p_{ABAQUS}^{elastic-plastic}$ and experimental p_{test} buckling loads are in parentheses.

As shown in Table 7, the elastic assumption yielded an increase of 53.98%-135.55% in the magnitude of the buckling load over that of the elastic-plastic assumption. A fairly large difference existed between the results obtained according to the purely elastic assumption and those of the experiments. This finding indicates that numerical predictions based on the purely elastic assumption are extremely nonconservative and are not suitable for engineering applications. However, the differences between the elastic and elastic-plastic results for 0.4-mm-thick spherical shells are always higher than those for 0.7-mm-thick shells. This implies that the failures of spherical shells vary gradually from elastic buckling to elastic-plastic buckling as the wall thicknesses increase. It is more reasonable to include plastic material properties when performing buckling analysis on a medium-thick shell structure.

As shown in Table 7, the elastic-perfectly plastic predictions deviated from the elastic-plastic predictions by as little as 6%. Very good agreement was obtained between the elastic-plastic and elastic-perfectly plastic results. The maximum difference between a prediction from the elastic-perfectly plastic assumption and that from the experiment was only 8%. This confirms that the buckling of a shell is greatly determined according to its stress behavior, particularly its yield [27]. It could be inferred that aside from the elastic material properties, the buckling load of a shell strongly depends on the yield strength of the material. This finding extends those of Bluchat [9, 10], confirming that the elastic-perfectly plastic assumption can be made in the buckling analysis of shells, and tends to result in extremely accurate predictions.

4. Conclusions

In the present work, the results of experimental, analytical, and numerical study into the buckling behaviors of spherical shells are presented, as well as the effects of constitutive modes on the buckling loads of these shells. The experimental buckling load increased monotonically with an increase in t_{ave}/r_{ave}, which was as little as 15.07%-24.55% of the elastic buckling load determined using Zoelly's equation. The experimental collapsed modes of all the shells were identical; all of them assumed the form of a local dent, which is typical of shells of revolution with a positive Gaussian curvature.

Geometrically and materially nonlinear buckling analyses were performed on the spherical shells for deterministic imperfections. Very good correlation was obtained between the numerical buckling loads and the experimental ones. The path of each spherical shell had an unstable characteristic typical of shell structures. All the shells buckled within an elastic-plastic range. The buckling and postbuckling modes of all the analyzed shells were similar and assumed the form of a local dent, which was in very good agreement with the experimental results.

The effects of constitutive models on the buckling of spherical shells were demonstrated numerically according to the buckling load. The failures of spherical shells varied gradually from elastic buckling to elastic-plastic buckling as the wall thicknesses increased. Very good agreement was obtained among the elastic-plastic, elastic-perfectly plastic, and experimental results. The elastic-perfectly plastic assumption resulted in a highly accurate prediction. The elastic assumption yielded a fairly large increase in the magnitude of the buckling load above the elastic-plastic assumption and experiment.

This work therefore indicates that the real load-carrying capacity of a spherical shell can be obtained numerically from measured geometric shape and average wall thickness, as well as from the assumption of elastic-perfectly plastic material properties. The current approach appears to be effective for other shells of revolution with typical meridional profiles, such as cylindrical and conical shells, as well as for shells of revolution with nontypical meridional profiles, such as barreled and egg-shaped shells. However, some limitations merit attention. Although the predicted buckling loads and final failure modes were verified experimentally, the critical buckling modes were not examined through testing. Moreover, the manufacturing process caused some variance in the wall thicknesses, and that variance exerted an effect on the buckling of spherical shells; however, this effect was not studied. These limitations require further investigation in the near future.

Acknowledgments

This work was supported by two grants from the Natural Science Foundation of Jiangsu Province, China (BK20140512, BK20150469).

References

[1] J. Blachut, Experimental perspective on the buckling of pressure vessel components, Appl. Mech. Rev. 66 (2013) 010803-1-010803-24.

[2] J. Błachut, K. Magnucki, Strength, Stability, and Optimization of pressure vessels: Review of selected problems, Appl. Mech. Rev. 61 (2008) 060801.

[3] B. B. Pan, W. C. Cui, An overview of buckling and ultimate strength of spherical pressure hull under external pressure, Mar. Struct. 23 (2010) 227-240.

[4] B. B. Pan, W. C. Cui, A comparison of different rules for the spherical pressure hull of deep manned submersibles, J. Ship Mech. 15 (2011) 276-285.

[5] J. Blachut, G. D. Galletly, D. N. Moreton, Buckling of near-perfect steel torispherical andhemispherical shells subjected to external pressure, AIAA J. 28 (1990) 1971-1975.

[6] J. Błachut, Locally flattened or dented domes under external pressure, Thin-Walled Struct. 97 (2015) 44-52.

[7] J. Błachut, A. Muc, J. Ryś, Plastic buckling of cones subjected to axial compression and external pressure, J. Press. Vessel. Technol. 135 (2013) 011205-1-011205-9.

[8] J. Błachut, O. Ifayefunmi, Buckling of unstiffened steel cones subjected to axial compression and external pressure, J. Offshore Mech. Arct. Eng. 134 (2012) 031603-1-031603-9.

[9] J. Błachut, Optimal barreling of steel shells via simulated annealing algorithm, Comput. Struct. 81 (2003) 1941-1956.

[10] J. Błachut, Buckling of externally pressurised barrelled shells: a comparison of experiment and theory, Int. J. Press. Vessel. Pip. 79 (2002) 507-517.

[11] B. B. Pan, W. C. Cui, Y. S. Shen, T. Liu, Further study on the ultimate strength analysis of spherical pressure hulls, Mar. Struct. 23 (2010) 444-461.

[12] B. B. Pan, W. C. Cui, Y. S. Shen, Experimental verification of the new ultimate strength equation of spherical pressure hulls, Mar. Struct. 29 (2012) 169-176.

[13] C. Quilliet, Depressions at the surface of an elastic spherical shell submitted to external pressure, Phys. Rev. E. 74 (2006) 046608-1-046608-6.

[14] H. Schmidt, P. Swadlo, Part C-Shells of revolution with Arbitrary meridional shapes-Buckling design by use of computer analysis, ECSC contract No. 7210-SA/208: Enhancement of ECCS design recommendations and development of Eurocode 3 parts related to shell buckling, Final Report, Universität GH Essen, FB Bauwesen-Stahlbau, 1996.

[15] GB/T 228. 1: Metallic materials-Tensile testing-Part 1: Method of test at room temperature, Chinese Standard Institute, china, 2010.

[16] ISO 6892-1: Metallic materials-Tensile testing-Part 1: Method of test at room temperature, International Organization for Standardization, 2009.

[17] T. Von Kármán, H. S. Tsien, The buckling of Spherical Shells by External Pressure, J. Aeronaut. Sci. 7 (1939)

43-50 (doi: 10.2514/8.1019).

[18] J. J. Healey, Hydrostatic tests of two prolate spheroidal shells, J. Ship Res. 9 (1965) 77-78.

[19] R. Zoelly, Über ein Knickungs problem an der Kugelschale, Zürich, 1915.

[20] CCS. Rules for the classification and construction of diving systems and submersibles, China Classification Society, china, 1996.

[21] NASA SP-8032. Buckling of thin-walled doubly curved shells, National Aeronautics and Space Administration, Washington, 1969.

[22] H. Schmidt, Stability of steel shell structures: General Report, J. Constr. Steel Res. 55 (2000) 159-181.

[23] EN 1993-1-6: Eurocode 3-Design of steel structures-Part 1.6: Strength and Stability of shell structures, CEN, Brussels, 2007.

[24] K. Hibbitt, S. Inc, ABAQUS-Theory and Standard User's Manual Version 6.3, USA, 2006.

[25] P. Jasion, K. Magnucki, Elastic buckling of clothoidal-spherical shells under external pressure-theoretical study, Thin-Walled Struct. 86 (2015) 18-23.

[26] P. Jasion, K. Magnucki, Elastic buckling of classini ovaloidal shells under external pressure-theoretical study, Arch. Mech. 67 (2015) 179-192.

[27] M. Barski, J. Krużelecki, Optimal design of shells against buckling under overall bending and external pressure, Thin-Walled Struct. 43 (2005) 1677-1698.

Table 1

Testing values of the wall thickness and radius for spherical shells (minimum, maximum, average, and standard deviation)

	t_{min} (mm)	t_{max} (mm)	t_{ave} (mm)	t_{std} (mm)	r_{min} (mm)	r_{max} (mm)	r_{ave} (mm)	r_{std} (mm)
t0.4-1	0.382	0.476	0.422	0.022	73.903	74.485	74.248	0.174
t0.4-2	0.396	0.496	0.432	0.024	73.843	74.517	74.163	0.170
t0.4-3	0.378	0.488	0.426	0.024	74.067	74.285	74.157	0.046
t0.4-4	0.382	0.436	0.401	0.010	74.304	74.754	74.548	0.133
t0.4-5	0.382	0.476	0.414	0.016	73.817	74.501	74.185	0.158
t0.7-1	0.650	0.754	0.708	0.024	74.231	75.005	74.710	0.249
t0.7-2	0.614	0.766	0.715	0.024	74.391	75.291	74.926	0.242
t0.7-3	0.644	0.746	0.723	0.02	74.282	75.102	75.023	0.142
t0.7-4	0.652	0.756	0.724	0.019	74.300	75.062	74.840	0.184
t0.7-5	0.648	0.762	0.716	0.021	74.317	75.001	74.983	0.252

Table 2

Thickness (in mm) at 13 equidistant points along 8 meridians for a t0.4-1 spherical shell

Longtitude no.	Lattitude no.							
	A	B	C	D	E	F	G	H
1	0.416	0.422	0.420	0.41	0.426	0.458	0.426	0.412
2	0.436	0.410	0.408	0.404	0.436	0.416	0.410	0.408
3	0.426	0.426	0.398	0.382	0.422	0.408	0.394	0.396
4	0.428	0.432	0.412	0.464	0.410	0.422	0.398	0.4
5	0.402	0.396	0.418	0.388	0.402	0.398	0.408	0.398
6	0.425	0.415	0.418	0.42	0.419	0.416	0.432	0.431

(续)

Longtitude no.	Lattitude no.							
	A	B	C	D	E	F	G	H
7	0.406	0.466	0.408	0.408	0.392	0.396	0.396	0.418
8	0.414	0.434	0.432	0.432	0.456	0.47	0.476	0.424
9	0.398	0.438	0.418	0.406	0.416	0.416	0.446	0.414
10	0.428	0.446	0.406	0.414	0.424	0.42	0.458	0.414
11	0.456	0.446	0.436	0.45	0.446	0.45	0.472	0.454

The thicknesses at the North-Pole and South-pole are 0.418 and 0.462 respectively.

Table 3

Material properties of 304 stainless steel obtained from uniaxial tension tests (E-Young's modulus; σ_{yp}-yield strength; n and k-strain hardening parameter)

	E(GPa)	σ_{yp}(MPa)	n	k
t0.4-c1	193.1	250.9	0.108	4.154
t0.4-c2	188.4	241.4	0.101	3.896
t0.4-c3	190.5	246.2	0.091	4.319
t0.4-average	190.7	246.1	0.100	4.123
t0.7-c1	187.2	288.5	0.081	4.291
t0.7-c2	180.3	292.0	0.088	4.733
t0.7-c3	197.1	294.2	0.118	4.972
t0.7-average	188.2	291.6	0.096	4.665

Table 4

Experimental (p_{test}), analytical (p_{zoelly}), and numerical ($p_{ABAQUS}^{elastic-plastic}$) buckling loads of spherical shells. The analytical and numerical values were normalized by the experimental values and are in parentheses

	p_{test}(MPa)	p_{zoelly}(MPa)	($p_{ABAQUS}^{elastic-plastic}$(MPa)
t0.4-1	1.708	7.586(4.44)	1.745(1.02)
t0.4-2	1.956	7.968(4.07)	1.946(0.99)
t0.4-3	1.773	7.749(4.37)	1.708(0.96)
t0.4-4	1.330	6.795(5.11)	1.332(1.00)
t0.4-5	1.594	7.313(4.59)	1.708(1.07)
t0.7-1	3.178	21.089(6.64)	3.155(0.99)
t0.7-2	NA	21.384(NA)	4.317(NA)
t0.7-3	4.496	21.809(4.85)	4.716(1.05)
t0.7-4	4.692	21.976(4.68)	4.397(0.94)
t0.7-5	3.974	21.412(5.39)	4.006(1.01)

Table 5

Number of the FE elements for each spherical shell

	t0.4-1	t0.4-2	t0.4-3	t0.4-4	t0.4-5	t0.7-1	t0.7-2	t0.7-3	t0.7-4	t0.7-5
S4	6746	6643	6820	6298	6264	6430	6348	6287	6436	6447
S3	1064	448	1110	1134	1064	1118	1212	1180	1170	1216

Table 6
First yield load p_{ABAQUS}^{fyd} values of spherical shells and the ratio of the first yield and critical buckling load $p_{ABAQUS}^{fyd}/p_{ABAQUS}^{elastic-plastic}$

	p_{ABAQUS}^{fyd} (MPa)	$p_{ABAQUS}^{fyd}/p_{ABAQUS}^{elastic-plastic}$
t0.4-1	1.466	0.840
t0.4-2	1.407	0.723
t0.4-3	1.531	0.896
t0.4-4	0.907	0.681
t0.4-5	1.528	0.895
t0.7-1	2.392	0.758
t0.7-2	3.401	0.788
t0.7-3	3.904	0.828
t0.7-4	3.905	0.888
t0.7-5	3.402	0.849

Table 7
Buckling loads of spherical shells obtained from elastic and elastic-perfectly plastic models. Values in parentheses were normalized by the elastic-plastic and experimental buckling loads, respectively

	$p_{ABAQUS}^{elastic}$ (MPa)	$p_{ABAQUS}^{elastic-perfectly\ plastic}$ (MPa)
t0.4-1	3.146(1.80, 1.84)	1.722(0.99, 1.01)
t0.4-2	3.389(1.74, 1.73)	1.823(0.94, 0.93)
t0.4-3	2.941(1.72, 1.65)	1.630(0.95, 0.92)
t0.4-4	2.051(1.54, 1.54)	1.332(1.00, 1.00)
t0.4-5	3.174(1.86, 1.99)	1.712(1.00, 1.07)
t0.7-1	5.930(1.88, 1.87)	2.953(0.94, 0.92)
t0.7-2	9.549(2.21, NA)	4.206(0.97, NA)
t0.7-3	10.174(2.16, 2.31)	4.483(0.95, 1.02)
t0.7-4	10.357(2.36, 2.21)	4.383(1.00, 0.93)
t0.7-5	9.035(2.26, 2.27)	3.953(0.99, 0.99)

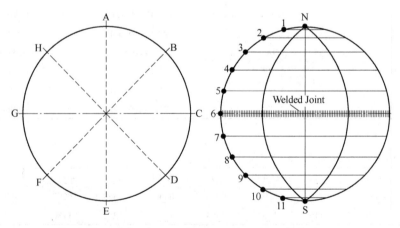

Fig. 1. Typical distribution of testing points for wall thickness.

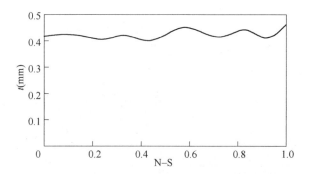

Fig. 2. Overall average wall thickness profile from the North-Pole to the South Pole for a t0.4-1 spherical shell.

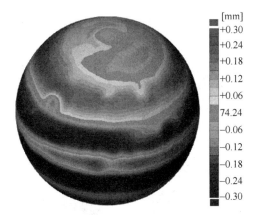

Fig. 3. Contours of local radii of curvature for a t0.4-1 spherical shell.

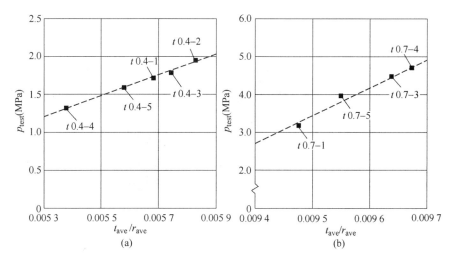

Fig. 4. Plots of experimental buckling load versus ratio of average wall thickness (t_{ave}) to average radius (r_{ave}) of spherical shells; a = 0.4-mm spherical shells, b = 0.7-mm spherical shells.

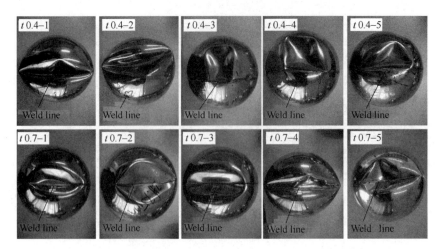

Fig. 5. Views of spherical shells after collapse caused by external hydrostatic pressure; All final failure modes assumed the form of a local dimple.

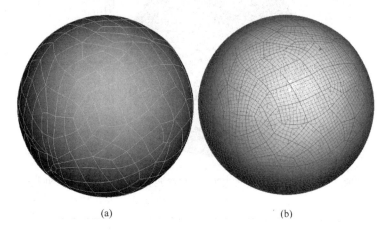

Fig. 6. Scanned CAD model (a) for a t0.4-1 spherical shell and its mesh (b).

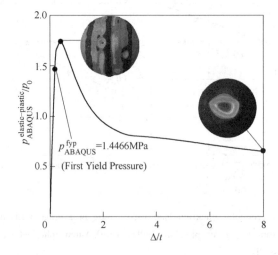

Fig. 7. Equilibrium path, critical buckling mode, and postbuckling mode of a t0.4-1 spherical shell.

9.2.4 二通意见答复与修改稿

(1) 编辑与专家意见

Comments from the editors and reviewers:

The revised manuscript reads much better. I have the following comments:

(i) Have the thickness of flat plates been measured before manufacturing of hemispheres?

(ii) Any comments how accurate was the scanned geometry?

(iii) Has the scanned data been checked against data produced by any other measuring technique?

(iv) How 90 measuring points of wall thickness were extrapolated to some 6000 FE elements?

(2) 专家意见答复及修改说明

1) 专家意见回复信

Ref: TWST_ 2016_ 349_ R1

Dear Editor,

Thank you very much for your email with reviewers' comments to our paper "Buckling of spherical shells subjected to external pressure: A comparison of experimental and theoretical data". We have made some revisions to our paper according to the reviewers' suggestions. And also we have formed the explanations to questions which reviewers were concerned in their comments.

Please find attached word documents of the revised version of our paper together with responses to the comments of reviewers respectively. If there is anything else, please just let me know.

Many thanks for your attention and looking forward to your response.

Faithfully Yours

Mr. Zhang

Research Assistant of Mechanical Engineering

Jiangsu University of Science and Technology

2) 专家意见答复及修改说明

Responses to the reviewers' comments

1. **Reviewer's comments**: Have the thickness of flat plates been measured before manufacturing of hemispheres?

1. Response: The thicknesses of flat plates have not been measured before manufacturing of hemispheres. Nevertheless, details of thicknesses of all tested spheres have been provided in the manuscript. Whether including the thicknesses of flat plates or not has no effect on the researching results.

2. **Reviewer's comments**: Any comments how accurate was the scanned geometry?

2. Accepted: We have added comments on how accurate was the scanned geometry in the manuscript, as follows: The scanned accuracy is not more than 0.02 mm reffering to operating manual provided by Open Technologies Corporation.

3. **Reviewer's comments**: Has the scanned data been checked against data produced by any other measuring technique?

3. Response: The scanned data has not been checked against data produced by any other measuring technique. Nevertheless, the data of 44492 to 64385 points were measured for each spherical shell. It appears that this scanning method could obtained a highly accurate geometry.

4. **Reviewer's comments**: How 90 measuring points of wall thickness were extrapolated to some 6000 FE elements?

4. Response: The average constant wall thickness obtained from measurements for each spherical shell was assumed in the numerical analyses, which has been mentioned in our manuscript. This assumption has been implemented by Blachut et al. and resulted in a good agreement between experiment and theory:

J. Błachut, G. D. Galletly, D. N. Moreton, Buckling of near-perfect steel torispherical and hemispherical shells subjected to external pressure, AIAA J. 28 (1990) 1971-1975.

P. Smith, J. Błachut, Buckling of Externally Pressurized Prolate Ellipsoidal Domes, J. Press. Vessel. Technol., 130 (2008) 244-254.

(3) 修改稿

Buckling of Spherical Shells Subjected to External Pressure: A Comparison of Experimental and Theoretical Data

Jian Zhang[a,b], Meng Zhang[a]*, Wenxian Tang[a], Weibo Wang[b], Minglu Wang[a]

[a]Jiangsu University of Science and Technology, Zhenjiang, Jiangsu, 212003, China

[b]Chinese Ship Scientific Research Center, Wuxi, Jiangsu, 214082, China

* Corresponding author:
Meng Zhang
E-mail: zmeng1227@163.com
Tel & Fax: +86-51184401142

Abstract: This paper focuses on spherical shells under uniform external pressure. Ten laboratory scale models, each with a nominal diameter of 150 mm, were tested. Half of them were manufactured from a 0.4-mm stainless steel sheet, whereas the remaining five shells were manufactured from a 0.7-mm sheet. The geometry, wall thickness, buckling load, and final collapsed mode of each spherical shell were measured, as well as the material properties of the corresponding sheet. The buckling behaviors of these shells were demonstrated analytically and numerically according to experimental data. Analyses involved considering the average geometry, average wall thicknesses, and average elastic material properties. Numerical calculations entailed considering the true geometry, average wall thicknesses, and elastic-plastic modeling of true stress-strain curves. Moreover, the effects of purely elastic and elastic-perfectly plastic models on the buckling loads of spherical shells were examined numerically. The results of the experimental, analytical, and numerical investigations were compared in tables and figures.

Keywords: spherical shell, 304 steel, buckling, external pressure, numerical solution

1. Introduction

For more than 100 years, research has been published on spherical shells subjected to uniform external pressure. Knowledge about this type of loading has been widely applied in various engineering fields such as those involving underwater pressure hulls, underground pressure vessels, and underpressure tanks [1, 2]. In particular, the spherical configuration is broadly considered an ideal structure for the pressure hulls of deep submersibles. This is due to the extremely efficient stress and strain distributions in the material [3, 4]. Although the theoretical elastic buckling loads are high, the spherical shells have been found to be highly imperfection sensitive and be strongly affected by plastic material properties. The experimental buckling loads are even lower than the theoretical ones.

The difference between theory and experiment has prompted numerous studies regarding the buckling of spherical shells loaded by external pressure. For example, Blachut et al. presented a series of experimental and numerical studies concerning elastic-plastic buckling of spherical [5], torispherical [6], conical [7, 8] or barreled shells [9, 10] under external pressure. In most of their studies, the material was assumed to be elastic-perfectly plastic. The effects of initial geometric imperfections were also taken into account, which included eigenmode imperfections derived from linear elastic buckling analysis of the perfect geometries or deterministic ones derived from a limited number of measuring points. Moreover, Pan et al. performed a set of experimental and numerical studies on the ultimate strength levels of spherical pressure hulls used in deep submersibles [11, 12]. Their numerical models were elaborated on the basis of initial equivalent geometric imperfections in the shape of the first eigenmode and a local dimple. Their numerical predictions were verified by pressurizing four laboratory scale spherical hulls to collapse. More recently, Quilliet carried out elasticity theory calculations to predict the collapsed mode of a spherical shell [13]. Quillet's prediction resembled previously published experimental results. However, little attention has been paid to true geometry, including deterministic imperfections. And the effects of plastic material properties including or excluding yield strengths and hardening parameters on the buckling of spherical shells were rarely investigated as well. Further study is still necessary in this branch of mechanics.

For investigating the buckling of spherical shells loaded with external pressure, spherical shells were manufactured from 304 stainless steel sheets through stamping and butt-welding processes. The geometric and buckling properties of these spherical shells were demonstrated by a series of tests. The buckling and postbuckling behaviors were determined numerically and verified experimentally. The numerical analysis was based on deterministic imperfections obtained from measured geometric shapes and elastic-plastic modeling of true stress-strain curves. Furthermore, the effects of constitutive models, such as purely elastic and elastic-perfectly plastic modeling of material, on the buckling loads were studied numerically. This paper aims to provide a rational approach to predicting the real load-carrying capacities of spherical shells.

2. Materials and methods

This study involved sampling and analyzing 10 spherical shells to determine their buckling behaviors. A series of tests were performed to obtain the geometric and buckling properties of these shells in addition to their material properties.

2.1. Shell manufacturing and testing

Each spherical shell was manufactured using the tungsten inert gas butt welding of two coupled hemispherical shells, after which the excess of the weld has been removed by grinding and then been polished. Each hemispherical shell was cut and stamped from 304 thin stainless steel sheets with a nominal thickness of either 0.4 mm or 0.7 mm. Ten spherical shells with a nominal diameter of 150 mm were manufactured for the tests. Five of them were fabricated from a 0.4-mm-thick sheet and were denoted as t0.4-1, t0.4-2, t0.4-3, t0.4-4, and t0.4-5. Five other shells were fabricated from a 0.7-mm-thick sheet and were denoted as t0.7-1, t0.7-2, t0.7-3, t0.7-4, and t0.7-5. In addition, all the shells were not stress relieved during the manufacturing process because the ratios of the wall thickness to the nominal diameter were very low. Before the spherical shells were tested, the wall thickness and geometric shape were measured for all the shells.

First, the thickness of each wall was measured using an ultrasonic probe at 13 equidistant points along a meridian for eight equally spaced meridians, as detailed in **Fig. 1**. Each shell was measured at $8 \times 11 + 2 = 90$ points. The values of the minimum (t_{min}), maximum (t_{max}), and average wall thicknesses (t_{ave}), as well as the corresponding standard deviations (t_{std}), are listed in **Table 1**. Overall average wall thickness profile from the North-Pole to the South Pole for a t0.4-1 spherical shell and its thicknesses of all measure points are also showed in **Fig. 2** and **Table 2** respectively. The average variation between the maximal and minimal wall thicknesses was approximately 17%, which may be attributed to the stamping process. Second, the geometries of all the spherical shells were obtained using a three-dimensional optical scanner, developed by Open Technologies Corporation. The scanned accuracy is not more than 0.02 mm reffering to operating manual provided by the corporation. Each shell surface was scanned in the form of a point cloud and automatically transformed into a CAD model. Each model demonstrated the real geometric shape of the corresponding shell, which contained deterministic geometric imperfections caused by manufacturing processes. Furthermore, the minimum (r_{min}), maximum (r_{max}), and average radii (r_{ave}) of each shell were also obtained from the CAD model in addition to the corresponding standard deviations (r_{std}); these values are listed in the final four columns of **Table1**, while contours of local radii of curvature for a t0.4-1 spherical shell are presented in **Fig. 3**.

The spheres were empty and they were floating in the test vessel. This floating was expected to exert a strong influence on the buckling behavior of spherical shells. The net buoyancy values of the spherical shells were considerably high because their buoyant loads were higher than their dead-weight values. The net buoyancy was obtained by:

$$F_{net\ buoyant} = \frac{4}{3}\pi r^3 g\rho_{water} - \frac{4}{3}\pi(r^3 - (r-t)^3)g\rho_{steel}, \qquad (1)$$

where, r, t are the nominal radius and nominal thickness of a spherical shell, ρ_{steel} is the density of strainless steel, ρ_{water} is the density of water inside the vessel, g is the gravitational acceleration. Assume that: $r = 75$mm, $t = 0.4$mm for a t = 0.4-mm spherical shell, $t = 0.7$mm for a $t = 0.7$-mm spherical shell, $\rho_{steel} = 7930\ kg/m^3$, $\rho_{water} = 1000\ kg/m^3$, $g = 9.8\ m/s^2$. Therefore, the net buoyancy of a $t = 0.4$-mm spherical shell is 15.12N, whereas the results of calculation can approximately be 13.50N for a $t = 0.7$-mm spherical shell. To minimize this effect, each spherical shell was encased in a string bag connected to a ballast pig. The weight of the pig was slightly higher than the buoyant load of the spherical shell. The shell, bag, and pig were then immersed together in a cylindrical pressure chamber with a 200-mm inner diameter, 400-mm total length, and 20-MPa maximum pressure. The chamber (located at Jiangsu University of Science and Technology) entailed using water as a pressurizing medium. The pressure inside the chamber was controlled automatically by a programmable logic controller and measured using a pressure transducer. All the spherical shells failed suddenly with substantial decreases in pressure. Thus, determining the buckling load was very simple.

2.2. Material properties

In cases of uniform external pressure, the buckling behaviors of spherical shells are determined according to the compression stress-strain behavior of the relevant material. However, experiments to demonstrate such behaviors with thin-walled structures are extremely difficult to conduct. Therefore, the compression behavior of steel is assumed to be the same as its tension behavior. This hypothesis has been frequently used in the buckling prediction of various shells of revolution loaded by external pressure [7, 9, 14]. Thus, the material properties of steel sheets can be established by testing a series of flat tension coupons.

The coupons for this work were designed and tested according to Chinese Standard (GB/T 228.1-2010) [15], which is in line with ISO 6892-1: 2009 [16]. They were cut along the rolling directions of the same sheets that were used to manufacture spherical shells for ensuring accurate material data. Five coupons were selected for each thickness and subjected to uniaxial tension. Two of them were strain-gauged in the transverse and longitudinal directions to obtain Poisson's ratio (ν) for the material and to verify the extensometer readings. The average values were 0.277 for the 0.4-mm-thick sheet and 0.291 for the 0.7-mm-thick sheet. Other coupons were tested to obtain accurate stress-strain curves, which can be demonstrated in the following form:

$$\sigma = E\varepsilon, \quad for \sigma < \sigma_y \tag{2a}$$

and

$$\sigma = \sigma_y \sqrt[k]{\left(\frac{E\varepsilon}{\sigma_y} - 1\right)n}, \tag{2b}$$

where E is Young's modulus, σ_{yp} is the yield strength based on 0.2% proof stress, and n and k are the strain hardening parameters. The values of these coefficients, as well as the average values, are listed in **Table 3**. The testing coupons were numbered and named according to the thickness and coupon number; one name, for example, was t0.4-c1, where t0.4 indicates that the thickness of the sheet was 0.4 mm, and c1 indicates that the coupon number was one. The variance of coefficients for each thickness was very small.

3. Results and discussion

Previous studies have indicated that the experimental buckling loads of spherical shells are lower than theoretical predictions [4, 17]. This phenomenon may result from inevitable geometric imperfections and from nonlinear material properties. This problem of classical mechanics is far from being solved; the buckling analysis of spherical shells remains to be vivid and is still challenging.

This section reports how the buckling loads and final collapsed modes of a family of spherical shells were determined from hydrostatic tests. The results of analytical and numerical investigations into these shells are presented and compared with the experimental findings. The effects of constitutive models on the buckling load are discussed.

3.1. Experimental and analytical results analysis

The experimental buckling loads are listed in column 2 of **Table 4**, and graphed in **Fig. 4**. Photographs of the final collapsed modes for 10 spherical shells are presented in **Fig. 5**. Notably, the buckling load of the t0.7-2 spherical shell was not recorded because of an incorrect operation during the testing process. However, the final collapsed mode of this shell was still obtained. The buckling loads of the 0.4-mm-thick spherical shells ranged between 1.330 and 1.956 MPa, whereas the 0.7-mm-thick shell buckling loads ranged between 3.178 and 4.692 MPa. The buckling loads of the 0.7-mm-thick shell loads were more than twice those of the 0.4-mm-thick shell loads. This variance mainly affected by the ratio of the average wall thickness (t_{ave}) to the average radius (r_{ave}), as illustrated in Fig. 4. The experimental buckling load increased monotonically with an increase in t_{ave}/r_{ave}. As shown in Fig. 5, the final collapsed modes of all shells are identical, and all of them have the form of a local dent because of the high ductility of stainless steel and the initial geometric imperfections of the shells. This failure mode is consistent with previous experimental results regarding shells of revolution with a positive Gaussian curvature, such as those for spherical shells reported by Quilliet [13], for ellipsoidal shells reported by Healey [18], and for barreled shells reported by Blachut [9, 10].

A theory derived by Zoelly [19] predicts the elastic buckling load (p_{cr}) of spherical shells, which is obtained using

$$P_{cr} = \frac{2E}{\sqrt{3(1-\nu^2)}}\left(\frac{t}{R}\right)^2 \qquad (3)$$

where the wall thickness t, radius r, Young's modulus E, and Poisson's ratio ν are assumed to be average values of the experimental results (Tables 1 and 3). This analytical formula is widely accepted in ocean and aerospace engineering as a rule for designing spherical shells [4, 20, 21]. The results of Eq. (3) are listed in column 3 of Table 4, followed by the ratio of the experimental load p_{test} to the elastic buckling load p_{zoelly} in parentheses. As shown in the table, the experimental load of a spherical shell was as little as 15.07%-24.55% of that shell's elastic buckling load, confirming that the spherical shell is a highly imperfection-sensitive structure. A small imperfection may lead to a substantial decrease in the magnitude of the buckling load. Furthermore, the average ratio of the experimental load p_{test} to the elastic buckling load p_{zoelly} for 0.4-mm-thick spherical shells was approximately 3% lower than the ratio for 0.7-mm-thick shells. It appears that the nonlinear properties of spherical shells' materials may play a major role in the buckling behaviors of shells with various wall thicknesses.

3.2. Comparison of experimental and numerical results

Prior work has demonstrated the effectiveness of the finite element method in predicting the buckling behaviors of thin-walled structures. Schmidt, for example, suggested that the real buckling load of a shell can be determined using geometrically and materially nonlinear analyses of shells that include imperfections [22, 23]. However, most studies have focused on equivalent geometric imperfections, such as eigenmode imperfections, in numerically analyzing the buckling of spherical shells.

In this study, we carried out nonlinear buckling analysis for the same types of spherical shells as would be tested for deterministic imperfections. The analysis was performed using the modified Riks method in ABAQUS software [24]. The finite element model of each spherical shell was established according to the real geometric shape obtained from the experimental data. The shapes and sizes of the initial geometric imperfections were automatically included in the models. A fully integrated S4 and S3 shell was selected to avoid hourglassing and the number of elements was determined using mesh density convergence analysis in line with [25], shown in**Fig. 6 and Table 5**. The mesh of each spherical shell was generated freely based on its real geometry in the form of numerous small surface pieces, where the local apex area was included. In all the analyses, a $p_0 = 1$ MPa external pressure was applied on the whole area of each shell. To avoid rigid body motion, three random spatial points were respectively constrained in the three orthogonal directions. These constraints did not lead to overconstrained models because the pressure was equally applied. The steel was assumed to be elastic-plastic as described in Eq. (2). In addition, the average wall thickness (column 4 of Table 1) and material properties (Table 3) were defined in the analyses. This averaging assumption has been implemented by Blachut et al. and resulted in a good agreement between experiment and theory [5]. **Fig. 7** and the final column of Table 4 show the results obtained using numerical analysis.

Because the equilibrium paths, critical buckling, and postbuckling modes of all the analyzed shells were similar, detailed results are provided only for the case of t0.4-1. Fig. 7 shows the equilibrium path of a shell; the vertical axis shows the applied load normalized by the initial applied load$p_0 = 1$ MPa, and the horizontal axis shows the maximum deflection (Δ) normalized by the wall thickness (t). The path has an unstable characteristic that is typical of shell structures: At first, the load increases nearly linearly with an increase in the deflection up to a peak corresponding to the critical buckling load, beyond which the load decreases sharply. The same figure shows that the buckling and postbuckling modes are similar and assume the form of a local dent. This may have been caused by the initial deterministic imperfections of the shell. Comparing Figs. 5 and 7 show that the predicted final failure mode is highly consistent with the experimental one. In addition, as indicated in the final column of Table 4, very good correlation between the numerical buckling loads and the experimental ones was obtained ($\pm 7\%$). This slight difference may be attributed to small variations of the material properties for the steel sheets, in addition to the assumption of the average wall thickness used to perform numerical calculation. These findings indicate that the real buckling resistance of a spherical shell can be determined numerically on the basis of its true geometry as well as its average wall thickness and material properties.

In the same figure, the first yield load of t0.4-1 is plotted at the value of 1.466 MPa, which was obtained using the postprocessing procedure as in Ref. [8]. The first yield load was approximately 84% of the critical buckling load. At the first stage of testing up to this value, the spherical shell had an elastic characteristic. At the second stage of testing higher than this value, the spherical shell appeared to be elastic-plastic. This phenomenon was observed for all the cases shown in **Table 6**. For spherical shells, the ratio of the first yield to the critical buckling load, $p_{ABAQUS}^{fyd}/p_{ABAQUS}^{elastic-plastic}$, varied between 0.681 and 0.895. It is suggested that all the spherical shells could lose stability within the elastic-plastic regime. This finding is similar to those regarding medium-thick conical shells subjected to external pressure [7].

3.3. Effect of constitutive models

It is well known that the modeling of materials strongly influences the accuracy of numerical results. Most recent numerical investigations on the buckling of shell structures have assumed the material properties to be either purely elastic [26] or elastic-perfectly plastic [9, 10]. To examine this assumption, the effect of constitutive models on the buckling of spherical shells was investigated in the present study. The same numerical models as those mentioned in Section 3.2 were employed, except that the steel was assumed to be elastic and elastic-perfectly plastic. The material parameters were determined on the basis of the average values listed in Table 3; 20 models were accounted for. Because the equilibrium paths, critical buckling modes, and postbuckling modes of these cases were almost identical with the elastic-plastic results for t0.4-1 shown in Fig. 7, the effects of constitutive models were examined according to the critical buckling load only. Table 7 shows the buckling loads $p_{ABAQUS}^{elastic}$ and $p_{ABAQUS}^{elastic\text{-}perfectly\ plastic}$ obtained from elastic and elastic-perfectly plastic assumptions, respectively, and the values normalized by elastic-plastic $p_{ABAQUS}^{elastic-plastic}$ and experimental p_{test} buckling loads are in parentheses.

As shown in Table 7, the elastic assumption yielded an increase of 53.98%-135.55% in the magnitude of the buckling load over that of the elastic-plastic assumption. A fairly large difference existed between the results obtained according to the purely elastic assumption and those of the experiments. This finding indicates that numerical predictions based on the purely elastic assumption are extremely nonconservative and are not suitable for engineering applications. However, the differences between the elastic and elastic-plastic results for 0.4-mm-thick spherical shells are always higher than those for 0.7-mm-thick shells. This implies that the failures of spherical shells vary gradually from elastic buckling to elastic-plastic buckling as the wall thicknesses increase. It is more reasonable to include plastic material properties when performing buckling analysis on a medium-thick shell structure.

As shown in Table 7, the elastic-perfectly plastic predictions deviated from the elastic-plastic predictions by as little as 6%. Very good agreement was obtained between the elastic-plastic and elastic-perfectly plastic results. The maximum difference between a prediction from the elastic-perfectly plastic assumption and that from the experiment was only 8%. This confirms that the buckling of a shell is greatly determined according to its stress behavior, particularly its yield [27]. It could be inferred that aside from the elastic material properties, the buckling load of a shell strongly depends on the yield strength of the material. This finding extends those of Bluchat [9, 10], confirming that the elastic-perfectly plastic assumption can be made in the buckling analysis of shells, and tends to result in extremely accurate predictions.

4. Conclusions

In the present work, the results of experimental, analytical, and numerical study into the buckling behaviors of spherical shells are presented, as well as the effects of constitutive modes on the buckling loads of these shells. The experimental buckling load increased monotonically with an increase in t_{ave}/r_{ave}, which was as little as 15.07%-24.55% of the elastic buckling load determined using Zoelly's equation. The experimental collapsed modes of all the shells were identical; all of them assumed the form of a local dent, which is typical of shells of revolution with a positive Gaussian curvature.

Geometrically and materially nonlinear buckling analyses were performed on the spherical shells for deterministic imperfections. Very good correlation was obtained between the numerical buckling loads and the experimental ones. The path of each spherical shell had an unstable characteristic typical of shell structures. All the shells buckled within an elastic-plastic range. The buckling and postbuckling modes of all the analyzed shells were similar and assumed the form of a local dent, which was in very good agreement with the experimental results.

The effects of constitutive models on the buckling of spherical shells were demonstrated numerically according to the buckling load. The failures of spherical shells varied gradually from elastic buckling to elastic-plastic buckling as the wall thicknesses increased. Very good agreement was obtained among the elastic-plastic, elastic-perfectly plastic, and experimental results. The elastic-perfectly plastic assumption resulted in a highly accurate prediction. The elastic assumption yielded a fairly large increase in the magnitude of the buckling load above the elastic-plastic assumption and experiment.

This work therefore indicates that the real load-carrying capacity of a spherical shell can be obtained numerically from measured geometric shape and average wall thickness, as well as from the assumption of elastic-perfectly plastic material properties. The current approach appears to be effective for other shells of revolution with typical meridional profiles, such as cylindrical and conical shells, as well as for shells of revolution with nontypical meridional profiles, such as barreled and egg-shaped shells. However, some limitations merit attention. Although the predicted buckling loads and final failure modes were verified experimentally, the critical buckling modes were not examined through testing. Moreover, the manufacturing process caused some variance in the wall thicknesses, and that variance exerted an effect on the buckling of spherical shells; however, this effect was not studied. These limitations require further investigation in the near future.

Acknowledgments

This work was supported by two grants from the Natural Science Foundation of Jiangsu Province, China (BK20140512, BK20150469).

References

[1] J. Blachut, Experimental perspective on the buckling of pressure vessel components, Appl. Mech. Rev. 66 (2013) 010803-1-010803-24.

[2] J. Błachut, K. Magnucki, Strength, Stability, and Optimization of pressure vessels: Review of selected problems, Appl. Mech. Rev. 61 (2008) 060801.

[3] B. B. Pan, W. C. Cui, An overview of buckling and ultimate strength of spherical pressure hull under external pressure, Mar. Struct. 23 (2010) 227-240.

[4] B. B. Pan, W. C. Cui, A comparison of different rules for the spherical pressure hull of deep manned submersibles, J. Ship Mech. 15 (2011) 276-285.

[5] J. Blachut, G. D. Galletly, D. N. Moreton, Buckling of near-perfect steel torispherical and hemispherical shells subjected to external pressure, AIAA J. 28 (1990) 1971-1975.

[6] J. Błachut, Locally flattened or dented domes under external pressure, Thin-Walled Struct. 97 (2015) 44-52.

[7] J. Błachut, A. Muc, J. Ryś, Plastic buckling of cones subjected to axial compression and external pressure, J. Press. Vessel. Technol. 135 (2013) 011205-1-011205-9.

[8] J. Błachut, O. Ifayefunmi, Buckling of unstiffened steel cones subjected to axial compression and external pressure, J. Offshore Mech. Arct. Eng. 134 (2012) 031603-1-031603-9.

[9] J. Błachut, Optimal barreling of steel shells via simulated annealing algorithm, Comput. Struct. 81 (2003) 1941-1956.

[10] J. Błachut, Buckling of externally pressurised barrelled shells: a comparison of experiment and theory, Int. J. Press. Vessel. Pip. 79 (2002) 507-517.

[11] B. B. Pan, W. C. Cui, Y. S. Shen, T. Liu, Further study on the ultimate strength analysis of spherical pressure hulls, Mar. Struct. 23 (2010) 444-461.

[12] B. B. Pan, W. C. Cui, Y. S. Shen, Experimental verification of the new ultimate strength equation of spherical pressure hulls, Mar. Struct. 29 (2012) 169-176.

[13] C. Quilliet, Depressions at the surface of an elastic spherical shell submitted to external pressure, Phys. Rev. E. 74 (2006) 046608-1-046608-6.

[14] H. Schmidt, P. Swadlo, Part C-Shells of revolution with Arbitrary meridional shapes-Buckling design by use of computer analysis, ECSC contract No. 7210-SA/208: Enhancement of ECCS design recommendations and development of Eurocode 3 parts related to shell buckling, Final Report, Universität GH Essen, FB Bauwesen-Stahlbau, 1996.

[15] GB/T 228. 1: Metallic materials-Tensile testing-Part 1: Method of test at room temperature, Chinese Standard Institute, china, 2010.

[16] ISO 6892-1: Metallic materials-Tensile testing-Part 1: Method of test at room temperature, International Organization for Standardization, 2009.

[17] T. Von Kármán, H. S. Tsien, The buckling of Spherical Shells by External Pressure, J. Aeronaut. Sci. 7 (1939) 43-50 (doi: 10.2514/8.1019).

[18] J. J. Healey, Hydrostatic tests of two prolate spheroidal shells, J. Ship Res. 9 (1965) 77-78.

[19] R. Zoelly, Über ein Knickungs problem an der Kugelschale, Zürich, 1915.

[20] CCS. Rules for the classification and construction of diving systems and submersibles, China Classification Society, china, 1996.

[21] NASA SP-8032. Buckling of thin-walled doubly curved shells, National Aeronautics and Space Administration, Washington, 1969.

[22] H. Schmidt, Stability of steel shell structures: General Report, J. Constr. Steel Res. 55 (2000) 159-181.

[23] EN 1993-1-6: Eurocode 3-Design of steel structures-Part 1. 6: Strength and Stability of shell structures, CEN, Brussels, 2007.
[24] K. Hibbitt, S. Inc, ABAQUS-Theory and Standard User's Manual Version 6. 3, USA, 2006.
[25] P. Jasion, K. Magnucki, Elastic buckling of clothoidal-spherical shells under external pressure-theoretical study, Thin-Walled Struct. 86 (2015) 18-23.
[26] P. Jasion, K. Magnucki, Elastic buckling of classini ovaloidal shells under external pressure-theoretical study, Arch. Mech. 67 (2015) 179-192.
[27] M. Barski, J. Krużelecki, Optimal design of shells against buckling under overall bending and external pressure, Thin-Walled Struct. 43 (2005) 1677-1698.

Table 1

Testing values of the wall thickness and radius for spherical shells (minimum, maximum, average, and standard deviation)

	t_{min} (mm)	t_{max} (mm)	t_{ave} (mm)	t_{std} (mm)	r_{min} (mm)	r_{max} (mm)	r_{ave} (mm)	r_{std} (mm)
t0.4-1	0.382	0.476	0.422	0.022	73.903	74.485	74.248	0.174
t0.4-2	0.396	0.496	0.432	0.024	73.843	74.517	74.163	0.170
t0.4-3	0.378	0.488	0.426	0.024	74.067	74.285	74.157	0.046
t0.4-4	0.382	0.436	0.401	0.010	74.304	74.754	74.548	0.133
t0.4-5	0.382	0.476	0.414	0.016	73.817	74.501	74.185	0.158
t0.7-1	0.650	0.754	0.708	0.024	74.231	75.005	74.710	0.249
t0.7-2	0.614	0.766	0.715	0.024	74.391	75.291	74.926	0.242
t0.7-3	0.644	0.746	0.723	0.02	74.282	75.102	75.023	0.142
t0.7-4	0.652	0.756	0.724	0.019	74.300	75.062	74.840	0.184
t0.7-5	0.648	0.762	0.716	0.021	74.317	75.001	74.983	0.252

Table 2

Thickness (in mm) at 13 equidistant points along 8 meridians for a t0.4-1 spherical shell

Longtitude no.	Lattitude no.							
	A	B	C	D	E	F	G	H
1	0.416	0.422	0.420	0.410	0.426	0.458	0.426	0.412
2	0.436	0.410	0.408	0.404	0.436	0.416	0.410	0.408
3	0.426	0.426	0.398	0.382	0.422	0.408	0.394	0.396
4	0.428	0.432	0.412	0.464	0.410	0.422	0.398	0.400
5	0.402	0.396	0.418	0.388	0.402	0.398	0.408	0.398
6	0.425	0.415	0.418	0.420	0.419	0.416	0.432	0.431
7	0.406	0.466	0.408	0.408	0.392	0.396	0.396	0.418
8	0.414	0.434	0.432	0.432	0.456	0.470	0.476	0.424
9	0.398	0.438	0.418	0.406	0.416	0.416	0.446	0.414
10	0.428	0.446	0.406	0.414	0.424	0.420	0.458	0.414
11	0.456	0.446	0.436	0.450	0.446	0.450	0.472	0.454

The thicknesses atthe North-Pole and South-pole are 0.418 and 0.462 respectively.

Table 3

Material properties of 304 stainless steel obtained from uniaxial tension tests (E-Young's modulus; σ_{yp}-yield strength; n and k-strain hardening parameter)

	E(GPa)	σ_{yp}(MPa)	n	k
t0.4-c1	193.1	250.9	0.108	4.154
t0.4-c2	188.4	241.4	0.101	3.896
t0.4-c3	190.5	246.2	0.091	4.319
t0.4-average	190.7	246.1	0.100	4.123
t0.7-c1	187.2	288.5	0.081	4.291
t0.7-c2	180.3	292.0	0.088	4.733
t0.7-c3	197.1	294.2	0.118	4.972
t0.7-average	188.2	291.6	0.096	4.665

Table 4

Experimental (p_{test}), analytical (p_{zoelly}), and numerical ($p_{ABAQUS}^{elastic-plastic}$) buckling loads of spherical shells. The analytical and numerical values were normalized by the experimental values and are in parentheses

	p_{test}(MPa)	p_{zoelly}(MPa)	($p_{ABAQUS}^{elastic-plastic}$)(MPa)
t0.4-1	1.708	7.586(4.44)	1.745(1.02)
t0.4-2	1.956	7.968(4.07)	1.946(0.99)
t0.4-3	1.773	7.749(4.37)	1.708(0.96)
t0.4-4	1.330	6.795(5.11)	1.332(1.00)
t0.4-5	1.594	7.313(4.59)	1.708(1.07)
t0.7-1	3.178	21.089(6.64)	3.155(0.99)
t0.7-2	NA	21.384(NA)	4.317(NA)
t0.7-3	4.496	21.809(4.85)	4.716(1.05)
t0.7-4	4.692	21.976(4.68)	4.397(0.94)
t0.7-5	3.974	21.412(5.39)	4.006(1.01)

Table 5

Number of the FE elements for each spherical shell

	t0.4-1	t0.4-2	t0.4-3	t0.4-4	t0.4-5	t0.7-1	t0.7-2	t0.7-3	t0.7-4	t0.7-5
S4	6746	6643	6820	6298	6264	6430	6348	6287	6436	6447
S3	1064	448	1110	1134	1064	1118	1212	1180	1170	1216

Table 6

First yield load p_{ABAQUS}^{fyd} values of spherical shells and the ratio of the first yield and critical buckling load $p_{ABAQUS}^{fyd}/p_{ABAQUS}^{elastic-plastic}$

	p_{ABAQUS}^{fyd}(MPa)	$p_{ABAQUS}^{fyd}/p_{ABAQUS}^{elastic-plastic}$
t0.4-1	1.466	0.840
t0.4-2	1.407	0.723
t0.4-3	1.531	0.896
t0.4-4	0.907	0.681
t0.4-5	1.528	0.895
t0.7-1	2.392	0.758

(续)

	p_{ABAQUS}^{fyd}(MPa)	$p_{ABAQUS}^{fyd}/p_{ABAQUS}^{elastic-plastic}$
t0.7-2	3.401	0.788
t0.7-3	3.904	0.828
t0.7-4	3.905	0.888
t0.7-5	3.402	0.849

Table 7
Buckling loads of spherical shells obtained from elastic and elastic-perfectly plastic models. Values in parentheses were normalized by the elastic-plastic and experimental buckling loads, respectively

	$p_{ABAQUS}^{elastic}$(MPa)	$p_{ABAQUS}^{elastic-perfectly\ plastic}$(MPa)
t0.4-1	3.146(1.80, 1.84)	1.722(0.99, 1.01)
t0.4-2	3.389(1.74, 1.73)	1.823(0.94, 0.93)
t0.4-3	2.941(1.72, 1.65)	1.630(0.95, 0.92)
t0.4-4	2.051(1.54, 1.54)	1.332(1.00, 1.00)
t0.4-5	3.174(1.86, 1.99)	1.712(1.00, 1.07)
t0.7-1	5.930(1.88, 1.87)	2.953(0.94, 0.92)
t0.7-2	9.549(2.21, NA)	4.206(0.97, NA)
t0.7-3	10.174(2.16, 2.31)	4.483(0.95, 1.02)
t0.7-4	10.357(2.36, 2.21)	4.383(1.00, 0.93)
t0.7-5	9.035(2.26, 2.27)	3.953(0.99, 0.99)

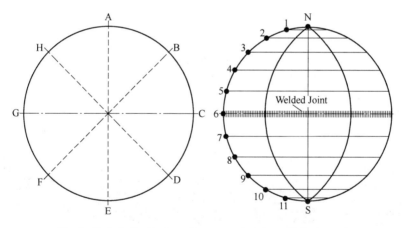

Fig. 1. Typical distribution of testing points for wall thickness.

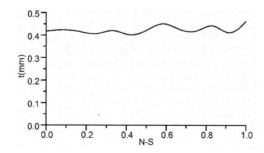

Fig. 2. Overall average wall thickness profile from the North-Pole to the South Pole for a t0.4-1 spherical shell.

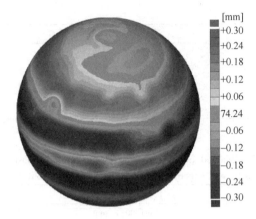

Fig. 3. Contours of local radii of curvature for a t0.4-1 spherical shell.

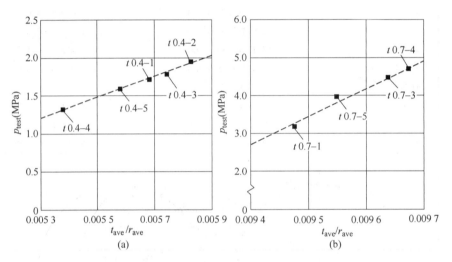

Fig. 4. Plots of experimental buckling load versus ratio of average wall thickness (t_{ave}) to average radius (r_{ave}) of spherical shells; a = 0.4-mm spherical shells, b = 0.7-mm spherical shells.

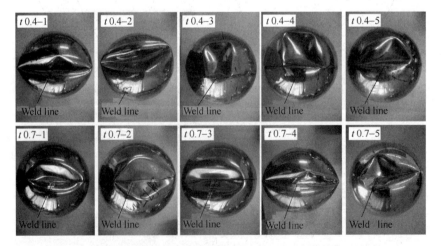

Fig. 5. Views of spherical shells after collapse caused by external hydrostatic pressure; All final failure modes assumed the form of a local dimple.

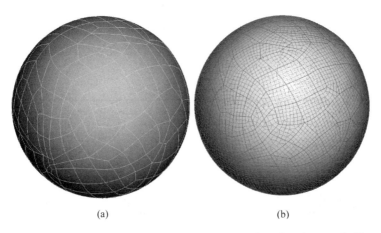

Fig. 6. Scanned CAD model (a) for a t0.4-1 spherical shell and its mesh (b).

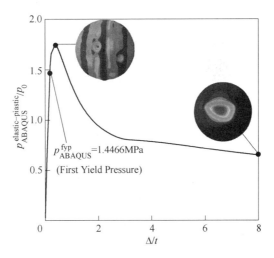

Fig. 7. Equilibrium path, critical buckling mode, and postbuckling mode of a t0.4-1 spherical shell.

9.2.5 稿件录用及后续

(1) 录用邮件

Ref: TWST_ 2016_ 349_ R2

Title: Buckling of spherical shells subjected to external pressure: A comparison of experimental and theoretical data

Journal: Thin-Walled Structures

Dear Mr. zhang,

I am pleased to inform you that your paper has been accepted for publication. My own comments as well as any reviewer comments are appended to the end of this letter. Now that your manuscript has been accepted for publication it will proceed to copy-editing and production.

Thank you for submitting your work to Thin-Walled Structures. We hope you consider us again for future submissions.

Kind regards,

Joseph Loughlan

Receiving Editor

Thin-Walled Structures

Comments from the editors and reviewers:

This is a good and well described contribution-pleased to recommend its publication as it stands.

(2) 修订

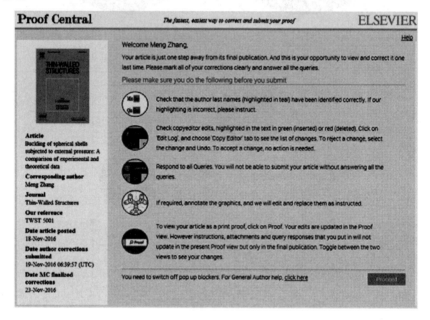

参考文献

[1] 张建,高杰,王纬波,等. 深海球形耐压壳力学特性研究[J]. 中国造船,2015(4):129-140.

[2] Zhang J, Zhang M, Tang W, et al. Buckling of spherical shells subjected to external pressure: A comparison of experimental and theoretical data[J]. Thin-Walled Structures, 2017, 111:58-64.

[3] 张建,唐文献,苏世杰,等. 硬土-软土插桩过程数值分析及验证[J]. 石油勘探与开发,2013,40(4):492-496.

[4] 张建,王国林,唐文献,等. 轮胎硫化过程数值分析及试验研究[J]. 材料科学与工艺,2012,20(4):20-25.

[5] Zhang J, Wang M, Wang W, et al. Investigation on egg-shaped pressure hull[J]. Marine Structures, 2017, 52:50-66.

[6] Zhang J, Wang M, Wang W, et al. Buckling of egg-shaped shells subjected to external pressure[J]. Thin-Walled Structures, 2017, 113:122-128.

[7] Williams H C. How to reply to referees' comments when submitting manuscripts for publication[J]. Journal of the American Academy of Dermatology, 2004, 51(1):79-83.

[8] Annesley T M. Top 10 tips for responding to reviewer and editor comments[J]. Clinical Chemistry, 2011, 57(4):551-554.

[9] Keshav S. How to read a paper[J]. Acm Sigcomm Computer Communication Review, 2007, 37(3):83-84.

[10] Socolofsky S A. How to write a research journal article in engineering and science[J]. Texas A&M University Journal, 2004, 1:1-17.

[11] 史帝夫·华乐丝. 如何成为学术论文写作高手[M]. 北京:北京大学出版社,2015.

[12] 比约·古斯塔维. 科技论文写作快速入门[M]. 北京:北京大学出版社,2008.

[13] Strunk Jr., William. THE ELEMENTS OF STYLE[M]. Harcont, 1918.

[14] Glasman-Deal, Hilary. Science research writing: for non-native speakers of English[M]. London: Imperial College Press, 2010.

[15] 国家图书馆《中国图书馆分类法》委员会. 中国图书馆分类法[M]. 北京:国家图书馆出版社,2010.

[16] 科学技术报告、学位论文和学术论文的编写格式:GB/T 7713—1987[S]. 北京:中国标准出版社,1981.

[17] 信息与文献 参考文献著录规则:GB/T 7714—2015[S]. 北京:中国标准出版社,2015.

[18] 文献类型与文献载体代码:GB/T 3469—1983[S]. 北京:中国标准出版社,1983.